Reinventing Local Media

Ideas for Thriving
in a Postmodern World

Volume II

Reinventing Local Media

Ideas for Thriving in a Postmodern World

Volume II

reinventing local media

Terry Heaton

Senior Vice President
Audience Research & Development

To Karen

Table of Contents

Acknowledgments

I must first thank my colleagues at AR&D, and especially president & CEO Jerry Gumbert, for the support I've received since moving to Texas in 2006. It's one thing to have ideas, but to be surrounded by great thinkers in bringing them to life is a real blessing. Long after I'm gone, AR&D will be recognized as the only company that really offered local media a vision during this time of great change. Our collaborative book, *Live. Local. BROKEN News. The Re-engineering of Local Television*, has challenged thousands of old media executives with a call for leadership in difficult times. I'm proud of that book; we all are.

I also want to personally thank the wonderful clients that I've worked with since joining AR&D. They've embraced ideas expressed in this book and taken positive steps in reinventing themselves. I love the people in Richmond, Lexington, Baton Rouge, Lafayette, Corpus Christi, Colorado Springs, Tucson, Montana, San Luis Obispo, Tampa, Charlotte, and elsewhere, and look forward to serving them in the years ahead, along with a host of new clients.

Once again, my dear friend Holly Hunter has kept me going with support and editing that is second to none. I'm blessed and fortunate to have her in my life, for she teaches me things every day.

Mostly, I want to thank Karen for her undying support. As a writer who works mostly at home, I can be a major pain, but she's handled me and my idiosyncrasies with grace and elegance. Thanks, too, to Tory and Alex for letting me work in peace.

To Brit, Clint, BF, Riss, and Chibi, thanks for your help and support, and to my wonderful family in Amman, may God bless you and keep you.

This is the most exciting time in communications history, and we've only just begun.

Foreword

Why is it that the embarrassing and painful moments of youth are those that are remembered most?

I was the "golly-gee" kid in elementary school, the guy who would rather skip than walk, loved to laugh and joke, and turned over every rock to see what was underneath. I was also deeply sensitive and aware of others and the power they had over me, because I wanted them to like me so much. I was the brunt of many jokes due to my naïveté, and embarrassing myself was the last thing I ever wanted to do.

In fifth grade, we were participating in a grammar exercise and practicing pronouncing words. The subject was the letter G and how it was sometimes silent, sometimes soft and sometimes hard. Mrs. White used the word "finger" to demonstrate a hard G in the middle of a word. "FING-gerrr," she said, followed by, "Say it to yourselves, 'FING-gerrr.'"

I missed the part about saying it to ourselves and, in my enthusiastic golly-geeness, hollered out, "FING-gerrrrrrrr."

Oops. The room was silent, and then erupted into laughter. As I turned bright red, there was no place to hide. It was one of the worst moments of my life. Thinking back on it, it's pretty funny, but the pain lingers, a reminder of rejection's hold over me even at age 64.

I'm drawn to this story today, because I find it odd that a guy with such a fragile ego would risk it all by putting on paper for all to read ideas that stem from visions that bubble and brew in my creative vat. What has happened to me that I would risk it all, again and again, to push forward in such a volatile, changing time? Why would I stand alone hollering "FING-gerrrr" for all to see and hear, all the time knowing that most people are simply going to laugh at me and continue going about their business as they have for many years?

Maybe it's that I don't care anymore what people think. There's truth to that, for sure, but I don't think it fully explains the last ten years of my life, the hundreds of essays, the hundreds of newsletters, the thousands of blog entries and tweets.

Perhaps it's that I just think I'm right and that my views are better than yours. I know I can come off that way sometimes, and I've heard complaints about my relentless beating of old media attitudes and behaviors. But that's really not me, at core. That would take a personality predisposed to braggadocio, and that's the opposite of the pedestal on which I hide. For a guy who imagines himself the least of all, it's out of character to stand up and brag.

The truth is I'm scared, just as I was back in fifth grade.

My favorite writer is Richard Adams of *Watership Down* fame. He wrote an obscure book long ago called *The Unbroken Web*, in which he gives his version of many ancient stories. In the foreword, he writes of a moving dimension where all creativity exists that floats above the planet this way and that. Sensitive people touch it and bring its wonders to the rest of the people who live "down here." This is the only thing that explains these ancient stories popping up at the same time on different parts of the planet before intercontinental travel was possible. I believe in the Unbroken Web, that creative ideas belong to everyone, and that we have no choice but to share them.

I think that drives me, because I see in there solutions to the problems impacting all of my old friends and colleagues in the news business. The fear that haunts me tells me we're headed for an enormous collapse, and my job is to warn everybody. That has the power to overcome my fear of rejection and allow me to stand alone hollering "FING-gerrr" when I know that the majority of people hearing it are going to laugh, scoff or otherwise dismiss what I'm saying.

I make no claims as a prophet and leave that to future generations to judge. I'm only following what my heart is driving me to do, and I make no apologies or claims.

This book is the second volume of my work. If you seek new ideas for the postmodern era that has begun, dig in. If nothing else, I'll at least make you think.

And every time you think you hear a little voice hollering "FING-gerrr," I hope you'll smile and not laugh at me.

The Triumph of
Personal Media
Over Mass Media

THE EVOLVING USER PARADIGM

In 1961, a high school track coach moved into the house next to mine and introduced my younger brother and me to track and field events like the high jump and pole vaulting. We had a big open field behind our house, which served as a buffer for the C&O railroad tracks that ran through the neighborhood. Soon we had built a sawdust "pit" for our jumping activities. We brought home long bamboo poles from a rug store a few miles away, and soon we were pole vaulting. "Coach" eventually got us the first fiberglass pole in Grand Rapids, and we certainly felt special.

I was on the high school track team as a pole vaulter, but I wasn't very good. That honor went to my brother, who went on to great things as a vaulter. There are probably many reasons why he was so much better than I was, but one thing is certain: by the time he got to high school, he'd been vaulting for several years. Experience impacts ability, and it's the same thing with most human endeavors.

In the digital world, for example, the amount of experience a user has changes the very nature of the transaction between user and software, and this is especially true online. It's what's so maddening for traditional media companies trying to react to change, because what's hot today is obsolete seemingly overnight. You can make a few bucks at something next week, but what will you do the week after that?

I call this the evolving user paradigm: the longer users use the Web, the greater the acceleration of the disruption they create. AOL was its first victim. America Online experienced growth so staggering that it served as the poster child for the bursting bubble that followed. Everybody was on AOL, or nearly everybody. Like Facebook today, it was THE gathering place in the 90s, a walled garden of wonders for those who were eager to explore this new thing called the World Wide Web.

The problem was that the longer you used AOL, the more you wanted to see what was beyond its walls. After a year or two, users wanted more, while AOL wanted to keep the money tree blossoming forever. So AOL became known as "training wheels" for the Web, and those with experience moved on. Broadband didn't destroy AOL; it was the evolving user paradigm.

Users of the Web get smarter with experience, which means their wants and needs evolve faster than our ability to keep up. It drives innovation and punishes those who wish things would just sit still.

In his wonderful book, *Everything Is Miscellaneous,* David Weinberger notes that no organizational system for information can possibly compete with a system, like search, that organizes information "on the way out." (1) Instead of wandering through the mall looking for something, you simply stand at the door and let the mall know what you're seeking, and, presto, there it is. No information portal that the human mind could conceive can compete with search, and that simple proposition is the fruit of the evolving user paradigm. Why? Because after you've "navigated" the various levels of any website, you begin to realize that the time it takes to do so could better be spent doing something else. Anxiety produces discontent, because we know intuitively that there has to be a better way. That demand drives innovation, and before we know it, there is a better way.

Novelty wears off. It's the evolving user paradigm.

"If I had it to do over, I wouldn't have done this (or bought that)." This, too, is the evolving user paradigm, for technology never simply stands still, and the people who use it grow in their understanding of it and of its unintended consequences.

Media companies are ongoing victims of the evolving user paradigm, because we spend our efforts trying to duplicate the money machine known as order-taking advertising. We mistakenly think that the established equilibrium of the past will, sooner or later, come to fruition online, and that is impossible when people who used to be our audiences are evolving faster than we are. We pay no (or little) attention to the user experience, because we're too busy multiplying the number of page views we can tout to advertisers. The cost of interaction that users must pay with us should be our most important metric, but it's often not even on the page. Hell, if we can shift six page views into seven, why not?

Steve Jobs is an expert at the timing necessary to keep users of his products coming back. Each iteration of an iDevice evolves with user experience and expectation. By the time competitors "copy" anything Apple does, iDevice users have already moved past what's being offered as "new." In the device development war, it's not so much who delivers better bells and whistles as it is who can match the pace of the evolving user paradigm. Apple does this brilliantly.

But in his zeal to create the perfect experience, Jobs is making a tactical error that could be costly. By running everything that makes it to an iDevice through his iTunes store, Apple is betting against the evolving user paradigm, and its archenemy, Google, has to be pleased with that. Google's core competency is to enable evolving users, and when users eventually run into the walls that Apple is building, Google will be there to take them forward.

As users evolve, they demand more from their experience, because they begin to understand how everything works. If technology won't help them work around the barriers they encounter, they'll simply move along, because they are hip to manipulation and, frankly, don't like it. This growing understanding of how it all works is perhaps the most disruptive element of the evolving user paradigm, because users increasingly are able to create their own experiences as technology becomes easier and easier to use. That's why Google is such a threat to the status quo.

As users of any particular software become more able, the software must evolve or run the risk of losing those users. Nobody understands this like Google and its immensely popular offshoot, YouTube.

You can browse YouTube's channels or libraries and follow those that suit your taste, but the engine that drives YouTube is search. It's the world's second largest search engine, and a necessary part of anybody's business that can tell a story using video.

YouTube is the playground of what J. D. Lasica first termed "the personal media revolution" in his seminal 2005 book, *Darknet: Hollywood's War Against the Digital Generation*. (2) The deep, dark secret of all media — and I apologize to those I'll offend here — is that it's just not that hard to make. Of course, there are levels of quality involved, but those, too, are being challenged by everyday people armed with inexpensive, but high quality equipment. This is especially true in the world of video media, and it's here where the evolving user paradigm is being played out for everyone to see.

Talent rises to the top, just like it always has, but YouTube offers an outlet for talent that's outside the scope of the traditional overseers. People like Shane Dawson and Philip DeFranco are making six-figure incomes by producing regular shows on YouTube, with Dawson's program being viewed 35 million times each month. That's bigger than the audience of, say, the finale of American Idol. So popular is Dawson with the junior high school crowd that Hot Topic carries Shane Dawson T-shirts.

Have you been to YouTube lately? It's evolved far beyond the world of bloopers, and with GoogleTV now waiting in the wings, YouTube is going to become an even more significant player in the media world. Michael Wesch, the Kansas State University anthropology professor who produced the profoundly insightful video *Web 2.0... The Machine Is Us/ing Us*, now offers a new video — a remarkable presentation of the evolution of YouTube (*An Anthropological Introduction to YouTube*) — that's well worth the hour it takes to watch it.

J. D. Lasica is still deeply involved in the world of personal media, and he told me that the evolving user paradigm will continue to disrupt the status quo.

The tools have become cheaper, more accessible and easier to use across a range of media. When I go to conferences now, I see lots of people whip out their Flip or Zi8 recorders to capture a moment or conduct an interview — something they never would have considered doing a couple of years ago. I tuned out of YouTube for a long time because of all the noise and fluff, but it's gotten serious about serving the public interest (while continuing to monetize the dog-on-a-skateboard videos). Look at the YouTube Reporters Center and YouTube Direct, a service that makes citizen reporting easier. I'm especially fond of sites like RockYou, Slide, Stupeflix and Animoto that give us new ways to tell a story beyond traditional photos or video.

More people are taking up the tools of citizen publishing, too, through free platforms like WordPress.org. With thousands of free open source plug-ins, citizen publishers essentially have a global army of developers working for them — for free. Amazing. So blogs and grassroots media are becoming not only more powerful and pervasive but professional, too.

Given all this, you might think that studying early adopters is path to success, and up to a point, that's true. However, a big chunk of all early technology adopters are the people who create technology, those lovable folks we call geeks. Their wants and needs are somewhat different from the average user, although I would argue that the gap is closing, because our educational system is cranking out more people with tech street smarts.

Web development and media creation are regular electives in most high schools these days. We have that "on the way up" meeting increasingly easy-to-use tools "on the way down," so I expect the evolving user paradigm to continue its disruptive ways for many years.

As Gordon Borrell says, "The deer now have guns. What do you do when the deer have guns? Get into the ammunition business." That's Google's business, and it should be ours, for the more users evolve, the less tolerant they become of anything we do that attempts to manipulate them to make a buck.

WE DON'T NEED NO STAGE!

A s a child growing up in Michigan in the 1950s, our telephone was connected to elaborate circuitry known as switchboards. The "operator" connected circuits as calls were made, and the technology to automate all that was just coming into being. These operators were often featured in television shows and films of the period, and they were just an accepted part of life.

A telephone call back then was a closed circuit from one point to another, and trust me, when the phone rang in my house, it was a very big deal. Depending on what you could afford, your circuit was often shared with others in what were known as "party lines." You'd pick up the phone to make a call only to discover that some other member of your "party" was using the line. Yikes!

So in telephony fifty years ago, the circuit and that which was being transmitted on the circuit were connected. The form was connected to its content, and this was the way of all communications. You could only watch Hollywood films at the theater. Ed Sullivan was on TV Sunday nights. Music was available on vinyl records. And so forth.

In 1960, scientists began experimenting with what's known as "packet switching" on telephone lines, where the data being transmitted was separated from the circuit and repackaged at the other end. Wikipedia describes it this way:

> *Packet switching* is a network communications method that groups all transmitted data, irrespective of content, type, or structure into suitably-sized blocks, called *packets*. The network over which packets are transmitted is a shared network that routes each packet independently from all others and allocates transmission resources as needed. Principal goals of packet switching are to optimize utilization of available link capacity and to increase robustness of communication. (1)

Packet switching is the foundation upon which the Internet is built. The breakthrough came when the Department of Defense used it to build ARPANET (Advanced Research Projects Agency Network), the precursor to the Internet.

This ability to separate form from content is at the heart of all of the disruptive technologies and innovations that we have in communications today. Former FCC Chairman Michael Powell referred to it during a formal chat with students at Stanford University in 2004.

> ...if you're the music industry, you're scared. And if you're the television studio, movie industry, you're scared. And if you're an incumbent infrastructure carrier, you'd better be scared. Because this application separation is the most important paradigm shift in the history of communications, and will change things forever....I have no problem if a big and venerable company no longer exists tomorrow, as long as that value is transferred somewhere else in the economy. (2)

While there are certainly questions as to whether value is transferring or disappearing, there's no doubt that venerable institutions are in trouble today as the result of application separation. The issue, however, is not how to protect oneself from this disruption, but rather how to move forward within it. And the problem for everybody in the world of communications is that once you separate "content" from the form in which it is presented, you give up the ability to monetize any subsequent forms of presentation. "Content" has no value in and of itself. The value is always with the presentation, and this is the real problem in an unbundled world.

It's the single most significant issue confronting the copyright industry and copyright law in contemporary culture, for the ability to separate form from content didn't exist when original laws were written or the concept of copyright was even conceived. If you wrote a play, you made money through a stage. If you created the news, you needed a printing press to monetize it. If you wrote and performed a song, you needed a record. If you created a movie, you needed a theater.

Since all of that has changed, the ability to make money from content of all forms must be connected to the original content itself and not the form in which its presented, and this will require a major shift in the paradigms governing copyright. Formulas for determining value that are based on forms of presentation are simply unworkable, for the Web routes around such roadblocks, viewing them as impediments to the mission of putting packets together with consumers of packets. What difference would it make, for example, if a film was pirated, if the value of that film was connected directly to it, rather than associated with the form in which it was presented? This is a significant business challenge, but not one that is insurmountable. It simply takes a new pair of glasses.

This is at the heart of contemporary debate, and it is evidenced in the decision by the NBCU/News Corp streaming video platform Hulu.com to pull its videos from the online streaming browser Boxee. It wasn't Hulu's decision, for Hulu is merely a form of presentation; Hulu's "content partners" asked for it. But Boxee is also a form of presentation, and while Boxee actually enhances Hulu's content by optimizing it for viewing on a television set, Hulu's content partners view it as another way to squeeze profit from copyright.

Hulu has also removed its content from the CBS-owned video aggregator, TV.com, and the logic here is the same. Hulu thinks it can create sufficient scarcity to force people to its own property, where it can then make money. If their videos go elsewhere, they want compensation, but this is contrary to the nature of the Web.

There are currently three ways to make money via copyrighted "content." One, the consumer of that content pays directly (movies, books, subscriptions, etc.); two, a third-party pays to present the content to consumers (syndication); or three, a third-party pays in order to access the eyeballs of those who are consuming the content (advertising). These three methods all stem from the laws of mass marketing, but the Web is not a mass-marketing medium, no matter how much traditional media moguls say it is or try to enact laws that make it so. The one-to-many model simply doesn't work online, because connectivity is horizontal.

There is no stage in the online world, and value propositions based on such are unworkable. Content has been freed from the limitations of the stage, and the sooner we all accept that, the sooner we can get on with the task of creating ways to pay for the costs of creating content.

We must find a way to attach a value to original content in such a way that, no matter how it is consumed, the copyright owners are compensated. That value must be fair and, in the meritocracy that is the Web, be able to produce profit, if the users (a.k.a. "the people formerly known as the audience") deem it of sufficient quality. Most people think this should come in the form of micropayments, but that concept assumes a virtual box office, a bottle neck that the Web would view as inefficient and route around. It would also require an elaborate rights management system to protect the copyright owner, and this has already been deemed unworkable by the music industry.

In "The Remarkable Opportunities of Unbundled Media" in 2005, I wrote of six ways to make money in a truly unbundled, application separation world, and these still make sense today.

1. Ads in or around the unbundled items
2. Expand distribution channels and the number and type of items offered

3. Charge for some unbundled items
4. Ads as unbundled items
5. Helping users rebundle
6. Smart Aggregators and Ad feeds

Of these, I believe number four and number six hold the greatest revenue possibilities for media companies. Already, consumer industries are creating their own media for distribution, and this will be a growing business, perhaps even harkening back to the day when advertisers paid for their own programs that were distributed via the fledgling broadcast networks. Number six is so potentially lucrative that it alone could support the artistic endeavors that drive media companies in a mass marketing world.

There is also considerable potential in number five, and this is what Hulu, TV.com and Boxee both help consumers do. Getting into this business is smart for media companies who want in on the new distribution models, but (so far), they're blinded by the old mass media scarcity concept, which is what produces the kinds of problems we're seeing with Hulu's "content partners." *If you seriously want a share of helping users rebundle, then you must be prepared to put your own material out there for rebundling by others, too.*

In Media 2.0, the stage is separate from the play itself, and enterprises that support this will prosper.

This is the only thing that makes sense to the Web, and what's stopping it is the fear of the copyright industry, a fear based in the misguided belief that it will destroy the money tree known as charging for every form of presentation. The only group that would be impacted by such a system are the lawyers paid to ferret out "offenders" who are simply trying to find a better way to serve the wants and needs of the people.

Like compound interest, residual payments for copyright are the Eighth Wonder of the World. They are built on assumptions that must be challenged in today's world, for they are formulas that support greed and nothing else. It's one thing to prevent other big institutional players from making money off the work of others — which is the intent of copyright — but it's entirely different when copyright law is used to prevent what essentially amounts to sharing. The latest silliness from the RIAA is that they "own" the music you buy, and that you are merely purchasing the right to listen to it. This is the ludicrous end of trying to control the forms in which products are consumed (I own the socks; you're purchasing the right to wear them). The people formerly known as the audience have figured out that the music's the thing, not the packages in which it comes.

The worst thing about such assumptions is that clinging to them prevents us from moving forward with the new.

Copyright owners should be able to set the price for consumption of their goods and services, but once that price is set, it shouldn't matter which channels or forms I choose to consume those goods and services. It's called commerce. You sell; I buy. It's mine. Application separation indeed changes everything, but it does not necessarily follow that it has to mean a loss for the people who create that which has been separated. This is doable for the artists of society, but artists are generally terrible business people, so the business of creativity has had very little to do with creativity or the artists themselves. It has become the purview of smart business people who view creative endeavors as their property.

NBC President and CEO Jeff Zucker is in the business of art, and his views are shared by those within his community. Hulu.com is one of his babies, and he is well-aware of this whole application separation business as it relates to his ability to make money for NBCU. In a 2007 speech, he made a statement that has been parroted by the mass media crowd ever since. Zucker said that the industry had to "effectively monetize" digital media "so that we do not end up trading analog dollars for digital pennies." (3)

There is a huge difference between analog dollars and digital pennies, but it has nothing to do with value, for analog dollars come in opaque boxes while digital pennies are transparent. This is a greater fear for the mass marketing world than the actual dollars versus pennies argument, for atomized and transparent content does not play well with blue smoke and mirrors — the kind of stuff that these businesses use to create wealth for themselves.

So Zucker's statement is more precisely that he doesn't want to trade opaque dollars for transparent pennies, and this is the problem for all mass media that is supported by advertising. Whether it's print or broadcast, the opaque nature of the sale is what allows the media companies to grow their businesses, and the more opaque, the better. The old saw about not knowing which 50 percent of the audience sees your ad is what has built media empires, despite the metrics of circulation or program ratings. There are uncertainties built into such measurements that can be exploited to hide realities that the publisher or programmer would rather keep hidden.

But application separation allows extreme precision, and this is both the great strength and the great weakness of the Web. The ability to serve and track ads separate from the pages on which they are served has changed the balance of power in the publisher-advertiser relationship, and those opaque dollars are flying out the window with remarkable speed.

With transparency comes the ability to determine costs, and this terrifies those whose business models are built on opaque sales. After all, if one can determine cost, one can determine profit, and that's a public relations nightmare that high margin companies can't afford.

Another problem for the "analog dollars and digital pennies" argument is that at the heart of the personal media revolution is a satisfaction with those pennies. It's a growth market for those with low barriers to entry, including costs. Mass media does not want to truthfully examine costs, for those costs support the infrastructure that allows for the making of money in the first place. A printing press used to be a license to print money. Same with a broadcast tower (and license). All that has changed, and to the new participants in the media game, those pennies look like a lot of money.

The stage has long been a necessary part of our culture, and in some ways, it'll always be with us. However, it's importance as the gathering place for crowds has been replaced by entirely new methods that cater to the wants and needs of the people formerly known as its audience

We don't need no stage anymore.

PROTECTING THE STAGE

M y two brothers and I played in a bluegrass band as teenagers in the early 1960s. We played at various coffeehouses, hootenannies, and gatherings around the state of Michigan. I loved the stage, and, rather than fearing the audience, I connected with them on many levels. We also played on the morning show on WZZM-TV every Friday, which is where I first tasted local television. I was a fortunate young man.

Life in a band is life on a stage, and the stage is always more important than the band.

In Kalamazoo, for example, we played on the same stage that hosted Peter, Paul & Mary and a host of major folk music acts from the period. It was The Side Door coffeehouse, and people patronized the place to participate in the music of the day. It was the stage that built the audience that paid the acts, and so it goes. The "stage" at WZZM-TV provided a much bigger audience, and the size of the audience determines the value of the stage.

The theater was one of the earliest forms of mass media, whether it was for entertainment or information. A soap box is a form of a stage. The newsreels of the mid-20th century kept movie-goers informed of the latest events from around the globe through the miracle of film. The world was getting smaller, it seemed, and the stage played a big role in that.

All mass media companies perform from various stages, and this metaphor is especially useful in understanding the disruptions to media and, especially, the advertising that used to support it. It's even more useful in understanding contemporary journalism and the arguments about values in the new world. Is the stage impartial, for example, even though the actors are not?

David Cushman, Digital Development Director at Bauer Consumer Media in England, noted in a June 2008 presentation that people aren't looking at the stage anymore; they're looking at each other, and this poses the real threat to one-way, traditional media. In mass media, Cushman wrote, the message is broadcast "at" the audience, but in social media, the message doesn't arrive. (1)

So in the network that is the Web, where empowered people (the people formerly known as the audience) can restrict outside access to themselves, the only way to transmit the message is through the conversation that exists inside the limits put in place by the people in the network. This is no easy task, especially when the people in the network are doing everything they can to block the message. It's also why arguments about forcing people to pay for journalism are ridiculous. Pay? No thanks. I'll do without.

Cushman's reference is to social media, and social networking is currently viewed as only a part of the whole. But remember the words of the creator of the World Wide Web, Tim Berners-Lee. "The Web is more a social creation," he wrote, "than a technical one." No one has described it better than Kevin Kelly in his seminal 2004 *Wired Magazine* article "We Are The Web." (2)

The Web continues to evolve from a world ruled by mass media and mass audiences to one ruled by messy media and messy participation. How far can this frenzy of creativity go? Encouraged by Web-enabled sales, 175,000 books were published and more than 30,000 music albums were released in the US last year. At the same time, 14 million blogs launched worldwide. All these numbers are escalating. A simple extrapolation suggests that in the near future, everyone alive will (on average) write a song, author a book, make a video, craft a weblog, and code a program. This idea is less outrageous than the notion 150 years ago that someday everyone would write a letter or take a photograph.

What happens when the data flow is asymmetrical — but in favor of creators? What happens when everyone is uploading far more than they download? If everyone is busy making, altering, mixing, and mashing, who will have time to sit back and veg out? Who will be a consumer?

No one. And that's just fine. A world where production outpaces consumption should not be sustainable; that's a lesson from Economics 101. But online, where many ideas that don't work in theory succeed in practice, the audience increasingly doesn't matter. What matters is the network of social creation, the community of collaborative interaction that futurist Alvin Toffler called prosumption. As with blogging and BitTorrent, prosumers produce and consume at once. The producers are the audience, the act of making is the act of watching, and every link is both a point of departure and a destination.

In the network, the stage is irrelevant, except when the people formerly known as the audience choose to make it relevant. Major news events make the stage momentarily relevant, for example, but news organizations can't survive on the revenue from such events, because they usually come commercial-free.

The owner of the stage can set the rules for the performers on the stage, but when nobody sees the stage, those rules can become a net liability.

This has staggering implications for journalism. If the stage is what gives the Fourth Estate its power to confront the powerful, then what does culture do without big, powerful stages? Moreover, if the burden of the message shifts from the stage to the people who used to make a living on the stage, do individuals in the network have the clout to change the world? The power of the stage protects its performers, but is the First Amendment strong enough for those who don't buy ink by the barrel? Does the work of journalists within the network reflect back on the stages of those who employ them, and if it does, is that really relevant? And what about ethical considerations beyond the stage?

When the Facebook policy of *The New York Times* was made public recently, it revealed the nature of the stage and what it expects from those who perform on it. Pay close attention to the need of the stage to "be" impartial.

> Another problem worth thinking about is how careful to be about Facebook "friends." Can we write about someone who is a "friend?"
> The answer depends on whether a "friend" is really a friend. In general, being a "friend" of someone on Facebook is almost meaningless and does not signify the kind of relationship that could pose a conflict of interest for a reporter or editor writing about that person. But if a "friend" is really a personal friend, it would.
> Should we avoid consenting to be Facebook "friends" of people in the news we cover? Mostly no, but the answer can depend on the situation. A useful way to think about this is to imagine whether public disclosure of a "friend" could somehow turn out to be an embarrassment that casts doubt on our impartiality (emphasis mine). (3)

The whole document is a textbook example of why mainstream media is increasingly irrelevant to the people formerly known as the audience. *The New York Times* needs to protect the alleged impartiality of its stage, but its messages don't get through to people, because they don't even see the stage anymore. So the *Times* is stuck. What it needs to do is let its employees loose, so that the *Times* can enter into all those discussions in the network. In so doing, however, it must give up the insistence that the impartiality of the stage is paramount, and that's unlikely to happen.

The stage is what matters to traditional media. It's the driver of its pursuit of impartiality. An impartial stage, after all, is home to others, including advertisers, and this is no accident. The purity of the stage for advertisers is a vital concern to the people who shell out millions of dollars to be associated with it. Martha White flour has been a sponsor of the Grand Ol' Opry for decades, because it values what the stage at the Opry represents. The artists are expected to live up to those values or risk never being invited back. Proctor and Gamble doesn't want its products associated with ranting and raving vulgarity, something it is assured won't happen on the stage of, for example, *The New York Times.*

Journalistic ethics are all about the impartiality of the stage, not the individual journalists. That's why the *Times* needs to influence the behavior of its employees in the network. Nothing can cast "doubt on our impartiality." Without an impartial stage, the paper believes its advertisers will bolt, so the decision is about business, not some holy calling assigned to people who are trying to document history.

The people formerly known as the audience expect an impartial stage. Why? Because we've told them that's the way it's supposed to be. The problem, of course, is that people don't believe it anymore.

So what are journalists to do in the network? Without a stage, there is no institutional wall of ethical protection. One, therefore, cannot pretend to be what one is not. This is the truth and the challenge of ethics in a networked world.

The stage says, "I am impartial."

The individual says, "I'm trying to be impartial."

Artificiality is a curse in the Network.

Your personal brand is everything.

This is why the values of honesty, transparency and authenticity are so important for contemporary professional journalists. The institution may be able to proclaim its perfection, but human beings cannot, so it's a matter of the expectations of the people formerly known as the audience. The time is coming when "the message" will be delivered through individuals in the conversation that is the network, This has already taken place on a certain level via the blogosphere, but many bloggers seem unable to resist the idea of replicating old media through their own efforts. Building a (media) business means building an audience and with an audience comes, well, a stage. Along the way, they run into the same problems that confront traditional media in its need to provide a sterile environment for advertising. Madison Avenue is terribly suspicious of bloggers, although that view has softened somewhat over the years.

TechCrunch is a stage. Gawker Media is a host of stages. The Huffington Post is a stage. The latter is actually a hybrid. Its writers each have their own smaller stages, but by combining their works in one place, they've built a bigger stage. This bigger stage exposes them to potentially new readers, and so it goes.

As each of these "new" media companies trots down the well-worn path of traditional media, they run into the same issues that plague the old-schoolers. The difference, of course, is that the new players don't have the overhead of the old boys, so their model is more easily sustainable. Nevertheless, the essence of the network is to shun stages, not so much for the acts they bring but for all the marketing messages that tag along. This is — and will be — the essential problem for media, for ad-supported content is a business model in decay.

The network is not one of stages but of tribes, and this is a better metaphor for new media. Tribes have leaders (or many leaders), and it is the leaders themselves, not their stages that give them authority. This has not gone unnoticed by Madison Avenue.

Wikipedia refers to the identifying and selling to leaders as "Influencer Marketing":

> Influencer Marketing, as increasingly practiced in a commercial context, comprises four main activities:
> - Identifying influencers, and ranking them in order of importance.
> - Marketing to influencers, to increase awareness of the firm within the influencer community
> - Marketing through influencers, using influencers to increase market awareness of the firm amongst target markets
> - Marketing with influencers, turning influencers into advocates of the firm.
>
> Influencer Marketing is enhanced by a continual evaluation activity that sits alongside the four main activities. (4)

This has dubious possibilities, and many smart advertisers are instead just joining the network as participants, some with remarkable success. Smart media companies will do the same thing, but the rules of engagement will have to change in order for the move to be effective.

There's a "creepy" factor that enters into marketing directly to individuals, as Joe Marchese recently pointed our MediaPost.

I think it's actually pretty simple not to be creepy. It's a lot like not being creepy in real life. Don't do anything online you wouldn't do in the real world. You wouldn't slap your brand on someone's back without asking that person's permission. You'd be creepy if you inserted yourself into a conversation, just because you overheard it, without being invited in. Just picture it for a minute. It really boils down to respect for people, their influence and their privacy.

And that is a plain language description of ethical behavior in a networked world, and rules by which journalists, independent or those who work for a stage, will have to live by downstream. It's not about protecting the purported impartiality of the stage anymore. It's about the conversation.

I catch myself wondering every once in awhile about what it would be like to be young and have a bluegrass band today. I'd love to have had YouTube, Facebook, and a bluegrass blog. Who knows? Maybe we'd still be pickin' and a-grinnin' today.

Or not.

PERSONAL WALLED GARDENS

In Frances Hodgson Burnett's *The Secret Garden,* Archibald Craven sealed up his wife's walled garden after her death and hid the key. (1) Being inside was too painful, for the memories of his wife were too difficult to bear. To Mary Lennox, however, it was a magical place, a safe harbor for her imagination and ultimately, her gardening skills. When she convinced Craven's sick son to go inside, Mary's magic impacted him as well, and he recovered from serious maladies.

So a wall around a garden serves different purposes, depending on who or what is inside. It can keep people or critters out and protect that which is inside, or it can invite others in and hold them there — protected from that which is beyond the wall.

The Berlin wall kept East Berliners in. The Great Wall of China kept invaders away from the Chinese Empire. Walls always serve one of those two purposes, with doorways of some sort regulating any coming and going.

This understanding is significant as one examines what's happening to media companies in the face of disruptive innovations, and it's even more important when looking far downstream, for sooner or later, all media companies will have to deal with a new form of walled garden that's becoming increasingly popular with the public, the personalized home page or "personal site."

Personalized Home Pages - Market Share (Comscore, January 2008)		
Service	Monthly Visitors	Market Share
MyYahoo	47,355,000	56.9%
iGoogle	21,987,000	26.4%
MyMSN	8,433,000	10.1%
MyAOL/Netscape	2,705,000	3.3%
Netvibes	2,545,000	3.3%
Pageflakes	203,000	0.2%
Total	83,228,000	100%

Take a look at these numbers from ComScore published by Tech-Crunch in January. MyYahoo is on top of the heap, largely because their personalized page has been around longer. What's significant is that MyYahoo is losing market share to the drag-and-drop AJAX technology of iGoogle (up 267%) and NetVibes, an extremely popular personalized home page without a major portal to drive traffic. iGoogle was Google's star performer last year, and it will continue to grow. Like everything else Google, iGoogle was built for users, not the company. It replaces the Google home page, so there's no advertising. It "belongs" to the users who build them. Here's the way Crunchbase describes the service:

iGoogle is a personalized home page that allows users to add tabs, themes and drag-n-drop widgets to their home page. The site has a whole bank of third-party widgets to choose from including widgets for news, tools, sports and lifestyle. Users can also add widgets for their favorite Google products including Gmail, Talk and YouTube. (2)

Other giant personal websites are MySpace, Facebook and other social networking entities. With widgets and developer applications, users generally control what's on the page, but not to the extent of iGoogle.

So why is this significant for media companies?

Media company websites are walled gardens with the mission of keeping people inside. The advertising ecosystem that the media company uses to make money is entirely within the walls, so it's necessary to keep people inside the walls to maximize revenue potential. This is why smart marketers will direct the traffic flow within the site, always offering more or forcing users deeper within the garden.

All mass marketing forms of media are, in essence, walled gardens with similar missions. In the early days of television, when there were only three networks, it was easy to keep people tuned in. And in the early days of TV news, image promotions ruled the roost, until more smart marketers discovered that topical promotions could "drive" viewers from one daypart to the next.

Newspapers rarely offer completed stories on one page, because turning pages is what's necessary to keep readers within its walled garden. Radio stations, magazines and even the Yellow Pages all exist as gardens with walls designed to keep people within (where they will be exposed to the ads).

This model is what I have long called "Media 1.0." It is the basic business model of traditional media, and it runs counter to "Media 2.0," that which is disrupting the old models.

So this personalized home page — and especially Google's growing model — is a serious threat to media, because these pages are designed to do just the opposite of media sites: keep others out, including advertisers. The more people have control over what they view as "their" information, the more they reject the relentless carpet-bombing of marketing. This is going to get worse and worse, because J. D. Lasica's "personal media revolution" is really a revolt against being treated like a punching bag for years by those who used their walled gardens to do whatever they felt like doing, the people be damned.

Personal walled gardens also function as media companies, because the social Web is where the people formerly known as the audience (TPFKATA) gather. Each page has an "audience," usually made up of the creator's friends, family and tribe members.

True "mass" is difficult to obtain, but this is where traditional media companies must focus their attention.

So this poses a serious dilemma for all ad-supported media, for how will such companies survive if access to these walled gardens is blocked?

This was first covered in an essay I wrote three years ago called "The Remarkable Opportunities of Unbundled Media." What I discussed then was largely theory, but the growth of personal web pages has turned theory into practical reality. The only thing that has changed is the urgency with which media companies need to embrace the concepts of unbundled media.

Unbundling will take place at the most basic levels, and technologies will flourish that assist people in rebundling according to their preferences.

Our response as media professionals has been to sigh and offer repurposed media items to the noisy crowd that used to be our consumers. This is a grave mistake, for it shortsightedly views the drift to unbundled media as a sideshow. It is not; it's the whole enchilada, and while we're busy toying with it, people we never imagined would be our competitors are grabbing market share. Can you say "Yahoo!"?

The problem is that while we're repurposing our content, the bulk of our attention is still focused on the creation of that which is bundled. That's where the money is, we convince ourselves, and so we don't ask the right questions.

Creating ways for people to access the content we create inside their walled gardens is only one part of the problem. The real conundrum is making money, because what "works" best in such a world is not that which is advertiser-supported. Advertisers themselves may actually find it easier to penetrate the walls than media companies carrying advertising, as demonstrated by the many applications created by advertisers for MySpace or Facebook. Trusted brands will find their way inside personal walled gardens, bypassing the traditional media venues formerly required to distribute their messages. Remember, even a personal web page is a form of media. The Web makes the middleman obsolete.

The world of personal walled gardens demands our attention and our study. Information widgets are a way to make our content available, so we desperately need to be in the widget business. The Weather Channel has a remarkable radar widget that I use on my iGoogle page. ESPN offers my sports news. I get entertainment news from E! Take the time to peruse the widget gallery that Google offers (they call them "gadgets") for personal pages with a single mouse click. Search "local news," and you'll find a host of local media companies making RSS feeds available via widget.

But such widgets are just a small corner of what's possible, if we only have eyes to see. Traditional media is brand-obsessed, and, to a certain extent, justifiably so, but our brands can also blind us to possibilities that others — mostly outsiders — can easily see. The mission is to make money and to do it in ways that make sense, whether associated with content we create, aggregate, or organize.

The possibilities for *relevant local* information are mind-boggling. How about a school lunch menu widget, a garage sale widget, a "things to do" widget, or even an obits widget? How about customizable widgets that draw from databases of local knowledge and information we maintain? As long as we limit what we can do to the content we create through our newsrooms, we'll miss real opportunities to be relevant to the people formerly known as the audience. (3)

The Web is an evolving entity, and we're currently in the third stage of evolution:

> Browsing
> Searching
> Sharing

The first two work with walled gardens that house knowledge and information. The latter, however, is the home of the personal walled garden, and this should inspire us, not scare us. Media companies should insist that every employee create a personal page, because you really can't understand the value of the entity until you're using it yourself.

Advertisers will pay for access to personal pages, and the only issue is how soon they'll discover they can do this without us. There is a window of opportunity, and it's all a part of the remarkable world of unbundled media.

And there's another reason we must explore this path: the most sacred of all personal walled gardens is a person's mobile device. We must tread lightly here.

Reinventing
Journalism

THE TWO STAGES OF JOURNALISM

I studied butterflies as a little boy growing up in Grand Rapids. Like other insects, these beautiful creatures begin life as larvae, what we call caterpillars, and some of them are downright ugly. I raised many varieties, because it was more fun to grow them than to chase them and kill them. A caterpillar doesn't become a butterfly until it passes through metamorphosis, a process that we don't fully understand.

Many things in life duplicate stages of growth, because we're generally process-oriented in the way we think and behave. One of them is journalism.

There's a difference between the news and an account of the news, between the event or a report about the event. Journalism is the trade that crafts the stories, the accounts, and the reports of the news, but the "story" is just a part of the process, and defining that process by its finished products alone is a significant tripping stone in discussions about the future. The news transcends all associated narratives. It simply is what it is.

When referencing an event, we call it "the story," and that is understood amongst all the practitioners of journalism. The problem is when we confuse our story — our account or report — with "the" story, because they can be two very different things. Stories demand completion, but the news never ends. It comes and goes in the timeline of life that we call history, but no news story ever really ends for everybody.

Stories require storytellers, and there are plenty of them around. That the best seem to choose fiction isn't by chance, for imagination is the common denominator of all good storytellers.

Joe Friday used to say, "Just the facts, ma'am," but Joe was a cop, not a storyteller. The moment Joe's facts get blended with a writer's prose, we have a problem. This problem has become acute in the age when anybody can participate in the fact-gathering process.

Collin Siedor was the best, most imaginative storyteller I ever worked with. The guy is simply a great writer and he always recognized the difference between "the" story and "a" story that he could tell. I recall a drowning in downtown Milwaukee one day that Collin covered. "The" story was the drowning, but Collin's piece was how the event disrupted the normally peaceful lives of those who live and work along the river. The beauty here was that Collin's story could be told in full fashion, within the context of the bigger story, and it's a great illustration of the difference between "the" story and an account associated with it. Collin's story was complete; it had a beginning, middle and end, while the story of the drowning would go on for days.

In discussions about journalism's future, we tend to overlook the reality that there are two stages of journalism — the gathering of the news and the creation of accounts of what has been gathered. The former is what has been completely disrupted by technology and the ability of anybody to be a reporter of the news. This includes everything from blogging to smartphone pictures and videos. The latter, however, is the "how" of journalism's presentation. It gets all of the discussion about how journalism itself will be supported, and that makes it hard to find solutions for an iffy tomorrow. Storytelling is still storytelling, but if we can separate presentation from gathering, options become much more visible.

A journalist is a keeper of a journal, a writer, a storyteller. This person functions in the finished product capacity, the one who writes an account of the news. In a recent piece for Salon, Dan Gillmor — the man who first wrote of "citizen journalists" in his seminal book *We, the Media* — asked the question "Who is a journalist? Does that matter?" (1)

Gillmor asked readers to help him come up with a name for people who are "creating valuable new information in the new-media ecosystem."

> This isn't only my problem, and it's more than just semantics. Asking the question in the right way has real-world impacts. So-called shield laws, for example, aim to protect whistle-blowers and the journalists whom they tell about government or corporate wrongdoing. Some states specify who counts as a journalist, which leaves out a huge range of people who effectively practice journalism nowadays; it also encourages a pernicious, back-door licensing of journalists. The right approach, if we need shield laws at all, is to protect acts of journalism.
>
> As digital media become ubiquitous and more and more of us communicate and collaborate online, every person is capable of doing something that has journalistic value. Quite reasonably, relatively few of these folks imagine themselves as journalists, and they'd laugh if you called them one.

The question is easier to answer if consideration is given to the difference between gathering the news and reporting it. Both are Dan's "acts of journalism," but it doesn't take a "journalist" to gather the news. People who pen narratives should be given no further rights for gathering the news than anybody else, and this will help us in the creation of laws and protections for the act itself.

The biggest special "right" granted journalists is access, and it's here where the challenges going forward will be greatest. In Lewisville, Texas last year, for example, the school board created special rules allowing principals to refuse interviews with anyone "if official press credentials are not presented or available." Blogger Steve Southwell says the rules are aimed at him and other bloggers in an effort to quash unfavorable coverage. Southwell does original reporting on his blog and requested interviews with three principals about campus policies for visits from religious organizations. Southwell's blog regularly takes on the Lewisville school district, and in passing the new rules, they've conveniently painted Southwell with a "non-journalism" brush and decided they don't need to speak with him. (2)

It's incidents like these — and there are many more than you might think — that highlight the problem of assigning access to a elite group in an age when anybody can function as the press. We're going to have to revisit matters like this as a culture, because people like Southwell — regardless of the reason — are functioning more like the actual Fourth Estate than those who hold the presumed right to call themselves that.

Viewing journalism in two stages also reveals that it is in the story-TELLING that the problems of trust and the press exist. It's here where journalists run into trouble over things such as bias, plagiarism and the like. Some biases can be revealed in the events one chooses to cover, but news events themselves have little inherent meaning until the gifts of the storyteller are applied.

Truth-telling is the quest of the journalist, according to tradition, but truth is often lost in manipulative attempts to "write from the middle," and so, again, it is the story element of journalism that represents the greatest difficulty in the process of writing the day's first draft of history.

News gathering in the age of participation has to be viewed as separate from the product of "the news," because the latter cannot be protected at the expense of the former. We need those pictures of the jet that just crash-landed in the Hudson, or the demonstrations in Iran, or the view inside the subway trains after terrorist explosions in Spain. We also need the kind of school board coverage that the Steve Southwells of the world can provide, because nobody else is doing it. We need to protect the people with fortitude, not only those who function as props on institutional stages like *The New York Times*.

I'm with Dan Gillmor completely on this. "Acts" of journalism must be protected, regardless of who performs them, but we can protect the acts without labeling everybody a journalist. In so doing, we're going to find cultural niceties disrupted, as access is redefined. It's easy, for example, to take a picture on private property with a cellphone, but publishing that picture brings other issues into play.

As an old TV guy, I think that cellphone cameras level the playing field between print and video journalism. A print journalist, for example, can simply walk into a place and begin taking notes, but TV reporters need to bring those damned cameras along. With smartphones today, one's not necessarily immediately identified as a "TV guy," but we're still ethically obligated to identify ourselves in most circumstances.

Similar images from a "citizen journalist" pose an interesting dilemma for video storytellers, but the taking of those pictures needs to be protected, because news gathering is only part of the process of publishing journalism.

The act of gathering the news mirrors the concept of Continuous News, for real time news presentation is different than that which is fully vetted and finished, as you'd find in a newspaper or in a TV newscast. "The" story is the event being covered. Nothing is presented as a story told with a beginning, middle and end, because the process of gathering the news is what's being made public.

This differentiation is what provides such an opportunity for traditional news organizations, because it's possible to create and present two different products. The real-time, unfinished form is ideal for the Web. It suits not only the need to provide something for free but also the free-form, distribute-everywhere, everybody's-connected, everybody's-a-participant nature of the Web itself. The drift to real time in advertising also suits such a product.

The finished product — the home to the storytellers — suits any payment option that media companies require to support their commitment to journalism in a more traditional format. Viewing journalism in its stages, therefore, helps communicate the message of two different products that we'll need in the future.

THE NEW NEWS CURATOR

My passion for the creative and my love for all things nature came from trips as a boy to the Grand Rapids Public Museum. I owe a lot to that place — especially the traveling exhibits that came to my schools — and I always thought it would be cool to work at a museum.

This is on my mind of late, because I've been increasingly encountering the word "curator" as it relates to new journalism. A curator is a person in charge of organizing an exhibition, and we're all familiar with the term as it relates to museums. A museum curator is the person responsible for what's displayed and how it's displayed, and the same is true for journalism's new curators. A museum exhibits the past; journalism exhibits the new, and so the term is highly appropriate.

Here's how Webster's defines the word: (1)

> Main Entry: **cu·ra·tor** ◀) ◀)
> Pronunciation: \\'kyùr-,ā-tər, kyù-'rā-, 'kyùr-ə-\\
> Function: *noun*
> Etymology: Latin, from *curare* to care, from *cura* care
> Date: 1561
> : one who has the care and superintendence of something; *especially* : one in charge of a museum, zoo, or other place of exhibit
> — **cu·ra·to·ri·al** ◀) \\,kyùr-ə-'tòr-ē-əl\\ *adjective*
> — **cu·ra·tor·ship** ◀) \\'kyùr-,ā-tər-,ship, kyù-'rā-, 'kyùr-ə-\\ *noun*

The word is increasingly finding its way into discussions of new media, because it emphasizes more the role of what's displayed than how it's displayed. Historical news curators are called "editors," but in contemporary discussions about what's happening with journalism, the role of the editor is often about how it's displayed more so than what's displayed. I'm referring to the vetting of reporters' work, the policing of copy and providing the "check and balance" that those critical of, say, bloggers like to use to argue for the supremacy of the old.

But the role of the curator in the news business is of vast importance today, and it will become even more important tomorrow. The "collection" that yesterday's editor had to display came from wire services, press releases, regional affiliations, group connections and, of course, her own staff. But the collection of today's curator is much, much broader, because the explosive growth of personal media has turned anybody into a contributor. This is why contemporary arguments about journalism continue to miss the mark. We're hung up on *how* news content is to be displayed, when we should be paying more attention to the collection itself.

One of the early users of the term "curator" for journalists is new media visionary, Jeff Jarvis:

> Every priesthood, it seems, is having a fit over loss of its centralized control: How dare people pick what they like without history degrees or share what they know without journalism degrees! The nerve! (2)

Except the irony in this comparison is that journalists need to learn better curatorial skills. Yes, in a sense, they've always curated information, collecting it, selecting it, giving it context in their stories. But now they have to do that across a much vaster universe: the internet. I hear all the time about the supposed problem of too much information online. Wherever you see a problem, I advise, seek the opportunity in it. There is a need to curate the best of that information (and even the people who gather it). We have many automated means to aggregate news (including Daylife, where I'm a partner). Curation is a step above that, human selection. It's a way to add value.

So the editor of the past and the journalist of the past had to curate news directly from sources of news and witnesses. Today's curator must also examine the "reporting" of millions of new voices in the mix. Don't think so? Where are people going these days during times of breaking news? Twitter, of course, where the fire hose of output is filled with all kinds of "reporting." And Twitter is but a small example of personal media.

In the "New News Organization" (NNO) model that Jarvis has come up with, the curator role is front-and-center. The image below is from Jeff's PowerPoint, and it shows the news ecosystem in a hypothetical market. The NNO aggregates and filters news coming from the community itself. This includes hyperlocal sites, blogs, social media sites like Twitter and Facebook, and much more. That filtering is the role of the curator. Jeff — and I think rightly — views the New News Organization as equally generating its own content and curating that which the community itself creates.

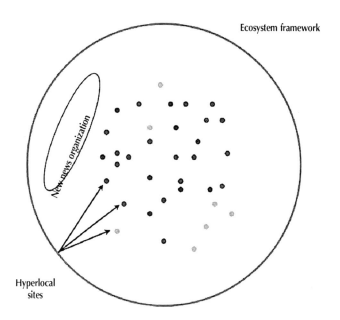

Curating the community is different than curating sources of vetted journalism.

1. It's continuous — When editors view the work of their subordinates, they're vetting completed stories. Curating the community, however, requires vetting the process of newsgathering, not the finished product. This means that some traditional vetting has to be done in-house, and not in the field.

2. It's unfinished and never-ending — Community news is real-time news, so there's never a "finished product" goal, except as it relates to the finished products of the enterprise doing the curating. But even when that is put to bed, the process of curating continues. To parrot the late Ellen Goodman: It's a bit "like being married to a nymphomaniac; Every time you think you're done, you have to start all over again."

3. It's harder — while I'm certain tomorrow's curators will get to know the people whose work they are curating, there's no question the job is more difficult than simply functioning as a editor over a staff of professional journalists. Decisions carry different consequences, because aggregating the community is never going to be like the manufacturing process for creating finished product news.

4. It's personal — One of the reasons it's harder is because it's personal. In today's professional journalism world, we're taught that we are NOT what we do, but as identity shifts to a blended reality, we WILL become what we do. Personal media will carry the identity of its makers, and I think this may be a bigger deal than we think. Personalities as part of the news? Who knew?

5. It's listening instead of broadcasting — Traditional media curators/editors are vastly more concerned about how THEY are reflected to the community, so most of our policies and procedures are about the outbound display of our exhibition. New news curators will have to be highly skilled at listening, because separating the gems from the noise will require the ability to gets one's arms around the enormity of that which is being created. My community recently went through a

snow event, and the school system was roundly criticized on Twitter for not responding quickly enough. A contemporary curator wouldn't know that unless they "listened" to the community of Twitter users.

6. It's a lasting value proposition — The value prop here is that "we will curate the fire hose that is 'news and information' and present it to you in an on-going, consumable fashion." This is the mantra of the New News Organization, and it should be ours already. This is the good news of being the new news curator. It guarantees relevance for tomorrow, because we're right in the thick of all the creating that's taking place across the community. It's as if the people formerly known as our audience are telling us what the news should be, and while that may seem a bit like the sheep leading the sheep to elitists, it is very much a part of the new world into which we are being thrust.

Curators — if future curating is to be a purely human endeavor — are the people to which philosopher Clay Shirky refers when he speaks of the fallacy of "information overload."

By the time that the publishing industries spun up in Venice in the early- to mid-1500s, the ability to have access to more reading material than you could finish in a lifetime is now starting to become a general problem of the educated classes. And by the 1800s, it's a general problem of the middle class. So there is no such thing as information overload, there's only filter failure, right? Which is to say the normal case of modern life is information overload for all educated members of society.

…So, the real question is, how do we design filters that let us find our way through this particular abundance of information? And, you know, my answer to that question has been: the only group that can catalog everything is everybody. (3)

"Filter failure" is a common theme of Shirky's, and he's absolutely correct. And this is the opportunity for the New News Organization and for all journalists of tomorrow. Technology can "filter," but it takes (at least so far) human interaction to turn filtered information into that which can be consumed and understood by others. Everybody may be participating in that, but to date, the best filters are those — such as Gabe Rivera's TechMeme, which groups together news items by idea or "meme" — by someONE who can provide an element of human knowledge and understanding.

I've recently been discussing the curating of YouTube with a former film student, Jimmy Harris, whose life is YouTube. YouTube allows users to "connect" various actions with Twitter and Facebook, so when Jimmy reviews a video via his YouTube channel, he automatically tells those who follow him via Twitter (@thebluearmy) or Facebook that "this clip is worth watching." In so doing, he's vetting the fire hose that is YouTube and filtering results for friends. There is a future business model here, I'm certain, and I hope Jimmy finds it.

To young people just beginning this adventure, my advice is always to "go forth and make media," because, well, they can. I do believe, however, that for some, the idea of beginning life as a curator has significant potential for the future, for the personal brands of all the writers will need the personal brands of all the curators to help people access their work.

And so the New News Organizations and the personal curators will exhibit the work for many others to see, just as the guy did who made my childhood so rich at the Grand Rapids Public Museum. Come to think of it, I owe my all to a rather large group of curators of all different stripes, although I never met them, knew their faces or even knew their names. The question for the journalists of tomorrow is Will that be sufficient for you?

Social Media Guidelines

S ocial networking sites have become an important point of contact for millions of people worldwide. Prior to sites like Facebook, MySpace, Twitter and many others, our contact with our audience was from us to them, as a mass. Social networking, however, connects everybody to each other, including us, and our future relevance as a news organization rests in how we respond. Not only can people we once considered our audience talk back to us, but they can also talk to each other at the same time.

This is changing the very nature of journalism and the journalist, for the creation of a detached and objective "first draft of history" that was the sole work of professional journalists is now competing with an on-going chronicle of events as written by all. We find it necessary to participate in both at this point, and we strongly question whether participation in the latter can be done following only the mandates of the former.

Let us begin by stating that any guidelines we publish will have to be flexible and adaptable, for this is a world that is evolving rapidly. What seems right today may be completely wrong tomorrow, so bear that in mind as we proceed.

Traditional media and social media may appear to be different sides of the same coin, but a closer examination reveals a more complex reality. If we were to assume, for example, that social networking was merely an extension of our roles and duties as journalists, we would be completely justified in considering the publication of anything on any website by an employee to be an extension of our own publication, whether it was print or broadcast. Moreover, if we were to assume that social networking was merely an extension of our personal lives, then we would be justified in bringing the same rules to bear that have applied to the private lives of journalists historically. As professional journalists, we've always given up certain rights to maintain the appearance of impartiality in our work. We don't work for political candidates; we don't march in social issue parades; and so forth.

Social networking is indeed both an extension of our work and our personal lives, but it is also a key component in the creation and maintenance of this new, on-going chronicle. We want and need to be a part of that, for the chronicle builds the first draft of history at the end of the day. To be sure, we could simply sit back, observe and write, but we also believe that journalism and journalists have a significant place in defining the agenda of what is or isn't to be included in that first draft. In order to be a part of that in the social networking world, we must participate in the process and not simply observe from a distance.

Another factor contributing to this document is our acknowledgement that social networking and social media are personal, not institutional. As much as we want and need for people to connect with us as an organization, the reality is that people connect with people on a different, more personal level than they do with institutions. This personal connection is a necessary part of participation in the daily chronicle of which we speak here.

We must further consider and acknowledge the growth of the independent voice in the contemporary evolution of journalism and that these voices represent constituencies but not necessarily traditional media organizations. They have the ability to be nimble, fleet of foot, adaptive and flexible in the pursuit of their work, and they move in and out of the social networking world with ease. While no one can be certain of the role these people will play in journalism's future, it's clear they currently have an advantage over those bound by traditional rules. We have two choices: We can let this growth continue unchecked or we can free our employees to join the competitive fray.

Finally, at certain points in the management of organizations, it is necessary to lead rather than manage, for the end is a moving target in this new world, and frankly, we have insufficient knowledge to create the necessary processional steps to get us from here to there at this time. Leading demands a degree of risk-taking and a willingness to get out of the way rather than oversee every step in the development process. That is what this document is intended to accomplish.

Therefore, the following guidelines are offered for the use of social networking and social media by employees of this news organization:

1. The integrity of the newsroom must be protected. The matter of integrity is currently being debated at the highest levels of journalism, but until any new values or codes of conduct are determined, we must rely on traditional rules in the defense of the tenets of ethical journalism, whether that be with the public or in a court of law. We do the best we can with regards to fairly and impartially reporting the news, and whenever and wherever you speak — as a representative of this newsroom — you must do so as representing those rules and traditions.

2. At the same time, however, we recognize that simply because you are an employee of this newsroom, it does not necessarily follow that every time and everywhere you speak, you do so as a representative of the newsroom. If, however, you choose this defense as justification for reaching beyond the accepted practices and tenets of contemporary ethical journalism in your interaction with people via social networking, you do so without the protection that accompanies living within those rules. In other words, you are on your own and cannot later try to represent that you were acting in accordance with the actual or implied approval of the newsroom.

3. We reject the suggestion that arguments and positions ex-
    pressed by professional journalists disqualify them from
    fairly and impartially reporting the news. We believe that our
    audience not only understands but accepts this, and we will
    not allow special interests to exploit the artificial rigidity of
    the matter of objectivity to interpret for us what we mean.
    Fair means fair and impartial means impartial. We do our
    very best, but we make no pretense of perfection, and nei-
    ther do we permit those with clear biases to call into ques-
    tion our effort simply because it furthers their position.

In the pursuit of truth, the concepts of fairness and impartially have
been falsely twisted to assume that truth somehow always lies between two positions. We reject this as only benefiting those who
wish to have their position considered equal to any other. We will
vigorously defend this belief, regardless of its controversial nature,
for we trust the public — our audience — to judge whether our
reporting adequately considers the beliefs of the minority voice in
matters of controversy.

Journalists answer to no one other than their readers. They will
decide whether we are living up to the standards they expect, not
a panel of experts, fellow journalists or the government through
its courts. Our pledge to them is fair and impartial coverage of the
news, not strict adherence to rigid beliefs imposed by special interests. Our voice is authentic and our methods are transparent.

-   You are all smart people. Use common sense when making
    friends or interacting with them, for what may seem inno-
    cent today could return to harm you or this newsroom in the
    future. If you discover an association that you believe might
    become compromising, simply end the relationship and
    move along. If such an association is brought to our atten-
    tion, we will investigate and make recommendations, but it
    is not our goal to control with whom you have relationships;
    our strong preference is that you police yourselves and make
    smart decisions.
-   Criticize your employer or your co-workers at your own risk.
    Likewise, publicly display untoward behavior or otherwise

embarrass yourself and your employer at your own risk. The Web is only private up to a point, and our organization is no different than others who will by any means disassociate themselves from public embarrassments caused by employees.

• Use social networking and social media to develop and nurture your personal brands. You are encouraged to link back to us wherever possible, for that strengthens our brand, but we accept that your use of social networking and social media potentially benefits you far more than it does us. However, we think that strong personal brands make for a strong traditional media brand. The success of publications such as The Huffington Post suggest an audience for people following the individual brands that make up the whole, and we would be foolish to stifle that without careful consideration of its potential long term benefits first.

In closing, let us reiterate the opaque nature of social networking's future as it relates to journalism and our belief that we need most of all to remain adaptive and flexible at this time. Social networking and the personal media revolution have already altered journalism forever, and regardless of where it's all going, our wish is to be relevant in the end. We need your help and cooperation to do that.

THE CHAOTIC NEW ORDER

We have a new puppy in our house, thanks to my youngest daughter moving in a few weeks ago. Her name is Chibi, which is a Japanese Manga term meaning "a small person" or "little one." She is certainly that, a long-haired miniature dachshund that will be about eight pounds when she's all finished growing.

And growing, she is. My daughter wishes that she'd stay at her infant size, because it's amazing how much she's grown in just two weeks. She's fully twice the size she was when we brought her home.

This longing to keep things as they are is a part of the human condition, and it's the source of all nostalgia. In 1986, Eddie Money sang, "I wanna go back and do it all over, but I can't go back I know." People could relate to the emotion of being trapped on a moving train. After the Paris Exposition in 1900, Henry Adams had the revelation that life had passed him by. He wrote that "the law of nature is chaos, while the dream of man is order," and for media companies today, our dream of order is becoming one depressing nightmare.

The World Wide Web is evolving before our eyes. Some are very comfortable with this, but the truth is that most are not. Our culture likes to take its time — time to analyze new things that come along, milk them for everything we can get out of them, and then move on to the next thing, thank you very much. The Web, however, is moving at light speed, its seeming chaos threatening to suck the world as we know it into a vortex of swirling innovation. We're afraid that it will either destroy us or leave us behind. Or perhaps even both.

In the beginning was the blog, and the blog was with the creators, and the creators thought it was good. But the creators wanted more, and so they sought speed and freedom from the wires that enslaved them. Broadband and mobility were their next creations. And the bloggers looked upon the Web and saw that connecting with others was its real virtue, and so was born the social network. But the social net was limited by profiteers, and the creators wanted more. And so the simple text world of Twitter was birthed and prospered, followed by methods of tying everything together. The creators looked upon this, too, and saw that it was good.

There are common threads throughout these innovations:

- Communicating
- Connecting
- Empowering
- Enabling
- Participating
- Growing

But perhaps the most revolutionary trend that these innovations are creating is the shift from then to now, finished to unfinished, perfect to imperfect, fixed to process. Welcome to the world in real time, what I'm increasingly comfortable with calling "the processing Web." The market for news and information that is packaged will likely always exist, although it will never again live in the stratosphere of the information hierarchy. Information in real time renders all that packaging unnecessary and a waste of that most precious commodity, a person's time. Make no mistake about it: Time is the real driver here; technology is but its servant.

The mainstream press has all kinds of problems with this, of course, and these problems are getting in the way of embracing what is here to stay. That bastion of all that is holy about the professional press, *The New York Times,* took a well-considered shot at blogs recently in taking the processing Web to task for reporting rumors, specifically that Apple was in talks to acquire Twitter. The *Times* piece — presented as a factual article and not a commentary — lifted quotes from Michael Arrington of TechCrunch that fit its predisposition on the matter, and led Arrington to correct the record online. His piece contains this gem:

> We don't believe that readers need to be presented with a sausage all the time. Sometimes it's both entertaining and informative to see that sausage being made, too. The key is to be transparent at all times. If we post something we think is rough, we say so. If we think it's absolutely true, we signal that, too, while protecting our sources. (1)

This is an apt description of the difference between the real time presentation of information and that which has been fully vetted and packaged. Go read the Arrington article, for it's a primer on why traditional media is painting itself into the corner of irrelevance.

Arrington references a seminal piece by Jeff Jarvis on the subject that is also must-reading for the interested. Looking at the same *New York Times* article, Jarvis calls it "product versus process journalism: the myth of perfection versus the beta culture."

> This is journalism as beta. I make a big point of that in *What Would Google Do?* — that every time Google releases a beta, it is saying that the product is incomplete and imperfect. That is inevitably a call to collaborate. It is — even from Google — a statement of humanity and humility: we're not perfect.
>
> Ah, but there's the problem: journalism's myth of perfection. And it's not just journalism that holds this myth. It is the byproduct of the means and requirements of mass production: If you have just one chance to put out a product and it has to serve everyone the same, you come to believe it's perfect because it has to be, whether that product is a car (we are the experts, we took six years to tool up, it damned well better be perfect) or government (where, I'm learning, employees have a phobic fear of mistakes — because citizens and journalists will jump on them) or newspapers (we package the world each day in a box with a bow on it — you're welcome). (2)

Jeff includes the diagram below that reveals the essence of process journalism. (3)

The new news process

This timeline refers to a "story" that is ultimately published in packaged form, but I think process journalism goes beyond that. There's no real need for packaging, because the audience is a part of the process of gathering the story. This concept is foreign to contemporary professional journalism, and it produces a unique cocktail of ignorance, condescension, and demagoguery from people who allegedly explore facts before reaching conclusions. There ought to be a law that you can't write about the Web, if you don't understand it.

I've been writing for years that the news business is evolving from a finished product to a process, so I'm obviously on the side of Jeff and Michael in this issue with the *Times*. As I tell clients, news has always been a process, but we've only let consumers in on the end of that process. The concept of Continuous News that we recommend to all of our clients lets those same consumers in on the news-gathering process. It's their way of participating in history with us, and we think that's a compelling reason for consumers to pay attention. We can even use this stream of thought to give people reasons to watch or read our packaged products and services. Along the way, our clients are learning all about unbundled media and the real time aspects of today's information world. Eyes are opening to the reality that waiting until everything is packaged for the six o'clock news or the morning paper is just an invitation to let somebody else seize the news agenda in our markets.

Moreover, the audience for online news is largely a Monday to Friday, 8 a.m. to 5 p.m. crowd, ideally suited to a news-as-a-process service.

Continuous News does not negate the need for packaged news. It's not "all or nothing," "one or the other." There is and will always be the need for that first draft of history. Humankind needs that record, but the record can be made after the public process. It will be complete, contain multiple points-of-view, and be pretty hard to manipulate by self-serving oligarchs, whether they exist in the public or private spheres of culture."

The processing Web is bigger than just the adventures of journalism, for its long-term ramifications impact every institution of our culture built on that which is packaged and perfect. Time is indeed the driver, for people are weary of their time taking a back seat to that of the institutions who claim to serve their needs. No profession is guiltier of this than the medical profession, and the calls for healthcare reform make it a logical candidate for disruption by the processing Web.

Online search gives time back to us, and for that we are grateful. No trips to the library, or scouring through the Yellow Pages or newspaper classifieds. No thumbing through cook books or browsing the encyclopedia that takes up space on the bookshelf. No visits to government offices to get forms, and no searching folders in a desk drawer to find that article you wrote five years ago.

The World Wide Web is a database, and any data that is entered can be accessed in real time. This is the path of all knowledge and information in the future.

My daughter knows that for as much as she's loved the puppy known as Chibi, the adult will bring her an equal, if not greater amount of joy. Dogs are like that. Life is like that. Opportunity is like that. May we all recognize it when it knocks at our door.

UNDERESTIMATING THE AUDIENCE

The debate about how we, as a culture, are going to fund journalism in the future is lacking discussion about certain assumptions, core beliefs about journalism that simply must be challenged, if we are to truly find our footing in a networked and distributed media world. These assumptions are fundamental to the profession of journalism and form its grand narrative. In postmodern discussion, a grand narrative — or metanarrative — is an comprehensive explanation of the experience and knowledge of a particular abstract idea. Wikipedia calls a *metanarrative* "a story about a story, encompassing and explaining other 'little stories' within totalizing schemes. (1)

Professional journalism's grand narrative is complex and multi-faceted, and it includes everything we take for granted about the business.

In his brilliant essay, "Audience Atomization Overcome: Why the Internet Weakens the Authority of the Press," (2) Jay Rosen explains that, in the age of mass media, the press was able to define the *sphere of legitimate debate* in the West, and that this is a key tenet of professional journalism's grand narrative. Rosen's central argument is that because the Web connects people horizontally, it undercuts the ability of the press to set the information agenda, and that this undermines its authority. This is the kind of assumption challenging that we all need.

> In the age of mass media, the press was able to define the sphere of legitimate debate with relative ease because the people on the receiving end were atomized — meaning they were connected "up" to Big Media but not across to each other. But today one of the biggest factors changing our world is the falling cost for like-minded people to locate each other, share information, trade impressions and realize their number. Among the first things they may do is establish that the "sphere of legitimate debate" as defined by journalists doesn't match up with their own definition.
>
> In the past there was nowhere for this kind of sentiment to go. Now it collects, solidifies and expresses itself online. Bloggers tap into it to gain a following and serve demand. Journalists call this the "echo chamber," which is their way of downgrading it as a reliable source. But what's really happening is that the authority of the press to assume consensus, define deviance and set the terms for legitimate debate is weaker when people can connect horizontally around and about the news.

But the Web is eating away at other "little stories" within the grand narrative that is professional journalism, all of which contribute to the issue of funding journalism tomorrow. Mass media is giving way to distributed media, and the Web is dramatically changing the make-up of the people formerly known as the audience.

For example, professional media begins with the crucial assumption that the people it serves — the masses, the audience — are uninformed, uninterested, emotional, and lacking in the intellectual capacity to sort through the complex issues of the day with sufficient clarity to make their own decisions in life, much less actually govern themselves. As knowledge is released upon the masses and access to information becomes easier and more widespread, the public has ways to inform itself that it never had before. This is new, and the elitist view that the press has of its audience has to change, or we will find ourselves eliminated from the growing stream that is news in the new world.

It would be easy to suggest that the press believes its audience to be stupid, but that implies a level of arrogance that may not be deserved. It's simply a matter of fact that any "elite" believes its existence necessary, because those not so fortunate as to be a part of the elite need them. This is fundamental colonialism, and it is at the heart of today's "second Gutenberg moment," for the masses are storming the bastille of authority that is based on protected knowledge.

It would also be easy to suggest that television's form of journalism is the principal offender in this arena. The need to "manage audience flow" throughout prime time, for example, gave birth to the late news "tease," an insulting form of unwanted interlude designed to manipulate viewers from one time period to the next. "Forty dead in an accident on highway 20, the details at 11" turns out to be pigs killed in a truck crash. But TV only copies the newspaper model of burying two paragraphs of a page one story on an inside page in an effort to expose eyeballs to the ads on that page.

Audience manipulation is a con game, and the audience is tired of being conned. And television news audiences have been telling us this for years. One visit to Nielsen to peruse the dairies of local TV news viewer will reveal just how much people hate being "teased" during prime time and during newscasts, and yet we consider this to be "best practices" in the creation of television newscasts.

In a fascinating article in AdAge about the current economic disruption, Jonah Bloom suggests that "Before Marketers Ask for Trust, Perhaps They Should Apologize." His words are also good advice for the people known as the press, for while most journalists deny it, we've been insulting people far too long.

While the roots of the professional press run deep, its principal author, Walter Lippmann, was an elitist social engineer. His early-twentieth-century debates with John Dewey set the underlying tone for professional journalism, and his books are a manifesto for the modernist, colonialist press. He referred to the public as a "herd" and wrote that for democracy to flourish, the herd's myths and emotions had to be put in check. An educated elite — and in Lippmann's mind, this included the press — was needed to lead.

Lippmann's personal and professional crony was Edward Bernays, the father of professional public relations. Like Lippmann, Bernays was a social engineer. Working on behalf of the business community, Bernays' beliefs dovetailed with Lippmann's and produced the seminal books *Propaganda* and *Manufacturing Consent*. "The conscious and intelligent manipulation," he wrote, "of the organized habits and opinions of the masses is an important element in democratic society." Who is to do Bernays' manipulation, if not Lippmann's educated elite. Who is to be its mouthpiece, if not the professional press?

The "objective" press that Lippmann envisioned flows from the colonialist essence of elitism. The promise to be "objective" is, in part, due to the view that people are incapable of determining the artificial center point between opposing points of view.

The "wall of separation" between news and sales is also another artificial attribute that exists, in part, because the audience can apparently be easily fooled by unscrupulous snake oil salesmen posing as journalists. The recent hubbub over Starbucks sponsoring "Morning Joe" on MSNBC is illustrative of the belief that the audience is incapable of deciding bias on its own and needs the protection of a press that is above reproach when it comes to conflicts of interest. In this area, the press has stood firm, while the audience seems vastly more concerned about political or cultural biases.

This belief, this core principle that an ignorant public "needs" its intelligent and, of course, helpful press is always present in the analysis of disruptive influences within contemporary culture that are impacting the press. It's why the United States Senate took the time to discuss the future of newspapers and why most observers from within the professional press establishment view the potential loss of newspapers as a threat to democracy itself. Hubris is a fruit of those who believe the ignorant need them.

The era of Lippmann and Bernays was the dawn of the industrial revolution. This can also be described as the age of the left brain in the human experience, for the process of manufacturing produced an economy based on mathematical margins and growth, one that rewarded the management of processes within the overall hegemony. If it existed, it could be measured, and if it could be measured, it could be managed. The worlds of Darwin, Freud and Jung fused with the worlds of Einstein, Edison and Ford, and science, logic and reason became the triumvirate gods of the culture.

If culture is to be "managed," somebody needs to do the managing, and this chore falls on the willing and self-serving shoulders of the cultural elite. Maintenance of such a status quo demands perpetuation of the ignorant class, for the health of the culture itself hinges on the authority of the managers, and that requires the obedient faith of the masses. Ignorance, therefore, is virtuous, for "they" are best kept in the dark on the deeper matters of the culture. This, too, is fundamental colonialism.

The bane of science is religion, with its ability to inflame emotions and inspire sacrifice. Early colonialists used religion to control the masses, but that began to change with the first Gutenberg moment. When the control mechanism of knowledge is placed in the hands of those being controlled, the result is very much counter culture. It's why John Wycliffe wrote, upon completion of the first common language English translation of the Bible, that "this book shall make possible government of the people, by the people and for the people," which Lincoln later lifted for his address at Gettysburg. The reformation was birthed from that paradigm shift, and from that burst forth the rise of the West. The willingness to risk in the name of knowledge grew from the faith of its practitioners, and what followed was an era of exploration and expansion that actually led to the industrial revolution and the rise of modernism in the first place. How ironic that, once empowered, a new elite, whose status is based upon (protected) knowledge, would wish to silence the very thing that helped put it in power in the first place.

It is through this veil — this colonialist grand narrative — that disruptive innovations brought about by technology and especially the Internet begin to make sense.

It's why professional journalism had to reject blogging. Here were everyday people in their pejorative pajamas writing about matters that — cough, cough — they were "untrained" to write about. The ignorant masses were raging against the institution. The rise of personal media and social media was originally the stuff of jokes and condescension, until they threatened to overtake the mainstream. None of the early bloggers had their sights set on taking over "the press," and yet that is how the threat was perceived. Why? Because the personal media revolution shattered the illusion of the ignorant mass.

It's why professional journalism rejects the current work of Gene Randall, for example, who is now doing corporate media as a way to support his family after CNN axed him several years ago. His report for Chevron (on YouTube) offset, from Chevron's perspective, a negative report on 60 Minutes earlier in the month. Randall has been vilified by former colleagues for "selling out," but his real sin is violating the grand narrative, because only the press can deliver the "real" story. The business community's relationship with the press is supposed to be symbiotic, but businesses are now a very real part of the personal media revolution, and Randall is seen as untrustworthy within the grand narrative.

When the fertile mind of J. D. Lasica first coined the phrase "personal media revolution" four years ago in his seminal work *Darknet, Hollywood's War Against the Digital Generation*, he was referencing a real revolt. Technology was enabling people to participate with media in a way that shifted the emphasis from a stage to a conversation. "We've entered an age," he told me, "where we continually shift between roles — as media makers, participants and producers, yes, but also as consumers and audience members." (3)

Lasica first wrote of this shift 12 years ago in a cover story for the *American Journalism Review*. "Net Gain" spelled out the opportunities that news organizations had to reinvent journalism for the digital age.

> Not only did news organizations fail to seize the historic moment, their very survival is now in question. Lots of factors contributed to the implosion: a disrespect for customers, as you say; the inability to reinvent newsroom culture, which rewards plodding, conservative approaches at the expense of risk taking and experimentation; the inability to embrace the values of participation,

transparency and openness that are at the heart of this historic shift in citizens' expectations and behaviors.

And yet, some nuance is called for. There are long-term forces at play that militate against mass media and toward unbundled, micro-chunked, fragmented personal media, the vast majority of which never becomes viral or widely popular. Craig Newmark did not set out to decimate newspapers' classified revenues when he started running online ads for free; yet, if he hadn't done so, someone else would have, and there's little the news industry could have done to head that off. The founders of Google could not have envisioned that search, and not content, would take the overwhelming amount of online advertising revenues.

So, some of this is what happens when you play your hand against tectonic forces. The real question is whether news organizations will team up with those forces — which are now becoming blindingly obvious — instead of continuing to play the same losing hand.

When Dan Gillmor wrote in his groundbreaking book *We, The Media* that "my readers know more than I do," (4) it was considered an affront to the mainstream. Gillmor, however, has been quick to point out that audiences have always been smarter than we give them credit for being and have always been more knowledgeable. What's different today is their ability to feed that knowledge to others through the software of the Web.

This new Gutenberg moment, however, is taking culture beyond even that, because knowledge that was once protected is now available to every day people. And so the grand narrative of the press that assumes an ignorant public runs smack into the horizontal connectivity of the World Wide Web and the explosion of heretofore protected knowledge that it contains.

Perhaps this ignorant mob isn't so ignorant after all, and that has staggering ramifications for the press of tomorrow. What would the press be like without this assumption? What would respect for the audience mean in terms of the "need" to provide balance? How would the "sphere of legitimate debate" to which Jay Rosen refers be defined in such a world? And, of course, who will fund journalism in a world where professionalism can no longer be used to define scarcity?

While no one can really answer those questions, it seems obvious that the values of honesty, transparency, and authenticity will be esteemed by all who participate in the craft of journalism in the years to come.

THE WEB'S WIDENING STREAM

Media companies attempting to reinvent themselves in the face of disruptive innovations must feel like they're playing cards with a 5-year-old who keeps changing the rules to avoid losing. How we wish the bloody thing would just sit still for a minute, so that we could study and adapt. It doesn't, however, and each week seems to bring something new that frustrates yesterday's "cutting edge" strategy.

"You can't do that," says little Johnny, his mind blocking our winning move. And while we stop to argue, Johnny has already made his next move. The privilege of playing cards with him comes with the price of always losing, or so it seems.

For media and the Web, it's not quite as bad, for the signs of change have been around for years. Despite admonitions to embrace new paths, media companies deliberately chose not to play, because the uncertainty of what appeared to be chaos was too great a price to pay. Today, we have media empires such as the *Associated Press* wanting Google to change the rules of search, so that they can come out on top. Rather than play the 5-year-old, we've instead become little Johnny ourselves.

During development of its "Longhorn" operating system in 2005, Microsoft adopted an RSS-friendly slogan that defined the company's view of the evolution of the Web:

> Browse
> Search
> Subscribe

The "Browse" phase of the Web was its first, and it's where the name of the desktop application known as the browser originated. The Web was seen as a series of roads leading to destinations, We hopped from site to site — or in the case of AOL, destinations within the site — and everybody was happy. "Visitors" to sites were welcomed through a front door, which became the most valuable online real estate in terms of advertising.

"Search" disrupted the paradigm by allowing people to access documents within a site without going through that front door. We were still visiting sites, though, because that's "where" the content resided. Search destroyed the value of the home page, and also allowed for advertising adjacent to search results — a way of monetizing content that existed only in link form on the pages of the search. If you wanted to buy ads next to football content, you didn't need to buy football pages, for example. You could simply buy ads on search results for football.

"Subscribe" blew everything apart, because users no longer had to even visit websites, assuming publishers were willing to make their content available in RSS form. Most major publishers refused to play the game, so media company RSS feeds have generally contained only a sentence or two, thereby forcing users back to the site of origin, where publishers can monetize pages. This irritating practice has kept publishers from exploring revenue possibilities in a truly subscriber-based environment, and it's the key thing holding back the development of RSS.

But a new paradigm is threatening all of the others and will eventually force all publishers into the unbundled media world. The staggering popularity of social media messaging via Facebook and MySpace "status updates" and, of course, Twitter is creating an information ecosystem that is a series of real-time streams. These streams come in short bursts, but when added to the RSS of Microsoft's "subscribe" phase of the Web, they form powerful, relevant and meaningful sources of knowledge and information for an increasingly networked world.

Edelman web guru Steve Rubel calls the "browse" phase "the destination Web," and he wrote last month that this era was drawing to a close.

> ...the numbers prove it.
> In March the average American visited a mere 111 domains and 2,500 web pages, according to Nielsen Online. What's worse, our attention across these pages is highly fragmented. The average time spent per page is a mere 56 seconds. Portals and search engines dominate, capturing approximately 12 of the 75 hours spent online in March. However, people-powered sites like Wikipedia, Facebook and YouTube are not far behind, snagging nearly 4.5 hours of our monthly attention.

Digital analyst Om Malik has been writing about this for the past couple of years and coined the term "Real Time Web" as the next evolutionary step in the Web.

> I believe that we are seeing a disruption of behavior in how people use the web. For now, it is still an early adopter phenomenon, but with 200 million Facebook subscribers and Twitter's rocket-like growth, it is only a matter of time before these two sources become major web content discovery engines. How these changes will impact Google's business remains to be seen, but one thing is for sure — many Web content discovery engines that exist as destinations (Digg, for example) are going to face challenging times. (1)

Venture Capitalist John Borthwick, whose company (Betaworks) has invested in this new infrastructure, views these streams as the new metaphor for the Web, making pages and other print media nomenclature obsolete.

> In the initial design of the web reading and writing (editing) were given equal consideration — yet for fifteen years the primary metaphor of the web has been pages and reading. The metaphors we used to circumscribe this possibility set were mostly drawn

from books and architecture (pages, browser, sites etc.). Most of these metaphors were static and one way. The steam metaphor is fundamentally different. It's dynamic, it doesn't live very well within a page and still very much evolving.

A stream. A real-time, flowing, dynamic stream of information — that we as users and participants can dip in and out of and whether we participate in them or simply observe are a part of this flow. (2)

Writing of Borthwick's metaphor, Erick Schonfeld of TechCrunch noted that the stream "does not replace Web pages or search...but it has the potential to completely transform them."

> ...the shift from pages to ever-widening eddies of information will have a dramatic downstream impact on many Web businesses, especially media businesses. This rising stream has the potential to fundamentally change the contours of media distribution on the Web. Large destination sites like Yahoo! and AOL, already weakened as distribution hubs by search and social networks, now face the prospect of becoming completely bypassed. No wonder AOL is sticking the stream in every part of its service, from its homepage to Bebo to AIM. (Yahoo! is grappling with the emergence of the stream as well, but so far still thinks it can hold onto its place as a central traffic and distribution hub). (3)

Schonfeld notes that the problem for consumers, of course, is information overload, but proponents of the stream feel that fear is overstated. Borthwick, for example, says the mission isn't to absorb everything or get to the bottom of a page; it's "a flow of data that we can dip into at will."

In 2007, the creative mind of Dave Winer birthed a concept that he called "rivers of news." Frustrated that news organizations weren't giving him what he wanted as a user, he created software that allowed him to place every story from the *New York Times* into a steady stream of content that he could dip into and out of whenever he wished. Borthwick's metaphor comes straight from Winer's innovation two years ago. Most people point to Winer as the person who birthed blogging and RSS, so his "news river" is a logical extension of earlier creations.

Two years later, the *Times* has launched an application it calls "TimesWire" that is, in essence, Winer's river of news. But what Borthwick, Malik and others are seeing is much more sophisticated and involves the blending of multiple streams to create a real-time user experience to keep abreast of all that is news, regardless of your definition of the term.

The question for media in all of this is how to be a part of the stream or, more importantly, how to monetize it.

Shortly after Winer's creation, I published an essay titled "News Is a Process, Not a Finished Product" that laid out the model of what we at AR&D call "Continuous News." Culled from my earlier work on unbundled media (including the seminal 2005 essay "The Unbundled Newsroom"), the concept follows the Microsoft "subscribe" categorization of the Web and presents news in blog format, the pioneer of which is the entertainment news juggernaut TMZ.com. A few month's later, the Project for Excellence in Journalism referenced the concept as one of the top trends for 2008.

News consumption has become continual, with news morphing from a "finished" product — a newspaper, a newscast, even a Web site — to a service that helps consumers "find what they are looking for [and] react to it."

One of the key reasons we support the Continuous News model is that its output, in RSS form, is ideally suited to the stream metaphor. As this new phase of the Web develops, we'll see innovations in how to filter the stream for individual consumption, and that's where the money will eventually be. For media companies to be a part of this, however, we're going to have to jump into it without holding back — using full-feed RSS, for example, instead of "teasing" people to get them back to our archaic portals.

Advertising will be another fundamental part of the stream, but the rub for media companies is that advertisers can enter the stream themselves, without the assistance of being attached to media content. This is the inevitable end of a truly unbundled media world.

The act of subscribing to any aspect of the stream is one of opting-in, and it may be at this point that media companies can either harvest data for subsequent mining or attach some form of ongoing user fees to pay for the cost of creating our content. Regardless, the stream is only going to get stronger and stronger in the months and years ahead, and we simply have to get into its current.

We should also be exploring filtering mechanisms for investment, because this is the new point of consumption for web users in an unbundled media world.

Johnny may be unpredictable and change the rules on a whim, but we always know that his motivation is to win. With the Web, the motivation is always to provide value to end users, so we ought not to be surprised by the evolutionary categories that spring up before us. The trick is to get in sync with where its all headed rather than try and drag it into something that's more convenient for us.

Only Superman, after all, can change the course of a mighty river. For the rest of us, it's just a wild ride.

JOURNALISM'S NEW VALUES

"Time is the new currency," Bob Jeffrey, CEO of J. Walter Thompson, noted in 2004, and it's no wonder. The amount of leisure time the average working American has is much less than that of previous generations. According to Roper, the average American worker had 26 hours of leisure time per week in 1973. By 2003, that was down to 19 hours. Less leisure time means we either need to pack more into it or find ways to cut the time that used to be required for specific tasks. This includes how and when we catch up with the latest news, weather and sports.

It's why people love their DVRs. Skipping the ads isn't so much about their lack of appeal as it is about how the ads waste time. Who needs the extra hour of prime time that's dedicated to ads? That's right. You thought prime time was three hours? In terms of actual programming, it's really only two.

This business of time is one of the great cultural drivers of the post-modern, post-colonial world, and it impacts nearly everything — from relationships to eating. We may wax nostalgic for the Rock-wellian family meal, but with every person in the house stretched for time, it's tough to make it a priority. If it isn't homework, it's soccer practice. If it's not the part time job, it's the dance class. If it isn't the overtime, it's the dash to the grocery store.

Our drive for more has come with a price, and that price is time.

The networked world in which we find ourselves is also a fruit of fewer hours in the day. I often hear, "Who has time for all that social web stuff?" but the truth is it's a lot less time-consuming to interact online, assuming socializing is on your regular agenda, than it is to attend gatherings that can actually be much less intimate.

To be sure, there are those who find deep problems with all of this. They are the cautious naysayers of the world, those who would have us all go back to simpler times. They feel strongly that we're all marching down a path to destruction in a licentious world gone mad with lust for more, more, more. They may be right, or it may just be fear of the unknown. The human mind's ability to access knowledge through the machine we call the Web is the world's second Gutenberg moment, and those who found comfort in the church in fifteenth-century Europe felt the same way back then. We've only just begun to explore what life will be like in a truly networked universe.

For journalism, this is truly a turning point. The hierarchical, colonialist "media" days are being replaced by what Jeff Jarvis and others are terming a "postmedia" world. Media is one-direction, from the source to the mass. Postmedia is a two-way street, and with it comes the need for new values that all journalists need to adopt. The authority of journalists can no longer be assumed, nor can the public trust. Like all one-way institutions, journalism has morphed into that which is self-serving, something a networked culture must reject. It's true that the rejection has been building for many years, but the growth of the machine has accelerated it to the point where it cannot be ignored.

Values determine the identity of organizations and people, and the sacred canons of journalist ethics themselves are badly in need of a makeover. Created to help guide us, they have produced a laughable caricature of themselves, for the people formerly known as the audience no longer believe our mission. Is that their fault? I don't think so.

And so we find ourselves in need of a course correct, if we are to remain relevant in the postmedia world.

Michael Smith heads the Media Management Center at Northwestern and speaks of a new set of values for journalism. What's interesting is that Smith equates these values to doing business, which is unlike the values that have driven journalism in the past. I find this strikingly honest, because "professional" journalism really has always been about business. For all the squawking about journalism needing protection from the bottom line, Walter Lippmann, the father of professional journalism, was very much driven by business. Moving the practice from one that's restricted to a detached newsroom to one that's actually seen as a business is a step forward.

In addition to the defining new norms for the internal newsroom culture, including who and what we celebrate, Smith says there are three values that we all must adopt.

> "**Speed** is number one," he told me in an interview. "Within 3 minutes of something happening, it has to be on the web." He acknowledges that speed doesn't mean recklessness, and that's where training and the restraint of an professional internal governor come in.
>
> "**Transparency** is number two," he continued. "There's so much information out there and such great suspicions about the media and their motivations, that the more transparent you can be, the greater the likelihood the audience will be accepting."
>
> "Number three is **authenticity**," Smith added. "That means trying to connect the end user — as well as you can — with the original source of information and getting the filters out of the way. (1)

All of these fit nicely into meeting the news and information needs of people with the conundrum of less time on their hands, and they all work together. As much as we'd like for people to sit through the depth of our labor — and as much as we may think that's necessary for the good of our culture — it simply isn't a part of the networked, postmodern, postmedia world. The assumption that the collection of our daily efforts places us on any form of hierarchical pedestal is very dangerous, for people are infinitely capable of figuring things out for themselves, given the above-stated values.

Speed obviously addresses this, but speed without transparency and authenticity is just rocketship on its way to nowhere. We can be so transparent about ourselves that people feel we're kin, but what good is it, if the information we provide isn't timely and authentic? And we can deliver the mayor's news conference live and unfiltered, so that people can judge for themselves, but this disrespects the not-so-small matter of time.

The speed with which information can be — and is being — transmitted these days is, not surprisingly, a source of pain for traditional journalists. Investigative reporter Charles S. Feldman and Howard Rosenberg, media columnist and former critic for the *Los Angeles Times* have written a new book that blames most of what's wrong in media (and, by proxy, culture) on the media's obsession with speed. They argue in "No Time to Think: The Menace of Media Speed and the 24-Hour News Cycle" that the level of inaccuracy and garbage in the press rises each time we go through another cycle of incremental speed increases, and much of their ire is aimed at the blogosphere. (2)

In an interview with CondeNast's Portfolio.com (ironically, on Jeff Bercovici's blog), the two authors complained about everything from blogs to cable news channels, but they make the case nicely that a solution is transparency. The two rightly discern that nobody's going back to the good old days, so they point to education as the solution. We need to be teaching children at a very early age about media, they suggest, and make a comparison with nutritional labeling. (3)

(Feldman) If the audience, if the viewer has a better sense of how the product is put together, what it's made of, where the biases are, what the hidden agendas are likely to be, they're still free to participate in it, but at least they have a fighting chance of understanding what they're looking at.

So these three values — speed, transparency and authenticity — work together to provide a check and balance system, which can be used to help us meet the news and information needs of busy people, and hopefully regain a measure of trust that we so badly need today.

In a blog post earlier this year, Jarvis wrote that "The first level of transparency in your dealings with the public is identity."

> I hold these truths to be self-evident:
> 1. The goal of the press is transparency. We want to shine sunlight on the powerful in public.
> 2. The press must be transparent. Not to be transparent is to be hypocritical. Opaqueness is not an act of trust.
> 3. *Public* means public. When something happens in the public, whether it is seen and heard by one person or by 100, it can now be seen and heard by the world thanks to any one of those witnesses. That's what public means. (4)

In the traditional world of media, personal transparency was anathema to the goal of maintaining an image of detachment and authority. This need to separate ourselves from the public we were serving is really what brought us down, and the evidence is in the decades old shrinking trust level demonstrated in research by the Gallup organization. People don't trust institutions anymore, and especially if they suspect a hint of self-serving in their behavior.

Two years ago, *Wired* editor Chris Anderson, posted six ideas about transparency that serve as a great starting point for any journalistic organization that wishes to implement the idea.

1. **Show who we are.** All staff edit their own personal "about" pages, giving bios, contact details and job functions [e.g., ED]. Encourage anyone who wants to blog to do so. Have a masthead that actually means something to people who aren't on it. While we're at it, how about a real org chart, revealing the second dimension that's purposely obscured in the linear ranking on a traditional masthead?

2. **Show what we're working on.** We already have internal wikis that are common scratch pads for teams working on projects. And most writers have their own thread-gathering processes, often online. Why no open them to all? Who knows, perhaps other people will have good ideas, too.

3. **"Process as Content."** Why not share the reporting as it happens, uploading the text of each interview as soon as you can get it processed by your flat-world transcription service

in India?…After you've woven together enough of the threads to have a semi-coherent draft, why not ask your readers to help edit it?

4. **Privilege the crowd.** Why not give comments equal status to the story they're commenting on? Why not publish all letters to the editor as they're submitted (we did that here), and let the readers vote on which are the best? We could promise to publish the top five each month, whether we like them or not: "Harness our tools of production! Make us print your words! Voting is Power!"

5. **Let readers decide what's best.** We own Reddit, which (among other things) is a terrific way of measuring popularity. Why should we guess at which stories will be most popular and give those preferential treatment? Why not just measure what people really think and let statistics determine the hierarchy of the front page?

6. **Wikify everything.** The realities of publishing is that at some point you push the publish button. In the traditional world, that's the end of the story. It is a snapshot in time, as good as we could make it but inevitably imperfect. The errors (and all articles have them) are a mix of commission and omission—we hope for the best yet brace ourselves for the worst. But what if we published every story on a wiki platform, so they could evolve over time, just like Wikipedia itself? (5)

Authenticity is a little more difficult to grasp, much less implement into the workflow of day-to-day news presentation. It includes such common sense practices as verifying the validity of both the source and content integrity of a document and being honest, real and genuine. In many ways, the more transparent you are, the greater the authenticity of your work.

There are many useful definitions of the word that will help us build our authenticity as a news organization.

Wikipedia: Authenticity refers to the truthfulness of origins, attributions, commitments, sincerity, devotion, and intentions

Princeton wordnet: genuineness, legitimacy (undisputed credibility)

Wiktionary: The quality of being authentic or of established authority for truth and correctness; genuineness; the quality of being genuine or not corrupted from the original; truthfulness of origins, attributions, commitments, sincerity, and intentions; not a copy or forgery

Secardeo.com: Authenticity typically means the integrity and trustworthiness of data or an entity

The idea of genuineness is what's so compelling about authenticity, and that requires being close to the action and delivering that action without the filters inherent in the gatekeeper concept of news. Technology and the cable nets have made live coverage commonplace, and people bring a certain expectation of that to news on the Web as well.

Tim Porter, long time newspaper writer, blogger and author of the new book *News, Improved: How America's Newsrooms Are Learning to Change*, sees another great benefit to authenticity and being our genuine selves in covering the news. "Somehow over the decades," he wrote, "somehow in the march toward bland professionalism (even at the smallest of papers) we drove the fun out of journalism — both for our readers and for ourselves." (6)

Few professions are as obsessively self-absorbed yet so stubbornly averse to honest self-criticism as the news media. This combination produces plethora of blather about the press, journalism and the future of all things media (to which I confess to contributing.)

This is why authentic voices of journalism ring so true. They emanate from people who care about news, care about community and care about finding — or preserving — the journalistic means to connect them.

Deborah Galant speaks in that kind of voice in her essay on Pressthink about the founding and flourishing of Barista, the hyper-local, blog-powered community news operation she started in Montclair, New Jersey, where she lives. Galant, a former non-staff columnist for the New York Times, writes about the joy of local journalism, of news writ small but smack-full of personality.

At AR&D client station KTBS-TV, Anchor Sherri Talley struck authenticity gold when two hurricanes went through East Texas earlier this year. She turned a web cam on herself at her desk, and offered chat software to concerned people via the Web. Hundreds of people tuned in to what was a raw, unedited version of an on-going news story. She made phone calls and invited guests to join her, including those staffers who normally worked only behind-the-scenes. It was strangely compelling, and its genuineness was one of the reasons.

Speed, transparency and authenticity are but the most visible of the new values of journalism in a postmedia world. People without a lot of time still need the news, but they want it quickly, from people they know and trust, and in a form that is demonstrably authentic.

We do well when we give it to them, but let's also remember the lesson of the first Gutenberg moment. For all the complaining from the clergy in Rome at the time, the printing press didn't destroy the church, only its absolute authority. There will always be a need for other forms of journalism, especially investigative work. Changes of this magnitude are rarely "all or nothing" things, although it may seem like it at the moment.

The new values of journalism don't replace the old, therefore. They merely modify the course.

YOUR PERSONAL BRAND

O ne of my large-market televisions station clients made an interesting discovery while developing a unique hyperlocal
news and information portal covering the community they served.
The station employed people to probe each community and make
contacts to establish themselves in these, often small, suburbs.
Along the way, they found many hyperlocal online publications
and discovered ads on one of them purchased by automobile salespeople.

Think about that for a minute. People who do business with auto
dealers often relate to their point-of-contact instead of the dealer-
ship as a whole, and good salespeople will usually "take" customers with them. This is true in many service businesses where
customers enjoy a personal relationship with an individual representing the company. And so, in this little suburb, car salespeople
are running their own advertisements, seeking to recruit new customers for, one presumes, their database of clients.

They are, in fact, practicing the art of branding themselves in the
community, and this is a bigger deal than it may at first appear. In
today's increasingly networked world, everybody who has a personal web page or web site is a form of a media company, reaching
out to others, whether tribal or the public as a whole. This is
changing the dynamics of identity, because a networked person's

identity is vastly more tied to what they do than it ever was during the modern era. The ability to shape one's identity is a big part of action-oriented branding, and this will be a part of every human being's life in the future.

But marketing guru Seth Godin warns that brands are always in the minds of the people who interact with them, and it's that interaction, not what you say about you, that matters. "What's a brand?" he asked in an email. "It's not a logo, or an ad campaign. It's a shorthand for the memories and expectations we have about our interactions with a product, service, organization or person."

He added that today, people interact with a thousand times as many brands as they did twenty years ago. "So before," he continued, "you could get by with vanilla or invisible. Today, no reputation, no trust, no sale." So reputation is a big part of your personal brand, and as Stephen Covey wrote in his *Seven Habits of Highly Effective People,* "You can't talk your way out of something you behaved your way into."

Godin agreed. "Brands are souvenirs of what happened," he told me. "So, if what happens with you is that you tell the truth, show up on time, exceed expectations, surprise me, delight me, trust me, inspire me and give good value, what sort of brand is that?"

Godin believes that a person's brand is already a part of the hiring process, "At least it is among employers you'd be willing to work for!" But one primary source of an individual's brand — social networking memberships — can lead to employment problems, for the indiscretions of youth can have long legs on the World Wide Web. A young person applying for a good job may be dressed to the nines, appear intelligent and mature, and leave a great impression, but if that person's MySpace or Facebook page (or YouTube video) reveals a different person, it can (and does) cause problems. The issue is which represents the person's brand, the interview or the identity projected on that person's web page?

So we are how people interact with us and the impressions they take away, and we need to understand that it's almost always in our best interests to put our best foot forward. This has profound consequences for culture, because a people always striving to do so — even in the name of enlightened self-interest — is a people predisposed to Life's ancient golden rule, which would be the opposite of what we have today.

Long ago, a person's identity was tied to their occupation, the place from which they came, the (known) family to which they belonged and other things, and the idea of a personal brand is taking us back to that time. In old England, surnames came from occupations, such as Smith, Miller, Carpenter, Weaver, Knight, Cook, Archer, Cooper (one who makes barrels) and many others. So upon introduction, much more than surface things was revealed. Identity in a networked world similarly reveals more, and this is why I use the term "brand."

Doc Searls doesn't like that word, because its origins in the marketing world were devious (How many different brand names can you use to sell the same soap?), and I don't disagree. But in my view, the marketeur today doesn't have as much say about the brand as does the consumer, and empowered consumers tell a different story than does the marketeur. In this, Godin is right when he says the brand is in the mind of the consumer.

Searls told me that in the future, our reputation will always precede us, because reputation in a networked world "is" our identity. This, he noted, is similar to the way life used to be prior to the industrial age, when the world of the community was much closer and people knew what they needed to know from others in the community. The industrial age, he noted, robbed us of individualism and our very identity by turning us all into nameless, faceless cogs in the machine and changed the way we relate to each other. "We need to take the best of how we relate in the industrial age," he said, "but go back to pre-industrial times and find a combination that works to the betterment of everybody."

Many will read into that the ideals of some unreachable utopia, but the reality is that nobody really knows what's possible in a networked world, although it's certain that it will be different in the information age than it was in the industrial age.

My 23-year old daughter, Brittany, is getting married in a couple of months. She has a marketing degree and works as a make-up artist at a local Nordstrom store. She's gifted in this area and really enjoys her job. Her fiancé, Clint, is an assistant manager at a nearby Game Stop. He's a serious gamer and the job is a perfect fit for him, too. So my daughter is Brittany, the make-up artist, and my future son-in-law is Clint, the gaming expert. There is much more to their identities, but these form a nice foundation.

In their networked worlds, they are each known as such. If someone in either's tribe needs make-up advice or products, he or she will turn to Brittany. Likewise, if someone needs knowledge or products in the gaming world, they will turn to Clint. In this way, their brands flourish and grow, because the people in their networks who choose to become customers in their areas of expertise have different expecations — higher and better ones, for their knowing Brittany and Clint as people — than customers off the street who are not part of their network. In the non-networked world, mass marketing is needed to put your message in front of as many "potential" customers as possible, but in a networked environment, your customer base is grown from the inside out. Each of the people in their networks have their own networks, and that's how word is spread.

Like the car salesmen mentioned above, however, Brittany and Clint can actually begin to market themselves beyond their networks by not only growing their network and sphere of influence but by advertising themselves to people beyond their networks. I have strongly encouraged them to do this, and I recommend it to you as well.

Here are ten things that you can do, at any age, to strengthen your personal brand:

1. Blossom where you're planted, because it leaves a good taste in the mouths of your co-workers and impacts your reputation. For young people especially, this includes your network, because one's network at that age often includes people you work with.

2. Build a database of customers and people of influence. Let technology do the heavy-lifting here, but these are the people who spread your reputation beyond your own reach. Get to know them. Remember them. Help them. Stay in contact with them. This strengthens your brand.

3. Spread the brands of others in your network, for it's the best way to motivate people to spread yours. Go to them as a customer, and let the shop owner know what you think. Help that person be the best they can be at their gift or chosen field.

4. Make personal business cards with your brand and spread them everywhere. Advertise yourself with people in person and online. Talk about what you do. Share your experiences and maybe even provide tips as part of your social networking. Everything you do, especially if it's negative, reflects on your brand.

5. Be a good person, not an ass. People are watching, and the last thing you ever want to do is prove yourself a jerk through your behavior while your intentions tell you you're really a good guy.

6. Get comfortable with yourself, even if it takes professional help. People intuitively recognize self-destructive or self-centered behavior, and it's a huge turn-off. If you use, for example, your Facebook page to constantly gripe about this or that, your brand will be that of a complainer and someone who enjoys life atop the old pity pot. You can't control what people think of you, but you can choose not to give them ammunition with which to interpret your brand as negative.

7. When someone asks for your help, offer it freely, for Life loves a cheerful giver, and your brand will continue to grow. This is also a hedge against those bad days (that everyone has) that contain bad behavior. People will know that's out of character and cut you some slack.

8. Devote some time each day to the study of your craft, and this is especially true for young people. You don't have to pretend to be an expert when you really are one.

9. Don't be afraid to be human. Nobody's perfect, although we all seem to think that we should be. Get off your own back, and soon you'll find it easy to get off the backs of others. You will make mistakes, sometimes pretty big ones. When they happen, admit them, turn the page, and move on. Tolerate your own imperfections and you'll discover how easy it is to tolerate the imperfections of others, and that is a good brand characteristic.

10. Be teachable and stay teachable, no matter how much (you think) you know. Run, don't walk, to those who can teach you and help grow your brand. Seek out such people and invest your time, for it will pay dividends beyond what you can imagine today.

Consistent and reliable behavior is also a great defense against those unscrupulous individuals who would use the network to harm a competitor's reputation. I trust the network — the tribe — to wade through such nonsense and award the benefit of the doubt to those who consistently prove themselves trustworthy.

The farther we get down the road of a networked culture, the more we're going to see our identity being shaped by what we do and how we interact with others in the network. In the industrial age, one's identity was more often associated with status than anything else. He lives in the big house up the street. She drives that beautiful Porsche. He's the youngest millionaire in town. Her family is old money. He doesn't have a pot to piss in.

Status also means "connections," and only those with the right ones can advance. In a networked environment, true meritocracy has a chance, and it puts the ability of a person to influence his or her reputation with the individual, for better or for worse. The Web levels playing fields, or at least it can. As the years go by, we're going to hear great weeping and gnashing of teeth from the people who used to "own" the playing fields of the industrial age.

Remember well the words of Tim Berners-Lee, the creator of the World Wide Web, who said many years ago that "the web is more a social creation than a technical one." The cultural disruptions that technology is creating are turning the old world upside-down, and identity is one of its greatest — and most exciting — challenges.

The business of personal brands in a networked world has implications for local media companies and how they relate to and with the people formerly known as the audience. As employees of these companies build their own brands (they are), the value of these brands will exceed that of the media company, especially as it relates to integrity, authenticity and trust. People won't need to "trust the history of our station (or newspaper)," because they'll have made a connection with individuals who work there.

In a networked world, media identity will be more tied to individuals and their identities and brands than to the corporate identity of employers, and this will be good for journalism. Gone will be the amorphous, elitist blob known as "the press," with its "trust me, because I'm the press" perspective. The trust of individual journalists will be the corrective measure that journalism needs to find its way in a networked world.

Journalists today would be smart to take their individual brands very seriously.

A REASONABLE VIEW OF TOMORROW

As the disruption to the mass media business models of tradi-tional media becomes more acute, more and more veteran journalists are beginning to ask how the business of news will be funded. Of course, this question comes from a belief that profes-sional news — that which is funded by advertising — is a per-manent institutional structure, and this is problematic at best. Now that advertisers are voting with their money, journalists are crying "foul" and desperately seeking another model to sustain what in-creasingly comes off as a sense of entitlement.

There was even a call for the licensing of reporters who do "real" journalism a few months ago by the deans of major journalism schools in a *New York Times* op-ed piece. Presumably, such a li-cense would separate "real" journalists into a class that would some-how command financial reward. (1)

This view of seeking governmental help of some sort is similar to that currently espoused by the record industry, whose suggestion of a music tax is as absurd as journalism's demand for a govern-ment-recognized status of some sort. Ethan Kaplan of Warner Records wrote that the concept of art (music is an "art") is "fun-damental to our identity as humans and our place in the world."

It's my opinion that before we start down the path of "how do you value digital artifacts" and "how do you value music," we also need to evaluate how we as a society value art. How do we as a government, a democratic society support artists to the point where the value of experience is enough to support the act of creation? How do (we) remove the fear-politics and the pro-ignorance in the US society to the point where art gains intrinsic value as a societal force?

Kaplan and others in the industry want to tax everybody to support music. This might be interpreted as interesting were it not so transparently self-serving. Music and artists don't need a tax, but the record *industry* does. (2)

Journalists face the same kind of problem, because — like our brethren in the music industry — we want our place in the culture preserved, regardless of behavior that contributed to the audience problems that led to revenue declines in the first place. Make no mistake about it; traditional media has an audience problem, not a revenue problem. Money follows eyeballs, and we seem incapable of understanding why the eyeballs are fleeing.

The people formerly known as the audience (TPFKATA) have been saying for years that they don't trust us, yet we have continued to operate as if they were just, well, wrong. And if we did accept that "some" media outlets were turning people away, we pointed our fingers at them instead of examining our own practices. Just as Jimmy Carter ranted against the American people in his infamous malaise speech, we chastise our former captives for their nerve in running away.

Like the record industry, which has gotten away with peddling garbage in the name of "art" for decades, journalists now find themselves racing at full-speed-ahead toward an ominous iceberg, and a collision is inevitable.

And while we watch the institutions of modernity struggle like this, culture continues to advance in a different direction. The disruption feeds itself, drawing sustenance from the lack of attention by institutional players, who'd rather fight for what they used to have than explore opportunities from within the disruption.

So let's take a trip down the path that traditional journalism refuses to explore and see what might be waiting, and we'll begin with that bane of the professionals — bloggers. Andrew Keen and his colonialist views of knowledge would have us believe that bloggers (a.k.a. "amateurs") are destroying the very fiber of our culture. Perhaps it is destroying Keen's view of culture, but it's far too early to tell if that isn't something that needs destroying anyway. Like King George III during the late eighteenth century, Keen and his crowd believe that the colonies/people are incapable of self-governance. This form of contempt bars any willingness to explore either the energy behind the blog revolution or its technological fruits, and this is a fatal tactical blunder by professional journalism.

Such contempt does not exist here, so the future begins with a fundamental belief that journalists, professional or otherwise, will be independent contractors, building individual brands based on the quality — and popularity — of their work. Already, established journalists are leaving their posts to become independent, and this will escalate for two reasons. One, smart, independent journalists can grab online niches not currently being served and eventually support themselves by aggressively pursuing local advertisers and perhaps entering into agreements with local media companies as independent contractors. Two, as bottom line pressure continues on local media companies, it'll become easier to justify paying independent contractors than employees, and this is especially viable in an increasingly commodified news environment.

This may not be good for all traditional media companies, but it's hard to argue that it would not be good for journalism. More independent voices — even those with opinions — would be a refreshing change in a world currently dominated by what many are now calling the "press-sphere," that united and established voice that determines and defines "the news" on any given day.

So let's make the leap and pose the obvious question: In a world of many independent voices, how will the public know what's important, if the press doesn't sort and stack it for them? The development of this paradigm is already well underway, thanks to the technology employed by, you guessed it, bloggers.

Techmeme is a website well-known by the technology media community, which includes a blend of professionals and amateurs. It's a remarkable aggregator of technology-related journalism, but the vast majority of "real" journalists have never heard of it. During a typical day, the algorithms of Techmeme search out the writings of its secret sauce "list" and group those offerings according to themes, or "memes," as the technology community calls them. Usually, the article that was posted first on any topic is given top billing, with all others grouped under a "discussion" heading. The remarkable thing about Techmeme is that a quick glance gives the reader an instant view of what's important at that moment in the world of technology writers. The software provides a seamless, constant editing of its sources to provide a very satisfying user experience.

With Techmeme, you don't need "the press;" you need only the writers. Tech media defies the rules of traditional media. It is as self-policing a postmodern non-organization as you'll find anywhere. Vetting is done by the group — and publicly, which is a refreshing change of pace from traditional media.

Techmeme was created originally as Memeorandum in 2005 by Gabe Rivera, a high-level geek (smile when you say that) with no prior web start-up experience. The simple brilliance of Rivera's software is its ability to detect patterns from the writers in its database via link-based algorithms, and this quickly raises "top stories" to the forefront. Much of it is based on the slippery and subjective term, "importance."

Rivera defined his idea of "importance" in an article in search engine land last year.

> Importance is determined by a number of factors. Citations can increase importance, so a post that accumulates inbound links can rise. Time is a factor as well. A headline that's appeared on the page for most of the day loses importance. Headlines usually fall off the page when the time component swamps all other factors. That's how old news gives way to newer news.

The software driving Techmeme has applications far beyond tech media, and Rivera has already launched aggregators for baseball, politics, and gossip. They're all excellent, and their RSS feeds are second to none in terms of keeping up with each niche vertical. Ballbug aggregates baseball news. WeSmirch handles gossip and celebrity news. And Memeorandum is a political news aggregator. He recently agreed to answer a few questions for us, with a specific eye towards the future adoption of his algorithms at the local media level.

Q #1: What's YOUR definition of a meme? (I think what I'm really asking is if it would be possible to substitute the word "issue" for meme in subsequent iterations of the concept — see question #2.)

Rivera: What's a meme? First, a detour: The good news is that Techmeme's "value proposition" is familiar: news. Techmeme is a news site, albeit one adapted to today's technology news realities. I originally used the term "meme" because that label is often used for news stories (and other things) that spread across the web. Since I describe Techmeme in terms of news and not memes, I'm free not to define it!

Q #2: The grouping of aggregated items to identify and follow a "meme" is the breakthrough of Techmeme and, frankly, what gives it its power. In layman's terms, how do you do that and could this be accomplished with, for example, issues in a local community??

Rivera: Techmeme's groupings are indeed key. The rationale: for many stories there are complementary points of view readily available on the web, so offering just one reporter's take shortchanges the reader. On the evening of February 3, for instance, Techmeme linked directly to Google's legal objection to Microsoft's Yahoo! bid and Microsoft's response to this alongside the usual media reports. Since all of these were giving shape to the story, a proper telling demanded direct quotes from and links to these sources.

Q #3: Local media companies use people — in the form of editors and producers — to aggregate and stack the community stories and issues, whereas you use technology to stack and sort based on what the tech community itself is saying. What's your view of mixing the two? Do we really need editors anymore??

Rivera: Human editors will always be needed. They even determine Techmeme's coverage, because Techmeme is just an automated process that rearranges content human editors have created and composed. Moreover, Techmeme relies on operating in the tech news space, a domain where certain technical characteristics of the online coverage (specifically, dense hyperlinking and temporal closeness of related stories) enable an automated process in the first place. Techmeme won't work at the local level.

Q #4: Authoritative writers in the tech space — those with substantial followings (TechCrunch, Scoble, etc.) — often drift to the "lead" position within any specific meme. Is that because they're actually creating the meme or because your software defaults to those with a big audience? What I'm asking, I guess, is how democratic is the system? Can anybody be the center of a meme??

Rivera: I'm not sure what a democratic news site is, but Techmeme's probably not it. It's difficult to offer a compelling view of news that gives everybody an equal voice, for many reasons. First, only so many writers have early access to much of the information that defines the news. And second, some people can tell a story far better than others. Neither will change any time soon. What makes Techmeme *more* open or dynamic or "democratic" is that it's nonetheless easier for new sources to make their way onto the page. The voice of a newspaper that introduces no new reporters will stagnate over the years. Techmeme is like a newspaper that hires a new staff reporter every month and offers daily columns from new outsiders.

Q #5: From your place at the cutting edge, what's the greatest error you see traditional media companies making during this stunning revolution in communications? What would YOU do, if you ran your local newspaper?

Rivera: I get the sense that instead of looking around the web to understand and internalize what's worked for others, far too many media companies have just applied a webby veneer to their existing product. More "rethink" and less "repurpose" is needed. Perhaps every local media operation should start by hiring at least one person intimately familiar with the dynamics of a very successful contemporary media site. So, like I said in #3, I can't help local media sites much. At least not for a few years anyway. (3)

Rivera's belief that there aren't enough voices at the local level to provide the scale needed to drive his algorithms doesn't mean that a similar model can't or won't develop in the near future. Independent voices are already springing forth everywhere, nurtured in the fertile ground of dissatisfaction expressed by the people formerly known as the audience, so the scale to which he refers may be closer than anybody thinks.

And while all of this is taking place, traditional media companies are still arguing about how best to hang onto the old model, one that quarterly reports indicate is unable to sustain so-called "real" journalism anymore. A reasonable view of tomorrow suggests that life for journalism — just as it always has — will find a way, and in fact, it is already taking place outside the view of those who have the most to lose by clinging to yesterday.

The Postmodern Culture

2009: THE GREAT BEGINNING

" Some of the worst things in my life never happened" is the lament of those whose imagination often leads to the elevation of life's molehills into mountains. Some people were born with the innate ability to get ahead of themselves, and while this has fueled creative advancement, it's also led to much human suffering. Anxiety is the flip side of creativity's coin.

Others rarely, if ever, spend time downstream and are often stuck in the rut of what happened yesterday. These are the people who can't let go, who remember the precise moment of each of life's wounds. Such looking backwards is the gift of those who guide the cause-and-effect, seemingly emotionless problem-solving of modern culture. Depression, however, is often its internal manifestation.

And so it is that both groups find themselves staring into the chaos of an unknown tomorrow, and this is a frightening contemplation for media companies, who are largely run by those who look backwards. Bean counting, after all, is based on what is known or can be known through a sophisticated obsession with the rear-view mirror, but if there's one certainty about tomorrow, it's that it will not even resemble yesterday.

This is bringing about the gut-wrenching realization for some of us that culture has passed us by, an intense feeling of abandonment that, if left unchecked, will wreak its havoc in the form of the institutional and personal depression that is already being felt in many circles.

Welcome to twenty-oh-nine.

I've been writing about the coming of this year since 2005, and nearly every thought has been ominous. Was it the stuff of mountains and molehills, or was it correctly reading the signs? I claim no special insight, for the signs have been there for anyone to see. I've used terms like deep darkness, dark clouds, and a cloud of locusts, all pointing to a perfect storm against local media in 2009 that I wrote about two years ago:

> National business is going away at an accelerating pace. Network compensation is all but gone. Stock prices continue to fall as investors' nerves give way to full-blown panic attacks. Staffs are being cut, and there will be no election or Olympics to offset declining audience shares and sales. Some companies may not make it…
>
> …By 2009, this storm may already have knocked down towers and crushed printing presses everywhere. The confluence of forces coming together is certainly destructive for the status quo…

You could say that I accurately predicted the bankruptcy of the media companies and the massive layoffs in the media sector, but as I said, these were "no brainer" calls, for pending calamity has simply been obvious.

This year, it's different. Something new has dawned deep inside of me that I wish to express as we're about to turn the page on 2008. I don't see darkness anymore. The caution lights have been replaced by green. I'm overwhelmed by the positive brightness of opportunity, and this has not been the case for the last five years. I'm not saying that 2009 will be a cakewalk, for the storm is upon us, but the skies aren't just dark anymore. The storm's finally here, and it's time to start thinking about what will be left when it's over. That's where my mind has been for the last few months.

Perhaps it's my view of culture, for I filter current events through the lens of postmodernism, a term that describes the massive cultural change in the West. If you've read my book or any of my old essays on the subject, you know that I believe that we're witnessing the influences of a second Gutenberg moment, and that the impact of this one will be greater than the impact of the first. Movable type and John Wycliffe's common language translation of the Bible released knowledge into the minds of the masses. It had been kept from Western Europeans by the Roman Church, which dominated premodern culture, and as the priesthood watched in horror, one fifteenth-century cleric wrote that "the jewel of the elites is in the hands of the laity." But that release of knowledge produced the wave after wave of cultural innovation that created the modern age.

So it is today that knowledge is once again being spread — through technology — on a level history has never seen. The jewel of knowledge is ripping apart the institutions of modernity, most of which exist based on some form of protected or restricted knowledge.

And so the culture is being turned on its head, for the fruit of the modern era was the Industrial Age and the fruit of the postmodern era is and will be the Age of Participation. "I experience, therefore I understand," is the mantra of the new age, and in this there is great potential for the West and its reborn institutions. Is there trouble on either side? Of course, but this is a time to keep our eyes fixed on the horizon, for we cannot steer a steady course with our attention focused on the waves that are buffeting the hull of our vessel.

I listened to an NPR discussion the other day on the state of the newspaper industry. One of the panelists lamented the loss of "real" reporting, to which Jeff Jarvis responded that journalism is actually going back to what it was before the artificial hegemony known as objectivity became the self-serving mantra of the elitist press. "This is a positive thing for journalism," argued Jeff, and I nodded my head in agreement. It felt like being time-shifted back 100 years to the debates between Walter Lippmann and John Dewey. Dewey trusted the people in a democracy; Lippmann did not, and it is that distrust that built "professional" journalism.

"The whole 'red state, blue state' nonsense is a creation of the press," Jarvis blared. Nobody ever asked the people if we wanted to be so divided, but that's what we have. Lippmann would've loved "red state, blue state," but Dewey would've seen the insanity of it. Lippmann felt the press should be an educated elite that helped shape life for the poor, disenfranchised rest of us. Dewey believed in the voice of the people, which he didn't think belonged with an educated elite. Dewey would've loved the blogosphere, that cacophony of voices that drives the neatly organized professional press nuts.

So here it is, the holiday season of 2008, which means 2009 is just around the corner. Fear dominates the media world like it never has before, and its paralyzing mist has frozen progress in its tracks.

David Carr published a fascinating piece in the *New York Times* recently decrying the media echo that the sky is falling. After rattling off a relentless list of bad news items, Carr made this remarkable observation:

> Every modern recession includes a media seance about how horrible things are and how much worse they will be, but there have never been so many ways for the fear to leak in. The same digital dynamics that drove the irrational exuberance — and marketed the loans to help it happen — are now driving the downside in unprecedented ways. (1)

Carr went on to quote Dan Ariely, author of *Predictably Irrational*, a book that explains why people do things that defy explanation.

"The media messages that are repeating doom and gloom affect every one, not just people who really have trouble and should make changes, but people who are fine. That has a devastating effect on the economy."

So it is with media's negative message to itself. We're stuck in a funk, waiting for some sign that it's okay to breathe again. For most, it's been a case of do more with less, which assumes a time ahead when we'll have more again. That is a dangerous assumption. What's really needed is a reinvention, and this should be our focus for the coming year. But reinventing by downsizing is different than reinventing based on opportunity, and this is the real challenge for all media companies in 2009.

It must begin with our business model, for that is what's broken. It's not a case of "business will come back when the recession's over," because there's not a shred of evidence to support that notion, so, at best, that's just wishful thinking. There's no doubt that the recession is influencing the death spiral of the newspaper industry, for example, but the industry's problems are much deeper. Business for mass media will never return to the glory days, because the "mass" is what has been disrupted. Those who choose to wait it out in hopes of such a return will be the real losers of the year. Instead, we need to be focusing on six things that will influence reinvention in 2009.

We must begin with our customers, both the people formerly known as the audience (TPFKATA) and the people formerly known as the advertisers. Lost in all the hoopla about "who's going to fund 'real' journalism" is the reality that we have chased people away in the name of serving them, for our service has actually been to ourselves. That's not to dismiss the quality work that's been done in the past, but the reality is that there is a huge difference between meeting the needs of the community and meeting the needs of shareholders. The whole world of marketing is built on the terms of warfare, where the fleeing masses are seen as an enemy to be conquered. Well, guess what? The audience has always known this, and now they have ways to escape our clever bombardment. Any attempt to serve the information needs of the public must be genuine, or it will fail in the end.

Our new business mission is the enabling of commerce in our communities, not the serving of advertising. Madison Avenue needs a static system to thrive, but Madison Avenue is also in disruption, and we need to see past it in order to create new value for our companies. The classified advertising upon which the whole newspaper industry was built began as a way to enable commerce in the towns and cities of the culture. We must return to those roots and creatively exploit technology to serve the business interests of the communities we serve. Those who do this — and especially first — will be those with the brightest of all futures.

We must make up our minds that the future is more important than today and have the courage to make decisions that bring new value to our companies, rather than clinging to old models. Media companies have given lip service to the concept of driving the car and fixing it at the same time, because the needs of the next quarter continue to outweigh the needs of the company. This has to change, and investors need to support that change. You may say, "Good luck with that," but the alternative is death, and that's permanent.

We will find successful any tactics that enable our customers to participate in the world that we used to have all to ourselves. That includes helping TPFKATA do what we do, and I'm not speaking of exploiting their content for our mass marketing gain. I'm talking about growing the disruption of personal media, for only in so doing will we have a seat at that table. We have knowledge they need, to say nothing of vast archives that can fuel new business for years to come. The postmodern world is one of participation, and we can do no better than to help people participate.

On the Web, we will find that Continuous News — our version of history in progress — is the best definition of our new mandate as media companies. And the extent to which we can make that ongoing process available in any unbundled form, the better and more profitable we'll be in the long run. News IS a conversation, and the pros have two missions in the conversation. One, somebody has to start it. Two, we can advance it, but to think we are the only people capable of delivering "the news" is to assign ourselves to the tar pits before we even take a step.

We should pay close attention to our incoming President's plan to make "ubiquitous Internet access" a key part of economic recovery, for if we are moving from the industrial to the information age, such access will be the economic infrastructure of tomorrow. Net neutrality and conflicts between the public and private sectors will be critically important as this initiative moves forward, but this infrastructure must be created. That means that in everything we do downstream, only the essentials of the web that we know today will matter, for as the years go by, today's web will seem increasingly primitive in comparison with what unfolds. The fundamentals won't change, however, and it is these fundamentals that require our attention as media companies today. We are woefully uneducated about such matters, and that must change.

We'll doubtless see more attempts to take companies private, more bankruptcies, more layoffs and more economic bad news in 2009, but we must keep these items in perspective, for 2009 is not the end but the beginning.

In recent weeks, I've been drawn increasingly to the autobiography of Henry Adams (*The Education of Henry Adams*), and especially his recollections of the 1900 Paris Exposition (World's Fair). The grandson of John Quincy Adams and great grandson of John Adams, Henry Adams was a man who ran in elite circles and ought to have known about the cultural trends that would eventually rock his world. However, he was unprepared for the helpless feeling that came over him, as he stood before The Dynamo in the Galerie des Machines. The twin 40-foot-tall generators symbolized the dawning of the industrial age, and Adams was humbled in their presence. He wrote of their godlike powers.

> ...to Adams the dynamo became a symbol of infinity. As he grew accustomed to the great gallery of machines, he began to feel the forty-foot dynamos as a moral force, much as the early Christians felt the Cross. The planet itself seemed less impressive, in its old-fashioned, deliberate, annual or daily revolution, than this huge wheel, revolving within arm's length at some vertiginous speed, and barely murmuring... (2)

Adams' book is written in the third-person, even though it's an autobiography, and the detachment of such prose serves well to describe the emptiness in his gut. "...lying in the Gallery of Machines," he wrote, "his historical neck broken by the sudden irruption of forces totally new..."

This is precisely the way most of us feel as we ponder the future and a new age. Industry has moved elsewhere, where the cost of labor is cheaper, and technology has stripped away many of the jobs that the industrial age required, so the very creations of the age are dispatching it without so much as a glimmer of concern. The Information Age — the Age of Participation — has just begun, and already there are amazing things happening in our culture.

Whereas the Industrial Age forced the creation of powerful city states (the labor force had to be centrally located), the Information Age allows us to be where we want to be. Watch for movement to friendly, peaceful surroundings, where the locals have been smart enough to build hubs along the information superhighway. Contrarians will argue that people working from home will be isolated, but from what? What new businesses will spring up to cater to American workers in the future?

Whereas modernity — that which drove industry — was built on the twin gods of science and reason, postmodernism sees limits therein, so we'll see a renaissance of religion, only it won't be built on hierarchical dogma. Of all the things I will likely miss when I'm gone, this is something I'd truly like to witness. At the end of the modern era, we see our culture lacking the internal governor that democracy requires, and I think you'll see this change as the years go by. Will it be built upon anything we've known in the past? I doubt it, for with Barack Obama's "ubiquity of access" comes ubiquity of knowledge, and that will benefit all of humankind.

Whereas the Industrial Age brought with it vertical silos of institutional knowledge, power and separation, we'll see more horizontal connectivity in the Age of Participation, and less hierarchical command and control. This will draw us together and reduce costs for everyone involved, and this, too, is a bright light ahead.

Whereas the Industrial Age brought us corporate marketing, the Age of Participation heralds the world of personal marketing and personal branding and a time of influence in expanding circles, rather than top-to-bottom. The time to gain traction in this world is today, for today's action will determine your place in tomorrow's culture.

The defense of cyberspace — the whole electromagnetic space — will become the top priority of government, for our enemies won't need bombs to destroy a connected society. But depending on the breadth of knowledge ubiquity, the whole matter of friends and enemies will be up for grabs.

So the problematic days of the precipice upon which we all seem to be standing are not an end, but an exciting new beginning, one that will push the citizens of the twenty-first century to new accomplishments, new values, new business opportunities, new leadership, and new wealth. What will be your role in the Age of Participation? What will be your company's? 2009 is a year to make those choices for ourselves, for a culture in transition is a time of incredible opportunity.

Years from now, people will look back and say, "I only wish I was around back then, because they had choices we don't have today."

Let's not get so caught up in anxiety or depression that we lose sight of that.

CHASING "THE" TRUTH

T ruth is an elusive prey. Is there one "truth" in any situation, or does more than one version of "truth" exist in human relations? These are the eternal questions of the philosopher, but so, too, the journalist, for we've been taught that the pursuit of truth is the trade's highest calling.

When a jesting Pilate asked of Jesus in the Gospel of John, "What is truth?" it was in response to His claim that He'd come to earth to represent "the truth." The phrase earlier in John's Gospel — "you will know the truth, and the truth will make you free" — has long been used by those who have a version of truth to sell (even journalists). However, that verse begins with an "and" and follows "If you continue in My word, {then} you are truly disciples of Mine; and you will know the truth, and the truth will make you free." So, to Jesus, "truth" was tied to His word and not some abstract reality. "Truth" could be known and understood only insofar as it was anchored in what He said.

So this "truth" business is dicey and culturally important, for whoever decides "the truth" can use it for their own gain. This is what

Jay Rosen references in his essay "Audience Atomization Overcome: Why the Internet Weakens the Authority of the Press." (1) The "sphere of consensus" to which he refers is "the truth," according to the professional press. How did we get this way? Who gave a group of unelected elitists the authority to determine truth for the culture as a whole?

In my early newsroom days, the leaders were all old newspaper guys (yes, guys), and I've always felt fortunate to have had that kind of foundation in my training as a journalist. I'm sorry, but you just can't learn in school the way you learn on the street.

One lesson I was taught early was "there are always two sides to every story," and we pursued this as a fundamental belief in the practice of journalism. That has evolved to a quest to determine which "side" is "the" truth or closest to it, for in the practice of contemporary professional journalism, according to Pew's Project for Excellence in Journalism, the "first obligation is to **the** truth."

> Democracy depends on citizens having reliable, accurate facts put in a meaningful context. Journalism does not pursue truth in an absolute or philosophical sense, but it can—and must—pursue it in a practical sense. This "journalistic truth" is a process that begins with the professional discipline of assembling and verifying facts. Then journalists try to convey a fair and reliable account of their meaning, valid for now, subject to further investigation. Journalists should be as transparent as possible about sources and methods so audiences can make their own assessment of the information. Even in a world of expanding voices, accuracy is the foundation upon which everything else is built—context, interpretation, comment, criticism, analysis and debate. The truth, over time, emerges from this forum. As citizens encounter an ever greater flow of data, they have more need—not less—for identifiable sources dedicated to verifying that information and putting it in context.

"THE TRUTH, OVER TIME, EMERGES..."

Implied in this statement is a belief that "a" truth exists, despite the fact that there are "two sides" to every story. This is a fundamental tenet of Modernism, the hierarchical need for an ordered reality that can, and must, be managed. It is also one of the basic elements of the rise of Postmodernism, for the deconstructionist, by daily practice, destroys the concept of a single truth and takes us back to the "two sides to every story" fundamental.

At Pearl Harbor in Hawaii, for example, there are American tours and Japanese tours, and they tell different stories. Why? Because there are two sides to the story of the bombing of Pearl Harbor. U.S. and Japanese history books differ on the event, but as the old adage states: "In war, the winner gets to write the history," so we assume our view is "the truth." To the deconstructionist, however, this is absurd, because there are two sides to "the story" in all wars. You can choose which one best suits or is needed to support your view, but you cannot deny that another exists.

In the Middle East, Israel's presence is unquestioned by the West, even though modern day Zion has existed only since 1948. To the Arabs in the region (most of the population), Israel's presence is "el-nakba," the cataclysm. Modern communications and a culture disincentivised to forget allow Arabs to advance their point-of-view, rather than simply accept defeat and the West's interpretation of history. This is the ultimate "two sides to every story" story, and it's unlikely to ever change. And it points to the difficulty, in today's flattened media world, for any government, including the U.S., to impose its will on another. Absent control of "the truth," colonialist attempts to rule the world seem more and more distant and unreachable.

This idea of multiple truths within the whole is a refreshing — and potentially world-changing — concept for journalism, and one that is increasingly the reality of the aggregate output of both professional and amateur journalism. It is not the "lame" practice of "he said, she said" journalism to which Jay Rosen referenced in his brilliant essay of the same title. "Truth," after all, is the quest.

> Today, any well informed blogger, competing journalist or alert press critic can easily find the materials to point out an instance of false balance or the lame acceptance of fact-free spin. Professional opinion has therefore shifted and among the better journalists, some of whom I know, it is no longer acceptable to defend

he said, she said treatments when the materials are available to call out distortions and untruths.

Truth, Rosen noted, is rarely the mid-point between two factions. "He said, she said" journalism allows the reporter the ability to maintain distance, rather than pursue the truth, which again, is the ultimate mission of the journalist. If the reporter who practices the genre is part of a dying breed, then what will take its place? (2)

Walter Lippmann, the father of professional journalism, wrote in his 1920 book *Liberty and the News,* a compilation of essays from *Atlantic Monthly,* that "truth" was the victim of a press that put it second to its own views of right and wrong in human relations. Facts, he determined, could save humanity. Lippmann was a brilliant thinker and one of the greatest minds of the early twentieth century, but what do you do when "facts" are a part of a multifarious reality? Whose "facts" do you choose as "the" facts, which, when discovered, lead to truth?

> ...the most destructive form of untruth is sophistry and propaganda by those whose profession it is to report the news.
>
> When those who control (the news) arrogate to themselves the right to determine by their own consciences what shall be reported and for what purpose, democracy is unworkable. Public opinion is blockaded. For when a people can no longer confidently repair 'to the best fountains for their information,' then anyone's guess and anyone's rumor, each man's hope and each man's whim becomes the basis of government. All that the sharpest critics of democracy have alleged is true, if there is no steady supply of trustworthy and relevant news.
>
> ...There can be no higher law in journalism than to tell the truth and shame the devil.
>
> ...The philosophy of the work itself needs to be discussed; the news about the news needs to be told. For the news about the government of the news structure touches the center of all modern government. (3)

Lippmann was a social engineer and believed strongly that an educated mind was the only hope for democracy. His views of the objective press were elitist, although certainly well-intentioned. The practice of professional journalism has followed Lippmann's ideals, and it's amazing that we've ended up in exactly the same place that we were before Lippmann wrote *Liberty and the News*. Those who control the news still arrogate to themselves the right to determine by their own consciences what shall be reported and for what purpose, so in the end, perhaps human nature is the enemy, for even "facts" can't be trusted to be as they appear.

Add to the "fact" that Lippmann's crony, Edward Bernays, the father of professional public relations, was an expert at manipulating facts. What do spin doctors spin, if not Lippmann's beloved facts. It is the alliance between these two institutions of the early twentieth century that cause most to be suspicious. What would Lippmann think, after all, if he could see the perpetual decline in confidence in his "facts-only" press as demonstrated by Gallup research going back 35 years? The spin doctors use the press today to convey their version of reality at the expense of all others, which is exactly what Lippmann was concerned about 100 years ago.

The older I get, the more I question this pursuit of a single, objective truth. In human affairs, the best we can get is various versions of truth, and then it is up to us to decide with which we choose to align. The problem, of course, is getting those who believe fervently in truth A to willingly consider truth B, but that is the new role of the press in today's mediated society.

Balanced news is about considering all sides, not presenting any one view as absolute. Fairness is another attribute for this pursuit. The public is clamoring for such, and while some of us think we're delivering just that, the evidence suggests otherwise.

Take the strange case of Sarah Palin. To the right, she is a sweet, although perhaps antagonistic, spokesperson for its views and positions. To the left, she is a mockery of intelligence. No one in the press — not one individual — has ever penned what I believe to be a fair or balanced piece about Sarah Palin. She is so polarizing that it simply does not exist. When editors choose to print pieces that make her look bad — even when it's her own words — are they not practicing exactly what Lippmann so despised? The

Washington Post published an op-ed piece she had written and was booed for giving her a platform, but it was simultaneously applauded as "alerting (the public) to what the radical right intends to accomplish if it's returned to office."

> Sarah Palin's column today in the *Washington Post* calling for President Obama to boycott the Copenhagen summit is pure malarkey. Which is why the *Post* was absolutely right to print it.

Likewise, when Fox News produces puff pieces that reveal her in the best possible light, are they not doing likewise? When audience counts are inflated and gaffes overlooked, are they not arrogating "to themselves the right to determine by their own consciences what shall be reported and for what purpose?"

Lippmann's big fear — although he came close to calling for it — was government regulation of the press.

> If publishers and authors do not face the facts and attempt to deal with them, some day Congress, in a fit of temper, egged on by an outraged public opinion, will operate on the press with an ax. For somehow the community must find a way of making the men who publish news accept responsibility for an honest effort not to misrepresent the facts.

Today, we find ourselves before Congress, asking for help to maintain that which Lippmann favored, an objective press that is pursuing truth in the name of facts.

As the industry of the news continues to evolve, this matter will be at its heart, and future generations will look back in wonder at what is taking place today. What is this "truth" that we are pursuing and how does it influence the life of humankind? Is it the role of the press or of the clergy, and if the latter, then where is its voice in the public debate?

To the philosopher and the postmodernist, one's truth is revealed in how one lives his or her life. Take a look around at our culture, its institutions and what it seems to value and ask yourself, "Is this the truth that I want representing me?" If it is, then all is well with you and yours. If it's not, however, then perhaps you need to be looking for new versions of truth, new versions of reality to pursue.

That calling is for each of us and not to be determined by others. It is my great hope that we'll figure that out before it's too late.

THE CHAOTIC NATURE OF CHANGE

This is one of my favorite photographs. According to Wikipedia, it was taken on May 4, 1990 at Wallops Island using colored smoke.

The swirl at the wingtip traces the aircraft's wake vortex, which exerts a powerful influence on the flow field behind the plane. Because of wake vortex, the Federal Aviation Administration (FAA) requires aircraft to maintain set distances behind each other when they land. A joint NASA–FAA program aimed at boosting airport capacity, however, is aimed at determining conditions under which planes may fly closer together. NASA researchers are studying wake vortex with a variety of tools, from supercomputers, to wind tunnels, to actual flight tests in research aircraft. Their goal is to fully understand the phenomenon.

The remarkable thing about the photograph to me is the image of order appearing at the edge of chaos. This is a fairly regular occurrence in our world, although most people don't have eyes to see it. That's because our minds are so fully in tune with the rules that our logic and reason have created that reality is obfuscated. We refuse or are unable to see beyond the red smoke. Order, we believe, cannot exist within chaos, and yet there it is.

This is a frightening prospect for a culture whose status quo is based on a different belief, for to the haves, the cultural elite — and especially those within academia — chaos represents the opposite of order, the devil to reason's god.

Is it really, or is chaos merely the process of change?

And what about our system of order anyway? Take a look around. If order is supreme, how do you explain events like our recent economic problems? Oh the usual suspects have their usual explanations, but minds like those of Umair Haque, Stowe Boyd or John Hagel view it differently. Haque's metaphor for our current economy is a "zombieeconomy," seemingly alive but not really. Our culture supports the status quo and not much else, and that's because order is really quite disorderly to those outside the velvet rope.

We search for answers to riddles like the economy within a paradigm of order, but if we can find the courage to step outside, we'll notice something completely different. Logical rules, it seems, aren't order at all; they simply codify the status quo. They're manmade in a world that is not, and therein lies the rub.

After Henry Adams' encounter with the dynamo (twin turbines) at the World's Fair in 1900, he wrote in his autobiography, *The Education of Henry Adams*, "The law of nature is change, while the dream of man is order." He wrote of staring helplessly at the machines of the industrial revolution and "meditating upon chaos," because he had lost his sense of order. An elite among the elite, Adams' education and status were completely incapable of grasping what he was seeing, and he wrote, "Nothing in education is so astonishing as the amount of ignorance it accumulates in the form of inert facts." (1)

"Facts" are necessary for order, but what are facts? Truth is the ultimate quest of logic and reason, but what is truth?

The change that Adams noted was chaos to him, but not to those who had created the machines. Chaos, therefore, is in the eye of the beholder, and that eye is colored by the knowledge and understanding behind it.

This is important to me in my work, because the fear of chaos is what freezes media managers in hopeless "solutions" to the disruptions that are ripping apart their world. These so-called solutions flow from that which is already known and practiced. Real innovation means real change, and change is chaos. "Managing change" is the oxymoronic business approach to a doorway marked chaos, and while an orderly process might make change little easier on everyone, it can cripple the desperate need to simply turn the page. In the midst of the downward spiral of disruption, the most logical path is often the most chaotic, grabbing old ways by the throat and crushing the life from them.

The way of nature is change, but the dream of man is order.

How does nature respond to change? When a violent storm tears a forest apart, what happens? Does the forest complain as it's being ravaged? No, it doesn't care. The forest responds as it must. All that dies feeds all that is new, and so the storm is simply a chaotic recycler. Reaction to change is the issue, not the change itself, and the forest can't react until the change has taken place. This is why Adams felt so insignificant 110 years ago. He'd lived an orderly life, one that gave him a false sense of control over circumstances of change. The dynamo blew it all away, and he didn't know how to react.

Humankind wants order, because we want to know when to duck. We want hard and fast rules, because order can be manipulated with the right connections, the right bloodline, the right amount of money, and so forth. Order, therefore, is all about self-preservation, and change doesn't give a crap about us. Rather than trying to manage change, perhaps we ought instead to be crafting our reaction plans. It is illusionary to think we have any power over change, a self-deception that haunts all of us. The only real power we have in times of change is how we react, and that should be our primary focus today.

What's happening in our culture today is an epic shift from the top-down order of modernism to the participatory age of postmodernism. As Jay Rosen notes in his brilliant "Audience Atomization Overcome: How the Internet Weakens the Authority of the Press," media audiences used to be only connected upward to the source, but the Web allows horizontal connectivity among what he calls "the people formerly known as the audience." But this "atomization overcoming" is far broader than just news audiences and the press; it reaches to every institution of the culture. (2)

Prior to the modern era, the hierarchy of the Roman Catholic Church dominated European culture. The invention of movable type placed knowledge available to only the elite in the hands of everyday people and created an entirely new elite based on education and the hierarchies it created. The "Gutenberg Moment" — with the foundational source code of the Bible and other ancient teachings — birthed institutions to serve the people, including those that have governed life in America since its beginning. It also made possible the machines and science of modernism, including that which is moving its own cultural influences to the side today: the Internet and its World Wide Web. We've entered the postmodern age now, one that is built on a second Gutenberg moment. Protected knowledge is again flowing into the minds of everyday people, hyperconnected by technology. Information has separated from the bundled forms of modernism, and this will change things forever. For. Ever.

It's important to understand that the modern era blossomed with religion and that churches flourished after the Protestant Reformation. Rome still had authority, but it was dramatically altered over time. Therefore, it would be foolish to assume that all vestiges of the modern era will disappear or that any form of "all or nothing" is an operational mandate for tomorrow. The postmodern — or "post-colonial" — culture is upon us, and to ignore it in the hopes of some nostalgic "return to yesteryear" is just foolishness.

Pragmatic postmodernism eats away at every foundation of the logic-and-reason-based modern culture. In Peter Lurie's brilliant 2003 essay, "Why the Web Will Win the Culture Wars for the Left," he nails perfectly how the Web guts modernism's core assumptions. (3)

> The content available online is much less important than the manner in which it is delivered, indeed, the way the Web is structured. *Its influence is structural rather than informational, and its structure is agnostic* (emphasis mine). For that reason, parental controls of the sort that AOL can offer gives no comfort to conservatives. It's not that Johnny will Google "hardcore" or "T&A" rather than "family values;" rather, it's that Johnny will come to think, consciously or not, of everything he reads as linked, associative and contingent. He will be disinclined to accept the authority of any text, whether religious, political or artistic, since he has learned that there is no such thing as the last word, or indeed even a series of words that do not link, in some way, to some other text or game. For those who grow up reading online, reading will come to seem a game, one that endlessly plays out in unlimited directions. The web, in providing link after associative link, commentary upon every picture and paragraph, allows, indeed requires, users to engage in a postmodernist inquiry.

He's referring to the practice of deconstruction, an academic term used to describe backtracking just about anything to reveal the complexity of its genesis, which often is one groups efforts to seize control over another. Again, order is the self-centered dream of man, while the way of life is change.

Anyone who has spent a lot of time online, particularly the very young, will find themselves thinking about content — articles, texts, pictures — in ways that would be familiar to any deconstructionist critic. And a community of citizens who think like Jacques Derrida will not be a particularly conservative one.

Derrida is an interesting fellow and one who would have loved Lurie's Web of links. A controversial French philosopher, Derrida argued that any text contains implicit hierarchies "by which an order is imposed on reality and by which a subtle repression is exercised, as these hierarchies exclude, subordinate, and hide the various potential meanings." Who imposes such order? Those in charge. "The winner writes the history of the war," the old saying goes. This is what Derrida meant.

So our attempts to escape chaos are based in both real and imagined fears, but to live and process one's life in such a state is to not live life at all, for as we used to say, "Shit happens." Blaise Pascal knew this when he wrote in his wonderful *Pensées*.

> We scarcely ever think of the present, and if we do think of it, it is only to take light from it to arrange the future…So we never live, but we hope to live; and, as we are always preparing to be happy, it is inevitable we should never be so. (4)

When unexpected change occurs, such as the sudden death of a loved one, preparation gives way to reaction, and that is the natural response to the chaos we experience. We grieve, which is the natural process of turning the page. In the end, the fortunate — like the forest above — move on, because that's the way of life.

For media companies in a postmodern world, the order that served us so well in the past holds us back from adapting to change. Do we manage the change as best we can, or is it better to simply embrace the chaos and let it tear us apart, if that's what's necessary? If our faith is in order, we'll hedge every bet and slowly move towards change. If our faith, however, is in our ability to respond to change, then we won't care what happens, because we'll be focused solely on what comes after.

If you run a television newsroom, for example, is it better to equip a handful of multi-media journalists and keep the bulk of the staff the way it is, or is it better to switch almost everybody to MMJs and deal with the consequences as they occur? The question cannot be answered without studying the motivation for the action, for if we believe that a staff of mostly MMJs will dominate our future, then the former is surely fear-based and self-centered, while the latter assumes a posture of acceptance and sets aside the fear of chaos in order to accomplish the goal. This is hard to do in a world where we are rewarded for the orderly management of processes and why fearless leaders are so vital to any industry in disruption.

The same is true with the paradigm shift in the world of journalism, from the finished "first draft of history" to the unfinished reality of real time news. Professional news organizations do very well with the former but not so well with the latter, because to do so would be to embrace the chaotic nature of the change. We're busy looking for ways to manage it, when the best path may be to simply turn the page.

Many, many professional journalists find themselves out of work today and blame everyone, including themselves. Blaming is a part of order, for when it is disrupted, our minds seek ways to discover the cause, because we think it can be logically fixed. This can be a waste of time, however, when it's never really the change that matters but rather how we react to it.

Perhaps the biggest failure in our logical thinking is that order somehow gives us control, but that, too, is a self-centered illusion. Life is so much bigger than our little corner thereof, and when we believe that we control anything related to it, we step out into the world fearful and deluded. Little things set us off, because they are micro examples of the much bigger fear of loss of control. The institutions of modernism play off that fear and offer themselves as serenity we can count on. The problem, of course, is that we can't.

The twenty-first century will blossom only to the extent each of us can leave the twentieth century where it belongs. I suspect, unfortunately, that it will take a generation.

PRIVACY DISRUPTED

Privacy, to say the least, is a touchy subject and one that is widely misunderstood as the Web keeps expanding our ability to connect with each other. A hyperconnected culture wants to go one way, but our senses of community and self want to go another. We expect maximum transparency from those who want a piece of us but refuse to let go of even a speck of what we keep behind locked doors. This is an intriguing proposition and one that the culture seems reluctant to honestly discuss.

The discussion, however, is long overdue, for the very core of our understanding of privacy is being disrupted, and we're not going anywhere until we resolve it.

Let's begin with a review the cultural advances of the West and each's dominant mantra for human growth and understanding:

1. Premodern era, pre-Gutenberg: "I believe, therefore I understand."
2. Modern, industrial era, post-Gutenberg, pre-Internet: "I think (and reason), therefore I understand."
3. Postmodern, postcolonial, postindustrial era, post-Internet: "I participate, therefore I understand."

As new eras became entrenched in Western Civilization, they modified but didn't remove that which came before. However, the dominant cultural mantra shifted entirely, because the key transition point for each was the release of formerly protected knowledge into the hands of the masses. Gutenberg's Bible gutted the authority of the Roman Catholic Church, prompting the famous quote, "The jewel of the elites is in the hands of the laity." The Internet is gutting the protected knowledge of the institutions that likewise govern culture today, and the result will be a vastly more participatory culture than history has ever known.

I have argued for years that the Age of Participation functions with different rules than the one it's replacing and that it's hard to understand how different the rules are, because we view them through modernist, top-down, command-and-control eyes. We have no choice, for the disruption is just now under way. I will never completely see that about which I write, but I have faith that my children will, perhaps in their old age. Between now and then, our culture will be at war with itself, because when a status loses its quo, there remain powerful remnants that will do everything in their power to make it otherwise.

The smart business person of today would do well to study fifteenth- and sixteenth-century Western Europe for clues as to what to expect. I will say that until I am no longer able to speak.

Which brings me to the matter of privacy.

When Facebook's Mark Zuckerberg told Michael Arrington in an interview that the "age of privacy was over," he was immediately vilified as a naive zealot, at best. He said that if he were to build Facebook today, the default position would be that everything would be public. To Zuckerberg, it's because society is changing.

People have really gotten comfortable not only sharing more information and different kinds, but more openly and with more people. That social norm is just something that has evolved over time.

"We view it as our role in the system to constantly be innovating and be updating what our system is to reflect what the current social norms are.

"A lot of companies would be trapped by the conventions and their legacies of what they've built, doing a privacy change — doing a privacy change for 350 million users is not the kind of thing that a lot of companies would do. But we viewed that as a really important thing, to always keep a beginner's mind and what would we do if we were starting the company now and we decided that these would be the social norms now and we just went for it." (1)

Most observers ripped Zuckerberg for his views, and Facebook has backed off since. However, Zuckerberg is absolutely correct, because a participatory culture cannot advance with modernist views of privacy. They are opposing forces that cannot be reconciled, and the collapse of the old view will be the biggest social change that future historians will note of the twenty-first century.

Jeff Jarvis has been exploring this matter for a new book. He sees the Facebook conflict a little differently:

> Facebook and Mark Zuckerberg seem to assume that once something is public, it's public. They confused sharing with publishing. They conflate the public sphere with the making of a public. That is, when I blog something, I am publishing it to the world for anyone and everyone to see: the more the better, is the assumption. But when I put something on Facebook my assumption had been that I was sharing it just with the public I created and control there. That public is private. Therein lies the confusion. Making that public public is what disturbs people. It robs them of their sense of control—and their actual control—of what they were sharing and with whom (no matter how many preferences we can set). On top of that, collecting our actions elsewhere on the net—our browsing and our likes—and making that public, too, through Facebook, disturbed people even more. Where does it end? (2)

Jeff told me that his epiphany came while studying life in Western Europe after the printing press, when culture was first becoming aware of "publics." He's writing the book, because he wants to help people feel more comfortable with being public, and that's a big, but necessary undertaking. Why?

In Jay Rosen's seminal essay, "Audience Atomization Overcome: Why the Internet Weakens the Authority of the Press," he speaks of our ability to connect horizontally and back "up" to the source, thereby weakening the authority of that source (I would argue **any** institutional source). (3) The source doing the pronouncing is no longer the sole determiner of truth or reality about itself or what it promulgates, because hyperconnectivity spreads that authority omnidirectionally. We can see how this is disrupting media, but it will also disrupt privacy, because the same mechanism that disrupts one top-down or one-to-many paradigm disrupts them all. If transparency is required of the one, it is required of all, for the connections run in all directions.

We may not think of privacy as "top-down" or "one-to-many," but that's exactly what it is. It's that "sense of control" about which Jeff wrote, one deeply centered in self-awareness and driven, at least in part, by fear. It's our effort to control information about ourselves for our own benefit. We are the top; everybody else is the down. We are the one; everybody else is the many. "Everybody and everything else should be transparent, but not me." We want the authority that we're getting, but we want no part of any responsibility that comes with it. This will eventually have to change, and that will be culture's problematic quest for decades. "It's nobody else's business" is a lame intellectual argument in a hyperconnected universe. People want and need to be connected, and increasingly, we'll have to connect in order to participate in life, and at that point, one's business, in a sense, does become everybody's.

In real life, when a customer walks into a store, the proprietor can take one look and make a pretty good guess about many things relative to that customer, including sex, age, race, marital status, children, income level, and interests based on where he or she looks. Online, however, we want to be able to shield that same merchant from the basic data she could get in real life. Moreover, we bring with us a record of places we've previously visited, which, we think, might give the merchant an edge in dealings with us. But complaining that the merchant can "see" this baggage is chasing the wind, for the customer doesn't "own" the record of where he's been and neither does the merchant; it's simply a part of life in the transparent world of hyperconnectivity.

This is why all the political gab about behavioral targeting in online advertising is demagoguery for political gain. The fears being fanned are deeply based in cultural command-and-control.

What we fear is that the merchant will somehow know that we've just been to the sex shop down-the-street, and that would reflect badly, not on our character but on the false front we wish to project. The Web doesn't do so well with false fronts, and yet this is what we want so badly to protect. Life, liberty, the pursuit of happiness, and the mask of anonymity. I don't think so.

So as Congress debates behavioral targeting, and the industries of media and advertising (they're the same, BTW) attempt to influence how it all comes out, perhaps a better use of our time would be in debating the core matters of privacy in a hyperconnected world. That, however, is a highly problematic exercise.

We can't know what genuine transparency would be like, because we live in an opaque world. To the fish, air is death. Our minds can't even comprehend omniscience, for the same mind that seeks all knowledge must give away what it has, and that is not exactly a human characteristic. We're in it for ourselves, every one of us. We want every piece of information about everybody else, yet we want to do so by keeping ourselves private. Omniscience demands that all knowledge be shared. Any thing else is intellectual dishonesty.

How on earth will we all agree to be transparent? Perhaps it will never happen, but at least we should be honest about it before dissing the debate.

We view every transparency issue through opaque eyes, so our assumptions about our data include umbrage at the mere suggestion that somebody else might have access to it. We want all the benefits of hyperconnectivity without paying even a snippet of the price. Is it not theft to demand transparency from those who serve us while hiding ourselves in a fortress?

We fear the loss of autonomy, and rightly so, but our fear comes, again, from this opaque view. What would some "power" do to/

with us, if that power had everything about us in the palm of its hand? This is modernist dystopia, best evidenced by George Orwell in the book *1984*. Big Brother had open access to everyone simultaneously, and used that power to crush individuality in favor of the totalitarian regime, The Party. The problem with this fear today is that it runs smack dab into Rosen's "Audience Atomization Overcome," for Orwell only saw connections up to and down from Big Brother.

Every time some new view of culture comes along, it is immediately judged and pigeonholed based on that which has already been. This is a modernist necessity, for to the logical mind, there is nothing new under the sun, only discovery. The creative mind is, in many ways, at enmity with the mind of reason, but both are allowed equal footing in the overarching all that is humanity. This itself is illogical, so "reasonable" people put themselves in charge.

The problem for us today is that it's no longer working. Industrial age ideas badly need replacement, but with what? Those same "reasonable" people want and need to drag us backwards, while others want to head in different directions. Who will decide? You can bet on one certainty for this century: as long as we're connected, we, the people, will decide. It can be no other way in the Age of Participation.

So is Mark Zuckerberg prescient or crazy? I think we need to listen to his views, but Zuckerberg also needs to be able to defend those theories and beliefs, which he heretofore hasn't done very well. He may, in fact, be on to something, but when he opens his mouth, it comes off as self-serving. We need to air the fears that we all have, but we must do so in an environment that doesn't automatically dismiss the unusual or distinct.

At the University of North Texas, where I teach an ethics class, I find young people much more amenable to openness than my generation, so the shift in how we view privacy — if it's ever going to happen — will likely take a couple of generations. Educating *for* the value of transparency against the cultural opaqueness of the industrial age isn't going to happen overnight. Slowly, but surely, however, it will come about, to one degree or another.

Many will judge this utter madness, but those judgments will come from logic and reason imbedded deep within the opaqueness of modernism's mantra of understanding. One day, historians will write that this served humankind well for generations, but that the quest for omniscience drove us elsewhere. Only then would war, hypocrisy and exploitation become remnants of an ancient past.

As Spock said to Captain Kirk just before his death, "The good of the many outweighs the good of the one. It is logical."

THE INTERNET WEAKENS AUTHORITY

In 2004, I delivered an academic presentation to J-school students in Tennessee that examined what would happen to culture as postmodernism's mantra of "I experience or participate, therefore I understand" became the norm. I've given this presentation to many audiences in the past six years, and I regularly hear from students that it is life-changing. It's based in fifteenth-century Europe at the time of the first Gutenberg moment in the West. My view is that every institution that governs the West today is threatened, mostly because they've failed in their charge but also because formerly protected knowledge is being disbursed to everyday people. I don't think we're honest with ourselves about how badly our system has failed, because we compare our poverty with others and conclude, "Well, it's not so bad."

Our economy remains on the brink with twenty-first-century thinkers like Harvard's Umair Haque believing the whole thing needs to be rebuilt.

It is no coincidence that so many industries are in trouble simultaneously and so fast. The growth of the Zombieconomy is a Jupiter-sized wake-up call to today's leaders.

Common sense environmentalist Terri Bennett is on a mission to wake people up, one at a time, because something's wrong with a country that contains 5% of the planet's population but produces 25% of its waste.

By studying census data put together by NPR, you can see that the income gap between the top one-fifth of the population and the bottom one-fifth has actually widened in 30 years. Every income level decreased except the top, and this has not gone unnoticed by the masses. As the rich get richer, the theory goes, they "lift" everybody else, but that's clearly not the case. Theories also provide little comfort to the unemployed.

Congress is working on legislation to extend unemployment benefits, but this is just political posturing and little else. Nearly 10% of the labor force is out of work as of this writing, but a CBS Marketwatch report notes the deceptive nature of U.S. Department of Labor statistics.

Many people have simply dropped out of the labor force statistics.

Consider, for example, the situation among men of prime working age. An analysis of data at the U.S. Labor Department shows that there are 79 million men in America between the ages of 25 and 65. And nearly 18 million of them, or 22%, are out of work completely. (1)

It is this sense of failure that's providing the energy behind the "second Gutenberg moment" that we are experiencing today. It isn't technology that's changing culture as much as it is the ability of people to act on long-held dissatisfaction. People, therefore, are the issue, empowered, connected and, yes, angry people. Nobody's "in charge" of the revolution underway, but more and more people are realizing that if we're going to fix what's wrong, we're going to have to do it ourselves.

Life was eerily similar in fifteenth-century Western Europe when the first Gutenberg moment materialized. The gap between the haves and the have-nots was staggering. Cultural dissatisfaction with the Roman Catholic Church was rampant when Gutenberg had the audacity to publish a Bible with his invention called movable type. The printing press disrupted the control mechanism by which the hierarchy of the time was able to keep things as they were. The Internet is doing the same thing today, and it will change things forever.

ATOMIZATION, A HIGHLY APPROPRIATE TERM

In January of 2009, Jay Rosen published his seminal essay, "Audience Atomization Overcome: Why the Internet Weakens the Authority of the Press." This brilliant argument focuses on what Rosen calls "atomization," or the concept that we, as the consumers of media, traditionally have connected only "up" to its source. (2) He wrote in an email to me that the word "atomization" isn't normally used in media circles.

> It was simply the best word I could find to describe the normal condition the mass audience is when the media are "mass." I had to use an unfamiliar word because I was trying to point out something weird that had come to seem normal, which is that the mass audience is connected up to Big Media but cut off—disconnected, atomized—from one another. Only with the rise of the web, and social media, can we see how odd this really is. For social media allows us to connect across to other people who share our interests as easily as we connect "up" to the media spectacle. So that's why I talk about audience atomization overcome. It points to the social isolation that was in the background during the age of mass media — so deep in the background that we couldn't easily see it.

Jay is not only right about media, but the concept can be applied to any institutional authority in our culture today. I take Jay's headline and remove a few of the words:

Audience **Atomization Overcome:** Why **the Internet Weakens** the **Authority** of the Press.

Many-to-many communications disrupts the one-to-many control dynamic of hierarchical modernism itself, and that will have ramifications far beyond just media.

Rosen agrees that this is changing our world. In a nutshell, he describes the great disruptor as "the falling costs for like minded people — those with the same interest, need, fascination, or problem — to find each other, share information, pool what they know, and publish back to the world, thereby attracting more people who share that same thing."

This is potentially world-changing.

"To see how it applies outside of news," he adds, "just picture how life has changed for the medical doctor as diagnostician when patients can find other patients with the same illness or taking the same medication and compare treatment options. It's not that the doctor's authority evaporates, but it cannot be established or maintained the same way. For there has been a shift in power. Atomization has been overcome. Multiply that by, oh…a million other ways it's happening all around us and you have yourself a cultural shift."

Atomization is the operating necessity of colonialism, the tap root of contemporary Western civilization. I often swap out the words "modernism" and "colonialism," because the latter is intrinsically woven into the former and is so inculcated into our society that it seems both natural and the way it's always been. From Wikipedia:

> Colonialism normally refers to a period of history from the 15th to the 20th century when people from Europe established colonies on other continents. The reasons for the practice of colonialism at this time include:
>
> 1. The profits to be made.
> 2. To expand the power of the metropole (mother country).
> 3. To inculcate the indigenous population to the colonists' world view and way of life.

Some colonists also felt they were helping the indigenous population by bringing them civilization. However, the reality was often subjugation, displacement or death.

This "taking what the cultural hierarchy offers" is what's so dramatically altered by our ability to connect horizontally. We may think our dissident views to be abnormal, because we're isolated, but hyperconnectivity alters that perception, and the result is a deeply empowered citizenry. This will have profound future implications for every institution of our culture. Media was just the beginning.

That's because if we honestly examine the colonialist motivation of institutions governing culture, we discover that each is based on how much "we" need "them." The lure of success and happiness is the bait, but, over the years, each has drifted to self-preservation as its fundamental mandate. The unwritten expression of each is colonialist, fear-based, and built on the idea of protected knowledge.

Institution of Government. You are unable to take care of yourselves, much less govern yourselves. You can find success and happiness only if we make it happen. You need us to make legal that which will make you happy and successful and to make illegal that which stands in your way.

Institution of Law. There are boogeymen out there to rob you of your success and happiness, and you need our protection. Besides, it's a complex society in which we live, and you need our help to simplify it for you.

Institution of Business. We provide the means for success and happiness. You need us to make the 'things' and services that will make you happy.

Institution of Religion. Only God "out there" can provide success and happiness, and you need us to bring Him to you.

Institution of Education. Only an educated mind can bring success and happiness, and we give you that and more, for what good is an education without certification? You need us to provide the credibility you need to work with others and bring about your success and happiness.

Institution of Media. Only we can make you aware of what will make you happy and successful. You need us to entertain, inform and enlighten.

Institution of Medicine. You cannot be successful and happy without a sound mind and body, and you need us to give it to you.

Institution of Finance. We provide the means for success and happiness. You need us to make the 'things' and services that will make you happy.

The overcoming of atomization weakens each of these institutions by disrupting hierarchies, just as Gutenberg's Bible did in the fifteenth century. A Bishop who could silence anyone by referencing

Scripture found his arguments weakened by someone who had studied the same text but didn't speak for the self-serving Church. This is why, upon completion of the first common language translation of the Bible in 1382, John Wycliffe said, "This book shall make possible government of the people, by the people and for the people." Wycliffe was branded a heretic, and 20 years after his death, "the Church" dug up his bones and burned them in a public ceremony. It didn't stop the revolution he'd launched, and the same thing is going to happen to other institutional authority in the twenty-first century.

One-directional authority — especially that which is based in deliberately protected knowledge — cannot maintain control for long, once that knowledge is acquired and spread throughout its constituency. All that we know today in terms how we govern our lives will evaporate and be replaced by something very different in the decades to come.

And so we have a big cultural problem, one that will increasingly disrupt and destroy the status quo, a status quo that will not go quietly. It will be heaven for some and hell for others, beginning as a war of words between populist anarchy and the law and order comfort of modernist command and control. We'll have warnings of danger ahead, if "we" permit this to continue, and those warnings will be accurate, for nobody knows what the outcome will be, just as no one could have predicted the outcome of the first Gutenberg moment.

One man's dystopia is another's nirvana.

In the end, though, humankind will gain, for the jewel of the elites is knowledge, and knowledge is the chief cornerstone of human advancement.

How the
Web Works

THE TROUBLE WITH TWITTER

Time is one of the most talked about subjects in anybody's life. It seems to drag on so slowly in the days of our youth, like me sitting in Mrs. White's 5th grade math class, and yet the speed with which it disappears in the latter years of life is truly astonishing. It's also a bit scary. I'll be able to test the old Beatles' tune "When I'm 64" in July, and time has become something very dear to me.

I don't know whether it's that or the reality that, as J. Walter Thompson CEO Bob Jeffrey puts it, "Time is the new currency," but I'm having issues with fully embracing the Twittersphere, because I just don't have the time. This, to me, is the biggest problem for Twitter — and the entire world that's growing up around it — because in the name of abbreviating communications, it actually makes it more time-consuming to pass along an idea or meme. I know that sounds absurd, but bear with me.

The 140 character world is many things to its denizens. I agree with Dave Winer that Twitter is an efficient notification system, and I believe, as he does, that this is its ultimate strength. Notification of what? Just about anything, including commercial messages. Twitter is unbundled media in the wild, and the money will go to those who figure out how to sort, filter, curate, aggregate and present all of those bits and pieces to help users get maximum use out of it all.

I recall an awful personal situation six years ago when I was a struggling writer, blogger and consultant. I had no health insurance and had a lump in my left breast that needed to be removed. I honestly didn't know what to do, and Jeff Jarvis convinced me to put a tip jar on my blog to let my friends take care of me. Sure enough, I got nearly $4,000 from hundreds of contributions in just a matter of days and was reminded of the angel's note to George Bailey in "It's a Wonderful Life:"

No man is a failure who has friends.

In today's hyperconnected world — with Twitter and Facebook — such an appeal would likely net even more. Back then, it was our blogs and our RSS feeds that connected us. Today's world has advanced so far beyond — and in such a short time — that it's truly astonishing. We have "friends" that we don't even know, thanks to the followers of the followers of the followers of those who follow us.

Twitter mimics broadcasting in some ways, which is why it has found such favor with mass media companies, celebrities, politicos and whatever. It's a fast and efficient way to (potentially) reach a lot of people, if those people are predisposed to follow its messages. Where the messages become unwanted, it's tricky, because those being courted can, with the simple push of a button, say "bye-bye."

And so we have a whole industry burgeoning that is attempting to lasso the beast of participatory media and bring it to its knees, and I'm fascinated by its potential. Prior to attending a conference in Naples, Florida last fall, I sent a tweet to my small group of followers to advise them of where I was going. Within a few hours, I'd received a tweet from a restaurant in Naples inviting me to stop by for a meal, with a 20% discount for mentioning the tweet. Smart, and an harbinger of things to come. A few weeks ago, I had a very bad pizza at the airport in Des Moines and tweeted about it, only to hear back from the maker with an apology and an offer for restitution later.

This is the real world of Twitter and its ultimate value, because Twitter is also a medium of conversation. It's why I've been recommending people participate since the beginning. As a tool for personal branding, it's very close to Facebook in value.

The trouble with Twitter for me arises when people whose work I follow closely use it instead of some longer form of communications to advance bigger ideas. Twitter is a very good discussion forum, although it's a crappy way to eavesdrop on a discussion, which is what I would love to be able to do. The 140-character limit, however, leads to a dependence on links, and this is why I say I don't have the time for it.

Rather than say what needs to be said, people have no choice but to reduce their view to a sentence and toss in a link. The inference is if I want to make sense of the thought, I have to go read or watch the link. This is nice for the spread of link love and for those involved in the discussion, but it's an incredible and time-consuming nuisance for those who wish only to follow a thought stream.

Jay Rosen is one of the most prolific users of Twitter that I know. I've been a fan of his for many years and am proud to say that I actually know the guy. Jay has taught me so much, and we've had some great give and take over the years. Today, however, I find that it takes more of my time and more of my concentration to keep up with some of the best of his thinking, because Jay has shifted his attention to places where he can find and interact with a different generation of people, places like Twitter, Tumblr, Posterous and YouTube. A few years ago, all I needed in order to follow his brilliant mind was to subscribe to his RSS feed. His blog, PressThink, was and is one of the most important in all of the blogosphere. The ideas expressed there have always been at the cutting edge of new journalism.

But I cannot keep up with Jay anymore, and that troubles me. I have three feeds of his in my RSS reader now. It's too much. I realize fully that it's my own fault, but Twitter does not make it easy.

His Twitter feed is tied to his Facebook page, where I also encounter his thoughts in 140 characters. I can't keep up, because, first of all, it's a full-time job. Secondly, where something he tweets does happen to capture my attention, I'm forced to follow a link in order to obtain context. Far more often than not, I find myself regretting such action, for it's Jay's opinion and thinking I seek, not that of some source material. The problem is I can't understand what he's talking about unless I follow the link.

In heady discussions, Twitter provides disjointed and disconnected thoughts to those not participating. The world of journalism needs Jay Rosen (and others, of course) to connect dots for us, because it is Jay's mind that is absorbing all of the various twists and turns that develop into a thoughtful examination of an issue. To be on the same page, I would not only have to stay with Jay for every tweet, but I'd have to follow those he's following and read everything he reads in order to fully comprehend what is presented in a single, 140-character message.

Perhaps there's a future market for that, but I just don't have time to do it. So I lose, and I wonder if it's just me. It's different when reading a thoughtful essay, where I can absorb everything and let that knowledge percolate in my own mind, where it will likely trigger other thought streams. Jay hasn't abandoned the long-form method of communicating, but he has certainly made a shift in how he advances ideas.

I do what seems to be working at the time and what feels fun and interesting. I also like to do things other people aren't doing, or don't see the importance of yet. Part of what's driving me now is a generational analysis. I don't think people of my generation or your generation are going to be the ones to solve the puzzle that the news trades are lost within. So I'm concentrating on reaching people in their 20s who have a much better shot at it. "Rebooting the News" has a tiny audience, but some of them are wicked smart young people who never bought newsroom culture in the first place, so they don't have to free themselves from it. That's why I have been putting so much into Studio 20 at NYU.

But there's another matter that I've come across that concerns me even more. In a recent PressThink essay ("How the Backchannel Has Changed the Game for Conference Panelists"), (1) Jay dropped in two links that require following rather than summarizing or quoting from the links themselves. This meant I had to follow the links in order to understand the piece more fully, and I believe this is a shift in prose that's directly attributable to Twitter. As I pointed out to Jay, I don't think he would have written the piece as such before Twitter.

So is Twitter influencing the longer form writing of those who use it day-in-and-day-out? Is the link to source material replacing the lifting of quotes from those articles to establish context? If so, this is a major shift in writing that I think we need to stop and think about, especially for those wishing to influence beyond a given circle of followers.

Of course, I could be completely wrong in all of this, but it doesn't change the fundamental thesis of this essay: that I simply do not have time — in my current life — to keep up with all the wonderful conversation of those I follow via Twitter. It is a major concern to me, because keeping up with the thought leadership in my world has been one of the most important aspects of my day-to-day existence. That is my trouble with Twitter.

Who will curate Jay Rosen (and others) for me?

THE ORDER OF THE WEB

Order is the essential ingredient in a modernist culture, where hierarchical authority is the skeleton around which everything is built. A century ago, Henry Adams wrote that "the way of nature is chaos, but the dream of man is order." However, order is really the dream of the haves, or those who can exploit it to become one of the haves. Order is a control mechanism, and while it serves humankind well in many ways, it best serves the status quo.

The Web disrupts many things, but its biggest cultural influence is that it disrupts hierarchical order. It does so by turning order on its head, for individuals have the power, not institutions.

One of order's weapons is restricted access, a little gem that is so prevalent in our culture that we take it for granted. Telephone answering systems, for example, are less about customer service than they are tools for restricting access. Ever try to speak with a real human being in, for example, the government's immigration department?

As consumers, we confront these restrictions every day, and most of us wouldn't dream of violating them. Why go through the "Employees Only" door, for example? Laws are written to protect the culture's systems of order. Ever heard of a TV show called "Law & Order"? However, occasionally something comes up where such barriers pose serious impediments for those in need, and we have to find ways around them. I've been in the media for a long time, so I know, for example, that the easiest path to the CEO is often to by-pass the company's restrictions and go through the public relations department.

Restricted access is upside-down on the Web, because it's not about institutions restricting access from us; it's about us restricting access from them.

The Web disrupts hierarchical order by creating an order of its own, because the infrastructure itself isn't hierarchical. Links challenge institutional authority by taking people to information's sources, essentially saying, "We don't need learned experts, because the expert's knowledge is at my fingertips." And if knowledge is just a mouse click away, there's no need to trust people whose knowledge grants them "expert" status in the culture. After all, they're generally in it for themselves anyway. This is a great threat to the status quo and the order it uses to maintain control, but what the modernist views as chaos is actually a different form of order, and the real question for culture in the twenty-first century is who or what will be the governor of all of this?

Those of us in media look at this disruption as our enemy, and justifiably so. The reality is that the technological innovations of the Web have birthed a certain irrelevance for traditional media companies, whose business model is built around advertising attached to (formerly) scarce content. Businesses don't need us anymore to reach customers or potential customers, and this is the real threat to all media. In this sense, the people formerly known as our advertisers are by-passing our system of order, and we should be concerned.

The Jerry Damson Automotive Group in North Alabama is my client. Ben Boles is the head of digital operations there, and he maintains six websites, 250 microsites, a blog, four eBay stores, four YouTube channels, a large Facebook presence, a video production company, email marketing software, and he serves his own online ads. In every way, Jerry Damson Automotive functions as a new media company, and a big one at that. Boles understands the Web like few others, and his primary focus these days isn't traditional advertising.

"Every minute of every day is spent thinking about the consequences of our decisions as it relates to Google," he told me recently. This remarkable statement is one that more advertisers will be making as they, too, grow in their understanding of the Web and how advertising can by-pass anybody's system of order.

> We begin each chunk (morning, mid-day, afternoon and evening) of the day with Google Analytics. The easy stuff is obvious — where does your web traffic live and what are they consuming? Google tells us this thru Analytics. But our custom tracking is what sets us apart and the live, real-time reporting of what works and what doesn't — when correlated with logs from our ad-server — paints the picture of what's working and what's not. We have tagged thousands of ads with custom tracking on websites all over the world to determine what is working and how sites are operating. In most cases, we can tell what's happening on someone else's website just as fast as they can from our data alone. It's that rich. Google Analytics facilitates this. (1)

Boles is far ahead of most, but others will catch up, for people like him are paving the way for a future generation of new strategies and tactics that enable commerce.

While this is certainly threatening to traditional media companies, the threat blinds us to fact that the same tools that enable Boles to reach across traditional advertising can also be used by us to reach across the hindrances that we face in taking our messages to the masses. Instead of always being buffeted by the disruptions, we should be using them to benefit ourselves.

Twitter is just one of many examples. The technology that runs Twitter is the most advanced notification system man has ever created, and we're just beginning to understand the many uses for such an application. The objective for media company participants is to gain followers, something that is easy to do when you have a big legacy property driving the train. But the secret of Twitter — and the real reason media people need to be using it — is not the people following any reporter; it's the people following the people who are following the reporter.

Let's take the case of a TV anchor with 5,000 Twitter followers. We can safely assume that those people are fans of this particular anchor, and it's also logical to assume that these people are likewise fans of the TV station for which the anchor works. Therefore, sending tweets to this group is another way of serving the same audience that the anchor already reaches on-the-air. It's a nice use of Twitter, but it produces a shoulder shrug and a "so what," until we look beneath the surface.

Twitter's own data reveals that the average active Twitter user has 100 followers. Therefore, the potential reach of our anchor is 500,000, if every follower retweeted something from the anchor. Moreover — and more importantly — those people are not necessarily fans of either the anchor or the anchor's TV station, so the act of retweeting by-passes the station's reach and adds a whole new weapon in the quest to "sell" that anchor to the broader audience. Twitter frees television personalities from bondage to the crumbs of the promotion department, and yet we fight it, "because it's more work." It disrupts the system of order that traditional media companies all accept as a way of doing business in the "real" world and exploits the powerful concept of friend referrals that is the bread and butter of a hyperconnected universe.

And it doesn't cost a dime.

Ben Boles is building microsites, because it helps him with organic results in Google searches. By creating sites based on the keywords that people already use to find cars in North Alabama, he is reaching beyond the Damson Automotive Group's conventional reach. Since he already runs his own server, the cost of these microsites is only the $6.95 annual fee from GoDaddy for the domain name that matches the keyword search.

This may seem like heady stuff, but it is practiced every hour of every day by people who understand that the Web has its own system of order and that it's built around the searching of an enormous database. As David Weinberger so brilliantly pointed out in his book *Everything Is Miscellaneous*, Google organizes information for people "on the way out" instead of the traditional system of organizing things before people begin looking. (2) Ever wonder why the bread bowls aren't in the soup section of the deli at the supermarket? Because somebody has decided that they belong in the bread aisle. One person's logic is another's foolishness, and this is Weinberger's point about organizing information on the way out. Let the searcher determine the organization.

This is the Web's system of order, and it's why vast portal websites, with information organized "on the way in" simply cannot compete with search.

Another disruption to order that traditional media companies refuse to participate with is RSS, really simple syndication. RSS is an XML application that separates content from the form in which it was originally presented. People who subscribe to an RSS "feed," therefore, can bring specific items from the database that is the Web to their own desktops. In other words, I can read a story from a media company without "visiting" that company's website. Most media companies offer RSS feeds to consumers, but very few provide what's known as "full feed," choosing instead to "tease" people in an effort to force them to the company's website in order to read the story. This is not how the technology was created to work.

Blinded by the laws of mass marketing, we seem unable to fully unbundle our "content" and release it into the wild. The belief is that we lose our ability to "monetize" that content, if we let it go, but this narrow view closes the door to revenue possibilities heretofore not practiced. Ads "as items" in the RSS feed of a traditional media company aren't viable, if everything in the feed is a link back to a portal website. This has to change.

And because RSS items each have their own link, they, too, can be passed around the hyperconnected world of the Web. This is another way to participate in the friend-based, referral-driven, real-time social Web. The world of RSS ads has yet to be created, but its creation is inevitable.

The Web has certainly disrupted things for media companies. Our orderly way of doing things — gathering an audience around our stage — has been trampled by a new order. At first, it appears chaotic, counterintuitive and impossible to understand, but it's really quite simple. Here are ten characteristics of the order of the web:

1. Hyperconnectivity produces an order that is horizontal, not vertical.
2. The routing of information is through connections, not one-to-many.
3. It is held together by a common goal, the acquiring of knowledge to better oneself or one's life.
4. The first rule of business is the accumulation of friends, not "consumers."
5. Friends like to be asked, not told, and if asked nicely, will respond accordingly.
6. Attraction works; promotion doesn't.
7. Unbundled items are easier to pass along to others than those that are bundled.
8. Its economy is based on links, for links have a real (dollar) value. It just hasn't been calculated yet.
9. Advertising is a form of content — information — that is subject to the order of the Web.
10. Its denizens, whether organizations or individuals, all function as publishers or broadcasters.

This is the essence of all that is Media 2.0. We are who we employ, for an accumulation of individual voices is stronger than combining those to produce only one. Where access is restricted for one, it may not be restricted for another, for such decisions aren't hierarchical; they are made one-by-one. This is the new order, and those who wish to prosper are required to play by its rules.

THE BACK END'S THE THING

In David Weinberger's fascinating book, *Everything Is Miscellaneous*, he writes that the ability to sort information "on the way out" of a website beats sorting "on the way in," and that this is a core competency of the Web. This back door approach to organization isn't what it appears to the casual observer. (1)

Yahoo!'s elaborate navigation helps users sort information on the way in (to its ad infrastructure), but Google allows people to enter search terms, which results in the sorting of information on the way out. Google makes its money by putting ads on everything that shows up in the searches, including an enormous number of the sites that the searches reveal organically. Weinberger brilliantly argues that what appears to be miscellaneous chaos actually turns out to be a neatly-ordered organizational system — only it occurs "on the way out."

This ability to "see" the value of the connections that take place away from what's obvious to the average user is what separates what I'll call "the Silicon Valley Web" from that which was built and promulgated by traditional media companies. Media companies intuitively are drawn to the front door, for that is the model of traditional success.

Several years ago, Cory Bergman and Steve Safran — both then of Lost Remote — and I participated in a panel at RTNDA, during which we each expressed the reality that "the Web is not TV." This had been a recurring theme of ours since we first encountered each other, and it was fun to share our thoughts together.

By now, you'd think everybody in traditional media (the Web is not a newspaper either) would understand this, but the longer I'm involved in this field, the less I think people really appreciate the depth of the differences between each. And that lack of understanding leads to all kinds of strategic and tactical errors, because traditional media companies — advertisers are guilty, too — continue to try and shove their existing models into a world that rejects them. Media companies will never reach their potential online until we deal with this fundamental issue.

At the core of the matter is design and, along with it, usability, for there is a world of difference between web people who work for media companies and those who've built the disruption of Media 2.0. I find this wherever I go, that while working in the same environment, the two groups seem to speak different languages.

Media companies design websites to advance their models, while the world of the Web designs sites to advance the lives of users. Media sites are built around a revenue model — their revenue model — while disruptor sites and applications are, again, built around users. Media sites "drive" and route traffic, so as to monetize every opportunity. Those disrupting the media world tend to avoid these traps, because they are more interested in serving the needs of, you guessed it, users. In the end, who will win?

So the statement that "the Web is not TV" is much deeper and, frankly, more important than some appear to believe. The direct pursuit of money online in the form of ad-supported content is, therefore, problematic at best.

At the October "Web Experience Forum" in Boston, web usability guru Jakob Nielsen noted in a keynote address that, as reported by Giga-Om (What if you ran an ad and nobody saw it?), "web design is doomed to failure unless we learn from end users. And one major lesson is that other than paid search, ads don't work."

"We call this banner blindness — people won't see ads at all," said Nielsen. "Ads might as well not exist as far as users are concerned, except for search ads." (2) The number of web users that so much as glance at banner ads, he added, is too small to even quantify.

The findings are no secret to web usability professionals gathered here, who obsess over how consumers use the web. But they're often ignored by ad buyers.

"For the longest time, the web has been in collective denial of this phenomenon," said Nielsen. "People still have this old media thinking: They think of the web being similar to TV because it's on the screen and visual. The main distinction is whether it's active or passive, not whether it's on a screen or not."

The findings of which Nielsen spoke are also ignored by media companies, because, well, ignorance is bliss in the blue-smoke-and-mirrors world of traditional advertising. After all, the networks are out there selling DVR "views" as ratings, because it boosts their numbers, even though everybody involved knows that nobody watches the ads. Do media companies really care? We're content to take advertisers' money without ever asking the obvious — kind of like looking the other way while debt becomes the core driver of business growth instead of equity (but that's another story, eh?).

How long will local ad buyers ignore the obvious? I wouldn't bet the revenue ranch that it will be forever, because the ad community is learning that the Local Web is cost-effective and efficient. This is the ticking bomb for the traditional media online ad model, for the "quality impressions" value proposition offered by local media companies won't mean much when advertisers are able to find those same people elsewhere for a lot less money.

We need to care about this, because the slow leak of revenue from our legacy platforms threatens a bursting of the dam entirely, and the paltry (by comparison) dollars coming from the Web through display advertising on our portals cannot possibly make up the difference. That's no exaggeration; it can't be done. The Web is not TV, and the Web is not a newspaper, so let's take a step back to try and determine why we behave as though it is and, more importantly, what we can do about it.

The Web was not built by the institution of media, and that's vital to understand. If media had created the Web, the ability to restrict access to create artificial scarcity would be built in, because this is the world that media companies know. It's how we make money. We create "mass" by teasing, driving or forcing people to scarce content, and then serve advertising to that group or charge them for the privilege of membership.

But the Web is about abundance, not scarcity, and if we're ever going to find the gold in "them thar hills," we're going to have to adapt new mining tools and skills. Hence, the Web is not TV.

So who did build the Web?

As Fred Turner, Stanford Professor and author of the book *From Counterculture to Cyberculture*, says, "The distance between the Grateful Dead and Google…is not as great as we might think." (3)

So it's those damned hippies that built the Web, or perhaps it's more accurate to say that its roots are in the counterculture movement of the 1960s, and anything fed through that nozzle is unlikely to behave in a manner conducive to the financial needs of the status quo.

Early iterations of the Web — as far as news and information are concerned — resembled that of newspapers, because the bandwidth available "worked" only for text. Hence, we make "pages." We sell "display ads." There's a "fold." And so forth. Yahoo! is essentially a giant newspaper, so it makes for a natural marriage with the newspaper industry, which has hitched its future to the portal.

But the Web is not a newspaper. I don't even like the term "pages," because it's so misleading. But that's what we have.

Television is just beginning to hit its stride online, after ceding a big lead to disruptors who understood the Web. Few media companies really appreciate what's happening at YouTube, for example, because all they see is the lack of ad money attached to all those videos. In so doing, they miss the communities being created on the back end and the value of being THE repository of everything video. If we've learned anything from the Web, it's this: new value creation doesn't have to even vaguely resemble old value creation.

So if the Web isn't TV or newspapers, then what of the news and information business? If media people were to step aside, how would the technology experts who built the Web communicate news and information? The answer is in our old friend — or nemesis — the blog.

Blog software was created in the social media world for personal journals, following the linear process of writing when you have something to say and then posting it for others to read — writing, posting, writing, posting. With the assumption that people were reading the journals, the latest entry always appeared at the top. The simple content management systems that drove the journals all delivered a "home" page with multiple items stacked on top of each other and individual entries of the journal displayed — with reader comments — on internal pages. As tech media developed, the industry adopted the blog format, generally because the content management software was sophisticated and usually free.

Then came professional blogging, and the writers stayed with the software and the format. Nobody thought anything about providing news and information in a descending stream, with the latest entry on top. But as the blogging world grew, so did the elegance with which the back end of the software communicated with the Web, and the differences between the software choices, like Movable Type and Wordpress, more often involved the back end and not how the content was displayed up front. This focus on the back end is what separates tech media from traditional media. Old media's online emphasis has always been on the front end and driving traffic to the orderly display of content within in order to make money.

Traditional media companies have adopted some of the interactive innovations of blog software, but it's all done in the name of keeping people on the site to make money. This overlooks what's happening at the back end, and this is where traditional media needs to take a lesson from the tech denizens of the Web.

Blog software talks to the Web in such a way that it fits all its nooks and crannies. The handshake is perfect. It's automatically unbundled. Its interactions work across thousands of applications. RSS output is second nature, because the mission was always about getting the message out instead of driving users in. Linking — both outbound and inbound — are part and parcel of blogging, because its creators understand that links, not page views, are the currency of the Web. Comments, tags, pings, automatic referrals to related sites, trackbacks and a legion of other plug-ins and applications "connect" blog software with the Web and its users. Blog software isn't about form or format; it's about the Web. It is the ideal form of communicating information online.

In a very real sense, this is the real mission of journalism, only this format wasn't built by professional journalists. Now that many pros are adopting the blog format, there's a blending of both worlds underway. But the big difference between the two — at least for most *local* media — is in the back end.

The fact that the innovators of the Web and their user-centric vision produced a form and format for transmitting news and information is a critical point, if one is to honestly examine where we are and, more importantly, where we're going. You can say all you want about the depth of information available via the portal model, but simple blog software will run circles around it in terms of meeting the information needs of users. Simplicity is at its core, and it does it well. You have a message. You want people to read it. You make it as easy as possible for them to do so, or they will go elsewhere. Unfed sheep will bolt to other pastures, and this is the crisis facing traditional media and professional journalism.

We think that bigger is better, that the more "sections" or "channels" we can attach to our URL, the greater the opportunity for revenue. There are two problems. One, we simply cannot make enough "pages" to carry the volume of display ads necessary to sustain the business, and, of course, this assumes those pages will all be seen. Two, even if they are seen, we run into Jakob Nielsen and his usability research. Nobody sees the ads on those pages anyway.

Local media companies need to design their brand-extension web entities to fit the medium of the Web, and we need to take a lesson from the technical press. TechCrunch and Engadget are the two monster sites of tech media, and both are presented in blog format. Are they "blogs" or media companies? What's the difference? Giga-Om is another successful tech media site in blog format, and there are many, many others. Other tech news sites use the blog format for internal pages but play with the home page. Take a look at The Inquisitr, which is actually built in WordPress, a popular and free open-source blog software.

Veteran tech writer Duncan Riley is the founder of The Inquisitr and wrote in an email that the top of the blogosphere and traditional media are beginning to blend, as tech media reaches into the old world and traditional media reaches into the new. "Most people who hit The Inquisitr wouldn't know they were hitting a blog," he wrote. "The Inquisitr is proudly a blog, but our mix of content is more towards a magazine or newspaper format, and our design changes over time have come to reflect this."

Riley strongly disagrees with statements by some that blogging is fading. "Blogging is still growing," he wrote. "It's just that the line between blog and traditional news site is now blurred to the point that many can no longer recognize the difference." The difference, most assuredly, however, is in the back end.

And then there's monster entertainment/gossip site TMZ.com, which is also presented in blog format. This subsidiary of AOL launched only three years ago and has even developed its own syndicated television program, which has now cracked the top ten in syndicated shows. It has no plans to change its basic format, because it works beautifully in sustaining its continuous news model.

TMZ.com's parent company, AOL, also uses the blog format for its general news and business news sites, presenting the front page in hybrid format.

The ad models for these sites vary, but they generally emphasize impressions in the right column and between items in the left column. Ads in this format don't compete with other ads, and that adds value to their positioning. Advertising here is linear, because the content of the page is always changing. Hence, it can be sold by daypart. As I've written previously, TMZ.com sells roadblock ads by-the-hour and makes a killing in so doing. We could and should be doing the same thing.

Most of these companies also monetize their RSS feeds, because they know that much of their content is consumed in that format, and this is another lesson we could learn from them. Most media companies use RSS to drive users back to their portal sites, but this is not the practice of tech media. Full feed RSS, where the feed itself contains the entire story, is another example of putting users first.

The blog format, or some variation thereof, may not be the be-all-and-end-all for local media companies, but we need to stop looking past it as a real vehicle for communicating with our users. Most of all, though, we need to take a big step back and *honestly* ask ourselves a few questions. Do we require people to dance through hoops in order to access what we're presenting? Do we bury content to serve ads that nobody sees? Is our content free to roam in the wide open spaces of the Web? Are we restricting our ad infrastructure to that which is only within our own walls? Is what we're doing online really useful to web users? Really?

If it isn't, we need the courage to start over, because the front end is increasingly irrelevant, and the back end's the thing.

THE COST OF INTERACTION

In the business world, the biggest number on the expense side of the ledger is generally the people that the business employs, so it's understandable that businesses — in their quest to improve the bottom line — will always be seeking ways to reduce that expense. The one who writes the checks gets to set the rules, unless there's an artificial barrier such as a labor union in place.

When profit is the motive, everything else is its servant, including the people who help generate that profit. It's capitalism at its finest, a world where "the market" determines everything and where the faithful believe "corrections" come from the markets themselves.

But forthcoming corrections will also originate beyond markets, because we're in the throes of a massive cultural shift — from the "I think therefore I understand" world of cultural modernism to the "I experience therefore I understand" world of postmodernism. One doesn't displace the other; it simply augments and, in some ways, re-routes the former.

Hierarchical systems are all on the table in a postmodern world, because the ability of people to access knowledge isn't blocked by barriers based on education or position in the culture anymore. The doctor is still the doctor, but the nature of his or her authority has changed, because the knowledge that gives the doctor a special place in the culture is increasingly available to non-doctors.

Likewise, the strategies and tactics of capitalism are also available for all to see, and we're on the cusp of an all-out revolt against many of them.

The market, if you will, is correcting itself, and much of it will be built around what's called the "cost of interaction." This is the value placed on what is required for a customer to interact with the product or service of a business. It's not a part of the price of the product or service; it's simply a charge that customers are required to pay that is off-the-books. Heretofore, businesses have not counted this, because the assumptions of modernism suggest it's unnecessary, but it is the centerpiece of the revolt that many are already experiencing, including media companies.

This cost of interaction is one of real currency, but not necessarily that which is counted by banks. This is why it slips past the business world.

There is no greater illustration of the cost of interaction than the complex telephone answering systems that are a part of every business from coast-to-coast (and beyond). The business assumes that interaction with callers can and should be on its terms, so it creates an elaborate sorting system that it believes will guide the caller to the right party or turn many queries over to automated systems. The investment has been worth it, because it has enabled companies to cut costs in its telephone interactions with the public.

Of course, nobody ever consulted the callers about this, so these systems are often nothing more than a source of extreme irritation for the people the business (hopefully) seeks to serve. What companies don't consider is that by forcing people to jump through these digital loops, they have raised the cost of interaction that everyday people have to pay. **They have, in fact, shifted the expense to the caller,** and while people may not be able to verbalize it as such, they are well aware of the frustrating price they're being required to pay.

The worst of all, of course, is our government. Have you ever tried to navigate through the Immigration and Naturalization Service

(INS)? If you ever find yourself with a free hour to waste, give them a holler.

There are some smart companies who have figured out ways that telephone communications technology can actually work to truly serve callers. One is American Airlines, whose new recognition program is nothing short of a godsend. As a frequent American Airlines traveler, the system recognizes my cell number when I call, greets me by name, and asks if I'm inquiring about the flight I have booked for that day. Instead of walking through a navigation system to find the gate for an outbound flight, all I have to do now is make that simple call.

The cost of interaction is paid everywhere, and it's usually a part of the company's expense control or the company's convenience. Not enough personnel in the check-out line at the grocery store? The cost of interacting with that store has gone up. Arrive on time for an appointment only to wait an hour to see the doctor? The cost of interacting with that office has gone up.

A few years ago, Bob Jeffery, CEO of J. Walter Thompson, noted that "time is the new currency." That, folks, is **absolutely true**, and time can actually have a dollar value attached with a simple mathematical formula. Inflation may not be dogging our pocketbooks at this particular moment, but this waste of time has a direct impact in a world where time is the new currency.

It is into this cultural tension that media companies are attempting to do business online with the people formerly known as the audience, people who demand better service than they got as passive participators in old world media. TiVo made it possible for people to skip commercials, something they deem a waste of their precious time. Television's response has been to increase commercial pod lengths and shorten programs, thereby digging themselves a little deeper into an anti-consumer hole. The networks have even gotten together to create a video-on-demand service where users *can't* skip the commercials. Nice try.

But the biggest place where the cost of interaction impacts media consumption is on the Web.

Media companies don't seem to understand that people are in charge of their web experience, and the greatest evidence of this unwillingness to understand is in the design of media websites. By shifting the finished product version of their output to the Web, news organizations have created elaborate portals that require clicks in order to access anything of interest. Assuming that the finished product is what people want, media companies all take part in a dangerously archaic model of content management.

The same newspaper industry that will deliver its finished product to your doorstep is now enamored with ways to make it difficult to access the same stuff online. The roadblocks come in the form of tactics to drive page views and increase revenue by forcing users through navigation systems and relentless links. Online, the cost of interaction for most media sites is much higher than we think, and it will ultimately impact our ability to reach the people we need in order to make money through advertising. The problem, according to web usability expert Dr. Jakob Nielsen, is that the home page is increasingly irrelevant. About 40% of people in 2004 visited a homepage and then drilled down to content they sought, and 60% used some form of deep link that took them directly to a page or destination inside. In 2008, according to Dr Nielsen, "only 25% of people travel via a homepage. The rest search and get straight there."

This is not just a matter of convenience for web users; it's a direct reaction to the cost of interaction charged by sites in the drilling down process.

The scrollbar offers a much lower cost of interaction than links, and yet we value only that which is "above" some artificial "fold" in a web document. This is nuts and an insult to people who increasingly don't have time to interact with us like that.

The broadcast industry is no different. Take away the anchor pictures from the home page of any TV station site, along with the graphics, the marketing, the colors and the ads, and what you're left with is basically nothing. It's just a bunch of links, and if time is the new currency, why are we wasting people's time by forcing them to find what they're looking for in this manner? This is the

Achilles' heel of media company web initiatives, for we only understand marketing through our own platform, and the bigger the platform, the more money we can make. This is known as the "walled garden" approach to web content, for everything we offer is within the "walls" created by our portal. In a nutshell, this is why Google will always beat Yahoo!, for Google's platform is the Web itself, whereas Yahoo! only controls that which is within its walls.

Google so respects the online cost of interaction that it willingly withholds ads from its home page, absorbing the cost of interaction into its own operating budget.

But there's more.

Don Day, Digital Media Producer for the KTVB News Group in Boise, Idaho, and a blogger at Lost Remote, recently published an insightful list of how the typical broadcast website stacks up against Google's basic rules for website design. This would be funny, if it wasn't so sad. (1)

Google has published a list of ten things that make a design "Googley" — and they really are universal. The problem today is that most TV sites have their own set of principles: (2)

Google: 1. Focus on people—their lives, their work, their dreams.
    TV: 1. Focus on promotion—our newscasts, our advertisers, our sweeps piece.
Google: 2. Every millisecond counts.
    TV: 2. Can we make it flash or use a bright color?
Google: 3. Simplicity is powerful.
    TV: 3. Are there enough ad units above the fold?
Google: 4. Engage beginners and attract experts.
    TV: 4. People will figure it out on their own.
Google: 5. Dare to innovate.
    TV: 5. Are we keeping up with the competition?
Google: 6. Design for the world.
    TV: 6. Design for the boss.

Google: 7. Plan for today's and tomorrow's business.
TV: 7. Focus on yesterday's legacy.

Google: 8. Delight the eye without distracting the mind.
TV: 8. Distract the eye while cluttering the mind.

Google: 9. Be worthy of people's trust.
TV: 9. People trust the anchors. Use big pictures of them.

Google: 10. Add a human touch.
TV: 10. Add a touch more clutter.

The problem is essentially this: the design model that nearly all media companies use on the Web was created by newspaper people as a reflection of a newspaper. From the non-existent "fold" to ad impressions by placement and beyond, nearly every online media term is a newspaper term. We make "pages." We sell "display" advertising. It is entirely a print paradigm.

And of course, the Web isn't print, and therein lies the rub. The pursuit of this model has caused nearly irreparable harm to media companies, and the longer we pursue it, the worse things will be tomorrow.

Television news and other forms of information media all adopted the same paradigm, because that's what was in place when they, too, got into this business of the Web. And so the landscape of media websites resembles the homogenized marketplace of any suburb, with its comfortable franchises and such.

We've studied the model to find ways to make it better, and today, most media company strategies are built on the assumption that this is the way it should be. Few within the industry actually question whether this is true.

The advertising industry adapted to the paradigm, because, well, that's just the way it was, but at no time did anyone ever truly step back and say, "This isn't going to work." Well, it isn't working, because newspaper websites are now experiencing a serious revenue growth problem — one created, you guessed it, by the inherent flaws of the design. These flaws have been masked by incredible growth — "new" money — but now they've come to the surface in the form of a missing key ingredient in mass marketing — frequency.

Steve Yelvington is one of the smartest new media thinkers around, and a newspaper guy through and through. In a blog entry on the subject, Yelvington wrote that frequency is the hard wall that media companies inevitably hit online. (3)

We can fix our sales incentives, train our people, tune our pricing and our packaging, and replace leadership as necessary. But at the end of the day we're going to hit a very hard wall. That wall is "available advertising inventory" that meets the advertisers' needs.

That inventory comes from audience, from reach (unique users) multiplied by frequency (pageviews per user).

And while the reach numbers may look good, the frequency numbers suck.

It's even worse than the raw pageview-driven ad inventory would suggest. An effective advertising campaign requires repetition of the message until you really, really understand that Geico is so easy even a caveman can do it. There's an old ad-biz rule of thumb that a message has to be repeated seven times to be understood. If your average user visits your site twice a month, how can you possibly deliver effective ad campaigns?

Yelvington believes that social networking applications can help, along with RSS feeds, frequent updates, games, newsletters and embed applications. There's no doubt publishers can increase stickiness with these tactics, but they all miss the point that maybe, just maybe, we've gone about this wrong from the get-go.

Moreover, there's evidence now that the reach of a newspaper site doesn't extend much beyond its basic circulation, which prompts local online revenue guru Gordon Borrell to suggest there are other factors at work:

> The reason their revenues are flattening and in some cases actually declining is that they've upsold all their print advertisers. They've hit saturation, and without "online only" salespeople they

have a difficult time reaching beyond the core product. In fact, according to the latest data I've seen, the average additional "reach" of a newspaper Web site beyond its core print audience is about 7 points. That's piddly, and that tells me we're looking at an industry that's pretty much defined the web as a way to serve its readers, not a way to reach out to new customers.

One of the reasons for that is that finished product news is all media companies know, and that requires a box that doesn't really play nice with the Web or with the people flocking online to access news and information without all the crap that goes with it. If we had set out to design a system for communicating with people online that began with a low cost of interaction, we would hardly have chosen our portal sites as a model.

A big part of the problem is that media people didn't create the Web. That was done by the tech community, as were all of the tools of personal media. They were designed with a couple of simple thoughts all built around the idea of using the technology to communicate: One, blog software (the term the tech community created to define **their** view of communicating online) needed to be easy to use. With a limited knowledge of HTML and style sheets, a person could easily create and maintain their own website. Two, that software needed to make a perfect handshake with the Web to insure a simple communication path and to allow for the easy finding and sharing of that communication. RSS is another non-media creation, one that was used to help the tech community accomplish their dream of simple communications.

Media websites were designed by traditional media types concerned about maintaining their brand in a multi-platform world.

Personal media software was designed by web people concerned about the Web, communicating, and the creation of new brands.

YouTube is another great illustration of the tech community's view of online television. No media company would have ever come close to innovating such a concept. Not a chance.

So here we are as media companies with two significant problems on our hands, both of our own making. One, we want the Web to mirror our own business model — that being mass marketing through content scarcity. We've forced the issue on this and we're shocked that it's not working. Two, every attempt we make to grow revenue in this paradigm raises the cost of interaction for the people we're trying to woo. Ultimately, this will be fatal.

If we believe that the consumer is god-like online, then we'll respect that by designing applications with a low cost of interaction. In turn, the elusive "audience" we seek will come our way as surely as the old proverb of the better mouse trap. It may seem courageous to step outside the box of our portals to do this, but in the end, it's just smart business.

Advertising/
Marketing

ADVERTISING LOSES ITS BALANCE

In his brilliant speech at the 2007 Supernova conference, former McKinsey and now Deloitte and Touche business guru John Hagel posed fourteen unanswered questions about business in the age of digital connectivity and information technology. The first was highly provocative: *"What if there is no equilibrium?"* (1)

Equilibrium in the business world is a stable situation in which forces cancel one another; a sense of balance; a state of sameness in which things are either completely still or moving at a consistent rate. "When a market is not in equilibrium, prices will rise or fall, or quantities produced will rise or fall in order to reach the point of equilibrium," according to Yahoo Answers. (2)

There is a symbiotic relationship between equilibrium and scale, for it is equilibrium's assurance that determines how well the market for a product or service will grow. Scale is the most over-used and over-valued business school term of the early twenty-first century, and its assumption as a necessity for making money confounds business experts trying to compete in the new world, where that which scales is free and revenue flows from the edges.

So Hagel comes along and asks the greatest business minds of the world a simple question, "What if there is no equilibrium?" It is a profound question and one that is especially troubling for the world of advertising.

When I began consulting with media companies about technology and content, the first question in every board room or conference room was "Okay, Terry, we hear what you're saying, but where's the money?" This has always been the cart before the horse, but the question was so common that I began to switch the focus of my attention from the content of new media to advertising, where I've made exactly the same observation that I made about media many years ago — that the vast majority of the writing about advertising these days comes from people within the advertising and marketing industries. As I did with media people writing about media disruptions, I find this to be misinformed and self-serving, for Madison Avenue — like institutional media — wants and needs to co-opt the Web to sustain its place in the culture.

That's not going to happen. The disruption to advertising is even more significant than the disruption to media, for the symbiotic relationship between media and advertising is such that the symbiote, the media, feeds off the host, advertising, so advertising's disruption is of greater importance to media than any content that media may create.

Every question about the funding of future journalism, for example, taps this core issue, for advertising doesn't "need" the symbiote anymore. Just as media has been disintermediated, so, too, has advertising. And the disruption to advertising is different than the disruption to media, because people are using technology to flee what they view as a relentless bombardment of unwanted messages. At least there is a demand for news and information.

What if there *is* no equilibrium?

An article last year in Online Media Daily was typical of the advertising industry trying to explain to itself the causes of the disruption. These efforts always lead to Hagel's question, because the assumption of equilibrium — with its laws of supply and demand — is strong.

J. Moses, CEO of Ugo Networks, a Hearst company, New York, said no one would have predicted that tools making it easy for advertisers to do their job would produce lower CPMs (cost per thousand page impressions) for publishers. "That largely has been caused by the enormous supply of inventory pushed through the market," he said, noting that Ugo's remnant inventory pricing dropped significantly during the past couple of years.

Compounding the issue, the rise of blogs and social media created an imbalance between supply and demand, which some said produced confusion when trying to price media. The promise of the Internet is accountability, but buying display ads is a complex process that makes it more difficult for demand to offset the abundance of supply. (3)

Media companies that base their business models primarily on ad-supported content are all suffering today. Bankruptcies are commonplace now, and those that are able to avoid such protection are doing so by gutting their operations. 2009 is looking like the year of the bloodbath for institutional media, but for all the squawking about content, audiences and disintermediation, it is the disruption to Madison Avenue that's really to blame. As advertisers shift their money to the Web, the industry runs smack into Hagel's question.

Advertising — and specifically the type of brand advertising that runs Madison Avenue — is built upon the scale provided by equilibrium. In defending the Interactive Advertising Bureau (IAB) from comments by MSNBC president Charles Tillinghast that IAB standards had led to online display advertising being commoditized, Randall Rothenberg, CEO of the IAB, wrote in his blog that Tillinghast was ignoring history.

Indeed, the accusation ignores the very reason IAB members ...developed the ad standards in the first place: to reduce the complexity and transaction costs associated with interactive advertising, and allow the medium to scale. (4)

Indeed, Rothenberg's standards assume a stable environment and a sense of balance in the developing market of internet advertising, but such an environment simply does not exist online — nor will it ever — and this is beyond problematic for media companies hoping to create online revenue the old-fashioned way.

Already, the paradigm is collapsing.

Gordon Borrell, whose Borrell Associates studies local online advertising, believes that local online display advertising has already peaked and that it is a losing proposition for tomorrow. The graph below shows that companies with digital strategies based on generating page views and ad impressions will not have a future, assuming such strategies are hoping to produce revenue growth.

US Internet User and Online Advertising Revenue Growth, 2007–2011
Source: Yankee Group and Interactive Advertising Bureau

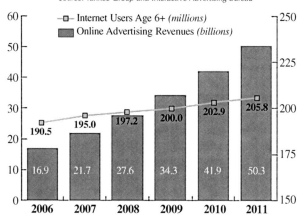

The online display advertising paradigm was pulled directly from the print industry, the group that originally designed the Web for media. Assumptions were made that simply don't apply, because the Web is not a one-to-many, mass marketing medium. It's a place where horizontal connectivity replaces the vertical, top-down model of communications. We weren't aware of this in the early days of the Web (or at least the media and advertising businesses weren't aware), so display advertising seemed a logical choice.

So dependent have media companies become on this that we've actually convinced ourselves that evidence to the contrary is simply wrong; at least that's the way we behave. Jakob Nielsen's usability studies have long shown that the eyeballs of users very rarely even see the ads, so the efficacy of the concept cannot possibly be what we hope it can be. And new research by Addvantage Media in the UK reveals that most people ignore display ads and especially on general interest websites. It's better for niche or specialty content sties, but those sites don't produce the kind of scale that Madison Avenue needs to function successfully.

Borrell noted in an email that the problem for Madison Avenue is a textbook disruptive technology scenario, namely that they make so much money running their core businesses that they think themselves too big or too important to deal with smaller interactive buys that don't produce the kind of scale normally associated with big money brand advertising.

> As a result, they have recognized the problem too late. Dozens of major interactive agencies have captured the business, leaving a lot of agencies with "interactive units" that pale in comparison to what the interactive-only agencies are capable of doing. It's a painfully familiar story with media companies that have tried, internally, to seize the Internet opportunity with existing staffs who inevitably try to mold the opportunity to fit the mothership's goals. Newspaper and TV web sites are chock full of news, weather and sports, while 88% (literally) of Internet users are NOT going to those sites, but instead flitting around between Google, MySpace, YouTube and thousands of niche sites that meet their needs.

Tim Hanlon, Executive Vice President/Managing Director of Viva-Ki Ventures and one of the most astute observers of big-picture advertising agrees. In an interview, Hanlon said that there used to be a relatively straightforward process for creating a message and finding places for it, but all of that has exploded. "The sheer complexity of opportunities makes Madison Avenue problematic."

> Madison Avenue is in the throes of the "death by a thousand cuts phenomenon." Lots of different opaque, black box services that agencies have done exclusively over the years are being chopped away by digital. These services are being made available to the common man, either through lower costs to entry or lower price points.
> The classic agency response is until it scales, it's not interesting. The scalable solution needs to be solved and agencies and

holding companies are in the best position to get there. The Mc-Donalds and Proctor and Gambles of the world need that. but what I'm concerned about is the rest of the marketing world. smaller brands, media properties, smaller agencies and the smaller dynamics such as social media or RSS that aren't immediately scalable and maybe never will be. To say that they don't exist or aren't important because they're not scalable is very dangerous.

Hagel's question is haunting. What if there is no equilibrium?

Equilibrium and scale matter much less in the direct marketing world, where it's all about finding interested people and delivering messages that generate business leads. This is the Web's specialty, and two of Borrell's projected growth trends — email marketing and paid search — involve direct marketing and lead generation.

Brand advertising has never been the Web's strength, despite Madison Avenue's wish that it would be, and Borrell thinks this is a big part of what's killing media companies.

I spent the last few months of 2008 visiting local agencies and studying the flow of marketing expenditures toward interactive media. Enormous amounts of money are being spent on website development and design, email marketing, search engine optimization, ecommerce functionality and database management. Because none of this is classic advertising, it tends to go right over the heads of agency managers.

The typical agency visit was dominated by the major media buyer and planner who brought in their "Internet experts" — typically junior people who said nothing during my visit — to discuss interactive advertising with me. When I questioned these experts, they were very knowledgeable about search engine marketing, somewhat knowledgeable about search engine optimization, and not knowledgeable at all about much else when it came to website development or interactive advertising. But they did know about the IAB ad standards and could cite the pixel dimensions quite clearly.

The needs of today's businesses are critical. Bankruptcy looms for many of them because of the economy. Now, more than ever, agencies need to do what they do best — help marketers sift through the "push" sales of media and determine the appropriate media mix that will affect sales... Most of these agencies today need to completely retool their organizations (though many of them would claim that they have, with their own in-house interactive units) to accept a different, technological-based understanding of marketing.

Borrell is spot on in viewing Madison Avenue's problem from the perspective of the people actually spending the money, for many of them are taking matters into their own hands. Nothing prevents any advertiser from becoming their own media company, shifting money away from traditional brand advertising to creating compelling content and serving it — along with their own ads — online. The mission is generating leads, for leads create real customers, and once you have a customer on your property, it's merely a matter of sales.

A large automotive client of mine in the South has built its own ad server and closely monitors every piece of data in developing strategies and tactics that it can control online. It's a textbook case of a local business using the tools available to anybody to drive its business in the online world. This company knows more about search engines than most media companies, and its use of tagging and data manipulation is so stunning that it causes real problems for the media companies in town, who wish the auto company would just buy branding space on their websites. That horse is so far out of the barn that it will never come back.

This client embraces social media and has developed successful — and highly cost-effective — ad campaigns via Facebook. They are only interested in leads, and they employ Google Analytics to study the movements of users as they come and go on their websites. They know which ad placements refer the most users to their sites, and because they serve their own ads, they are able to place advertising on any site that hosts traffic in the market, measuring the unique eyeballs that their ads cume. Each ad is fully tagged and contains unique code that allows the automotive company to examine bounce rates and determine where they're getting real return for their advertising dollars.

This is not good news for either the media companies or the ad agencies in town, but this is the future that Madison Avenue faces. The irony is that those who run media websites know all about using analytics to shape business. Why we can't use that knowledge to genuinely enable commerce for everybody in our communities is a real mystery.

The rise of personal media and the growth of businesses that cater to it — especially Google — is the real threat to local media downstream, for what J. D. Lasica termed the "personal media revolution" in his seminal book *Darknet, Hollywood's War Against the Digital Generation* includes both the people formerly known as the audience *and* the people formerly known as the advertisers. (5)

What if there is no equilibrium? The question applies to the neat, modernist world of yesterday and the businesses that have exploited it for gain through fundamental capitalism. As we are learning, however, the world of tomorrow — thanks mostly to the horizontal connectivity of the World Wide Web — doesn't play well with fundamental anything, and those who can get beyond their old assumptions are a yard ahead of everybody else.

THE PROBLEM WITH WEB ADVERTISING

Is it not self-evident that every human being has an inalienable right to avoid unwanted messages? This is a profound question for a culture that has evolved to become the world's salesman, for how does one sell without a perceived inalienable right to bombard others with those unwanted messages? If it's good for the culture, is it not good for its citizens?

These messages are called *advertising*, and you can find them anywhere you might find yourself, even in your own home. America is all about advertising, and the extent to which we all assume it's just a part of life is extraordinary, especially if you visit other countries.

As the twentieth century evolved, an unwritten bargain was struck between Madison Avenue and those who provide entertainment and information. The deal was that sponsors would pay for the programs that people watched in trade for the ability to drop messages into the programs. Hence, in the broadcasting world, the commercial was born. This was actually a good deal for everybody, including the viewers and listeners of these messages, because there was a clear understanding — especially early in the arrangement — that it was the sponsor's money that was actually paying for the program that the viewer was watching. In business, this is called a value proposition.

As a new century neared, however, this deal had been stretched to a point where the value proposition to viewers no longer existed. Commercial breaks had grown from a minute to four and sometimes five minutes in length. And a remarkable new paradigm emerged in motion picture theaters, where consumers themselves paid for the experience, only to be greeted with 20 minutes of commercials before the film actually started.

And now as disruptive innovations in technology surround us, how can anybody be surprised that people are using them to express their inalienable right and escape what economics guru Umair Haque calls the "carpet bombing of ads?"

Marketing is one of the most studied, scientific and sophisticated areas of our culture, and yet, it seems unable to take a step back and view with any honesty its impact on both people and the media. For if the deal between Madison Avenue and media is broken, who will pay for expensive productions and how will businesses get their (unwanted) messages out?

And as all of this was taking place, a new form of communications debuted, which was immediately seized by certain visionaries as a fertile ground for advertising. The first internet bubble occurred, because entrepreneurs bet that advertisers would rush to the Web. They didn't, and the crash that followed hurt a lot of people.

Slowly but surely, mainstream advertisers have now moved to the Web, where they've been greeted by revenue-starved — and therefore highly amenable — web publishers, including media companies with serious bottom line issues. Since the internet crash at the beginning of this century, web advertising has been a buyer's market, with advertisers determining the rates they will pay. This is about to change, as publishers are coming to the conclusion that their online properties are worth a whole lot more than what advertisers are willing to pay.

The decision by ESPN a few weeks ago to drop its association with third party ad networks was bold and sensational, but its significance seems to have escaped many, because not much has been said. That's too bad, because it was historic and unprecedented, a seminal moment when a publisher proclaimed, "I determine the value of my product, not you." The move will have a cascading effect on all media company web properties, which will ultimately be good for everybody, advertisers included.

ESPN has shut the door on ad networks, in part, because the measurements that determine value are so grossly out of step with what it costs to produce the environment in which advertisers can attract the attention of potential customers. How did this happen?

THE HISTORY OF WEB METRICS

Let's go back to the early days of the Web. There were two important factors at work that set the stage for a losing proposition for media companies. One, the earliest iterations of the Web were entirely text-driven, and who knows better how to monetize text than the newspaper industry? And so was birthed a set of newspaper terms that define the Web even today. We serve "pages." There's a "fold." Ad prices are determined by size and placement on the page. More content equals more pages, and so forth. Reach — or circulation — was the defining factor in making money.

Two, even though the Web mirrored the newspaper industry, the media companies making up the industry viewed the Web as the junior varsity, to be kind. This half-hearted perspective allowed the advertising industry to shift the newspaper metrics to a place that favored them instead of the media companies that owned the real estate in which the ads were served. ANY money was deemed found money, and so it went.

Even television stations adopted the print model without question and suddenly found themselves in the text publishing business. Many an observer noted — with an appropriately raised eyebrow — that TV reporters would have to learn proper grammar and correct spelling.

While all of these events are certainly understandable, given the circumstances, it does raise some interesting questions today.

If you read a newspaper, you are exposed to multiple pieces of content and all of the ads on the pages simultaneously. Your eyes can and do wander from place-to-place, scanning page-after-page, and this is a key part of the newspaper's value proposition. However, it simply doesn't apply online, which leads to our first false assumption about online media, specifically that content is served on pages. We may call them "pages," but they most certainly are not. And because we think of what a user sees in his or her browser as a "page," we cram as much as possible into that space, which frankly creates an environment of relentless clutter in which ads are in constant competition with other elements.

The page concept leads to other false assumptions. If these are not pages, then there is no such thing as a page "view." There is no "fold" either, a concept that has cost all media companies millions in online advertising revenue, because display ads (another newspaper term) below the nonexistent "fold" carry less value — as determined, I would add, by the industry itself. We stack all of our "good" content in the user's first browser view, thus digging two holes for ourselves. One, we make an unwritten statement that this is the only real value on the "page," and, two, we force users to pay the price of loading other "pages" in order to access more content. This, too, is an old newspaper trick, and the problem is that users can and do vote not to make all those clicks.

As stated earlier, online ads are often priced based on the "reach" of the website. the newspaper industry recognizes this as circulation, but ads sold based on circulation are far different from ads sold based on the reach of a website. Newspapers can pack in as many ads as they wish, simply by printing more pages and moving the content around. Online, however, more "pages" demand more content, and who's going to make it? So traffic to a website cannot be compared to newspaper circulation, because a web user is not exposed to the whole paper, so to say.

This is a good thing for the advertisers, of course, because the measurement of exposure to their ads is far more precise. The problem for media companies is that we've valued the ads based on the reach/frequency of the whole. Consequently, advertisers pay pennies online when they should be paying dollars. This is one of the reasons ESPN said, "Enough!"

Today, the revenue growth of online newspapers is shrinking, and much of it is due to the fact that there just isn't enough content to create the valuable ad impressions. Reach isn't the problem, but frequency is. A revenue strategy that is based in page views demands more pages for growth. It's that simple, and when you can't create enough pages to maintain growth, you have to raise prices, which is problematic in a buyer's market.

Another contributing factor is that the sales teams of traditional media have always been enamored with the size of their mass, despite the reality that much of it is based on, let's face it, blue smoke and mirrors. If one could apply web measurement standards to either newspapers or television (and they're trying), there's a real likelihood the legacy platform revenues wouldn't be anywhere near where they currently sit. For TV, blame the remote control.

DEMAND SHIFTS TO SUPPLY

What publishers need is a shift to the supply side, and here's one reason this is inevitable: The graphic at right is a projection from The Yankee Group on where online ad spending will be in 2011, just three years downstream. Even if the estimation is high by $10 billion, that's a lot of money for ads looking for a place to reside. Given today's metrics, it is impossible to accommodate that kind of money, although it's going to be there for the taking, because consumer behavior is shifting attention to the Web. By comparison, last year's total television ad spending — the granddaddy of all mass marketing muscle — topped $70 billion.

So even if more than half of that $50 billion goes to non-traditional forms of media (it will), we are still on the cusp of an enormous change in the value of online media company content, because there is no way we'll be able to crank out enough "pages" at today's prices to match projected revenue growth. It will have to come from price increases, for the pendulum will have swung to the publisher's side of the online value chain.

But will advertisers sit still for that using today's metrics? The answer to that will be determined by what kind of online advertising "works" in terms of branding or other kinds of ads, and so we're back to the original point of this essay.

Online publishers are going to have to work together to design advertising environments that will accomplish advertiser needs — without repelling consumers — and this has to begin with a new lexicon and new metrics that acknowledge that the Web isn't a newspaper or a television station. There are no "pages." There is no "fold."

"Browser view" becomes the central focus of design. The only thing that matters online is what the user sees at his or her end at any given point. Whatever is being viewed online is done so through a browser "window," and that is how we must approach monetizing our labor. We must strive for a one-ad-per-browser-view presentation, for that provides maximum value for both users and advertisers. This includes our own promotions, for we simply cannot compete with an advertiser for eyeball attention during a browser view and expect that any value is transmitted. The only things a user should "see" are content and a single marketing message. whether that be ours or an advertiser's.

The scrollbar is our friend. Since there are no "pages," we are free to work with the mechanisms inherent to the medium. In the print paradigm, the scrollbar is a nuisance that interferes with its objectives. That which requires scrolling has less value, so what's placed down the "page" is progressively irrelevant, including the ads. The scrollbar is not a nuisance; it's a valuable tool to help us in our mission of both providing news and information and supporting ourselves through adjacent ads. We simply need to design in a way that incorporates the scrollbar and give people content, not just a seemingly endless list of links.

Every ad placement has the same value, and it is high. The answer to the online frequency problem is to stop declaring that different placements have different values, because from an architectural standpoint, they don't. What should matter is the lack of clutter, which will dramatically increase the effectiveness of the message. Instead of disrupting the user's experience by blinding him or her with "engaging" ads, why not be respectful and kill two birds with one stone? As the pendulum shifts to a seller's market, we'll have the opportunity to raise prices, because all of our ad placements will be effective instead of just sitting there.

The cost of interaction is a paramount design fundamental. The portal website is colonial in nature, at a time and in a place where people are increasingly forcing their way out from under the thumb of cultural overseers. We may be enamored with the idea that people need us to guide them (pure colonialism), but the truth is they don't. The extent to which media companies stick with the portal concept is puzzling, unless the user has the ability to create the portal. The biggest problem with portals is they demand a high cost of interaction for users, who must follow preset navigation and childishly load page-after-page to find what they want. This is ultimately self-destructive, for the people formerly known as the audience (TPFKATA) are godlike in their control of information consumption.

At first glance, these concepts may seem foolish, but they are being implemented at sites like TMZ.com, where a "news-as-a-process" paradigm exists. Fifteen items are stacked in a left column, while ads are placed between some content items to the right. Only one ad can be found per browser view. The scrollbar is the navigation tool, and the cost of interaction is very low. TMZ makes a ton of money on Thursdays by selling roadblock ads by the hour to movie studios who want to drum up business for new weekend releases. Roadblocks, in this context, mean that every ad position in the entire user experience is dedicated to a single advertiser. It's very effective and a model that can be duplicated with any local media company.

Isn't it smarter, after all, to sell online ads by daypart? We know when people come and go, and we should price our traffic accordingly. We can sell roadblocks by the hour in the same way, for example, by offering them to a car dealer with a big weekend promotion upcoming. We'll make more money than we currently do, because every impression has equal value, and it's priced accordingly.

"Supply and demand is transformative," says Jarvis Coffin, CEO of Burst Media, one of the third-party ad networks trying to do business in a changing environment. "It shapes and reshapes value," he wrote in an email, "and it is doing so right now online with Ad Networks as its manifesting agent. For instance, ESPN.com's recent move to purge networks from its pages signals that value is undergoing a correction at the media brand end of the market: it says brand value is proprietary."

Coffin went on to note that the sudden explosion of vertical niche ad networks is "telegraphing that while value may be proprietary it is not exclusive: the media integrity of quality niche content online is real and must be reckoned with," which he views as a positive thing.

In the end, he concludes, it means increased pressure on ad networks to produce results. "No more setting up a table and selling umbrellas on the street simply when it's raining. It means regular customers and merchandise; which means an increasingly dependable marketplace; which means increased customer confidence."

Publishers need the same customer confidence, which isn't likely to happen with a continued emphasis on what we've known and practiced since 1995. So the pressure is not only on ad networks but also publishers, because, when all is said and done, we are the ones who must create advertising value for all that projected spending. You can't raise the price unless the value is there, but if it's there, we can demand and get what we want for the products we create.

Along the way, however, both the supply and the demand sides are going to have to deal with the scorched earth that their old paradigm has left behind, for the power that consumers now wield didn't exist when the original carpet bombing approach was in vogue. For everybody to win, treating web users with respect is job one.

THE HIDDEN DISRUPTION

The best scene in the 1975 film classic "Jaws" is when Chief Brody first sees the shark. I know you remember. He's at the back of the boat laying a chum line when the monster comes up right alongside the boat, opens its enormous mouth and swims away. Actor Roy Scheider's look was perfect as he jumped and moved away from the edge, and the script was even better: "We're going to need a bigger boat!"

This "bigger boat" revelation is one that's also occurring with a few media companies as they begin see the enormity of the disruption to advertising that's taking place. Yes, disruption to advertising, not content. Most executives simply point to the economy and expect some form of return when it gets better, but that's a very dangerous view of what's really taking place. Advertising isn't just shrinking; it's completely transforming, and with the transformation is coming a blooming irrelevancy for media companies who just "serve" ads. It's going to consume those who don't see the size of the problem. Simply put, we're going to need a bigger boat.

This kind of talk generally brings about the rolled eyes, coughs and guffaws, because there's still a great deal of money being spent on traditional brand advertising. These executives are happy with the present and view their mission as milking it for every possible dime. There's nothing wrong with that, but the extent to which it becomes our only focus is a trap, for two very powerful forces are at work that will change everything.

172

CONSUMER REVOLT

The first is the steady shift of consumers' time to the Internet, where they are in charge. A Harris Poll released in December and reported in Salon reveals that the time U.S. Web users spend online has doubled in ten years, from seven percent in 1999 to 13 percent in 2009.

> Harris said the increase in the past two years was "striking," and partly reflected growth in TV watched on the Internet and online shopping...
>
> People from ages 25 to 49 spent the most amount of time on the Internet (17–18 hours a week), whether at home, work or another location. Americans who were 65 and older spent only eight hours a week online, on average.
>
> Nearly a quarter of people aged 25 to 29 said they spent between 24 to 168 hours online per week. (1)

This is a significant cultural shift, for consumers now spend an average of eight percent of their week online, where they're able to avoid the tricks and manipulation of mass marketing. As Denuo CEO Rishad Tobaccowala noted in 2004, consumers are now in charge.

> ...2004 ushers in an "empowered era" in which "humans are God," because technology allows them to be godlike. The question Tobaccowala put to conference attendees is: "How will you engage God?" (2)

Despite what every good media company executive wishes to believe, people are simply fed up with the relentless carpet bombing of unwanted messages throughout their day. The Web is their salvation, a place where they can pursue the information and entertainment they want and need without this treatment. The marketing pyramid has been turned upside down; marketers must now obtain permission before approaching consumers.

I was recently surfing sports websites in search of stories about a particular game, and I noticed that even with pop-up ads, I pay no attention whatsoever to the message. My eyes focus on the "close" button, and that's exactly what I do. This is in keeping with studies by Web usability guru, Jakob Nielsen, who first identified the concept of "banner blindness." People simply ignore the ads on media company sites.

The point is that the longer people spend online, the more sophisticated they become as users, and that impacts what marketers can do with them. One of my baseline questions in Web research is "How long have you been online," because it determines much in how they can be approached. Things like the "price of interaction" that consumers must pay in order to interact with a website (e.g., clicking on multiple links to get to content) become real issues for long-time users of the Web. The assumption that we can tamper with such a thing is a sure path to turning people off, and that is a major issue in the evolution of advertising.

ADVERTISING IS CONTENT

The second "bigger boat" issue is actually more significant, and it's one that no media company executive wants to really accept. Simply put, the people formerly known as the advertisers are now becoming media companies themselves and directly pursuing consumers and potential consumers of their products.

Gordon Borrell has been studying the growth of an advertising category known as "Promotions" for many years. It's an area of growth, and one that hasn't really caught on yet at the local level (it will). The images from Borrell on the next page suggest that what's already happened at the national level is about to occur locally.

What this means is that local advertisers — the heart of the "business" of local media — are picking up the tools of personal media — easy-to-use software — to become a form of media company themselves. Twitter, Facebook and other social media applications allow businesses to deal directly with consumers, and allow consumers to deal directly with businesses that they like. This is transforming commerce, and it is a significant threat to media companies — unless they can find ways to work "with" the process.

Another factor at work in advertisers becoming media companies is the stunning recent growth of what's called "content marketing," the originator of which is generally regarded to be John Deere's 100-year-old *Furrow Magazine*. Subscriptions can only be obtained through John Deere dealerships, and the company's website asks, "Did you know…"

- John Deere publishes nine regional editions of *The Furrow* in the United States and three editions in Canada.
- Our editors are recognized as some of the top journalists in agriculture.
- *The Furrow* is believed to be the most widely read farm magazine in the world. It is published in 14 languages and is circulated in more than 115 countries.
- Our worldwide circulation is more than 1.5 million.

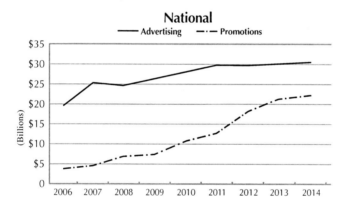

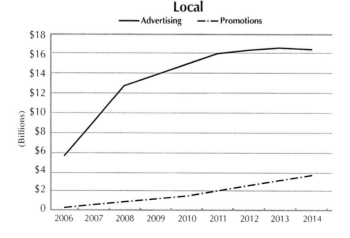

What you may not realize is that there is no mention of John Deere in the magazine, except for occasional ads. Since 1896, the company has used the magazine to generate business by developing ownership of the market on farming news and information. This is the premise of content marketing, and the low-cost, easy-to-use tools of the Web are undergirding dynamic growth in the market.

According to a new study by the Custom Publishing Council (CPC), the creation of branded content is at an all-time high. The annual study found that marketers poured more money into branded content in 2009 than ever before, double what it was in 2008.

"Due to rising demand, branded content has proliferated in recent years, expanding beyond its traditional roots of print publications and the Internet. The study shows substantial growth in our industry sector," explained Lori Rosen, Executive Director, CPC. "Perhaps even more importantly, 78% of respondents reported that branded content is more effective than advertising." (3)

The number one reason marketers choose this category is to educate consumers, and that's why it's felt to be so effective. It's not a method of directly marketing, but it does provide a very positive position in the minds of consumers.

Joe Pulizzi runs Junta42, a company he founded to help businesses create branded content for themselves. He's a "content marketing" specialist and a threat to traditional media, because money that his company generates or channels to others comes directly from the pool of money that advertisers used to spend on traditional advertising.

"Content marketing is the art of communicating with your customers and prospects without selling. It is non-interruption marketing. Instead of pitching your products or services, you are delivering information that makes your buyer more intelligent. The essence of this content strategy is the belief that if we, as businesses, deliver consistent, ongoing valuable information to buyers, they ultimately reward us with their business and loyalty.

Content marketing "works" on the Web, because it doesn't insult people by interrupting their experience. In this sense, it fits perfectly into the cultural shift to a post-industrial, post-colonial, post-modern, participatory culture. As the years go by, this kind of marketing is going to become increasingly important, and, as Pulizzi told me, the tools of personal media are making it happen.

> Everyone is a publisher today...I can communicate information in any industry with a computer and two minutes to set up a free blog account.
>
> In the past, publishing was exotic. It was expensive to deliver information to customers...be that by print, television, radio or in-person event. Now, anyone can do it...including brands. And they have to. Customers are gathering information to live their lives better or do their jobs better every minute of every day. They are ignoring more traditional advertising than ever before to get to that information. So, if the brand is not the content provider, how can they connect with the brand?
>
> Brands are now the new publishers.

The problem is that this kind of activity is taking place outside the view of media companies, most of whom are still trying to deal with content disruptions instead of those posed by advertising. Content is not the problem; advertising is the problem, and our websites — our boats — are simply not big enough to deal with it.

We have to either get a bigger boat through the creation of local ad networks, which take advantage of the growth of promotions and content marketing, or we have to get into the water and become disruptive sharks ourselves. We do that by teaching the people formerly known as the advertisers how to do everything we know how to do.

The disruption to advertising may seem hidden, but if that's truly the case, it is hidden in plain sight.

The Business
of Media

It's Always about the Money

When the Internet bubble burst early in the new millennium, many smart people learned the harshest of all business lessons: when the money's gone, there is no business. Great ideas aren't self-sustaining, and when the investors decide they've given enough, it's over, unless you can actually make money. Business is business, and while many of us frolicked in the coolness of innovation, those who paid attention to the bottom line were stressed to the max. In the end, it's always about the money.

Local media companies have frolicked in a world of easy money for decades — sitting back and taking orders from deep pockets who needed us to get their message out. Along the way, many mixed the mission of media with double-digit revenue growth and came to the conclusion that this was the way it was meant to be — that owning a printing press or broadcast tower brought with it some inalienable right to easy profit. This, of course, made us sitting ducks for disruption.

And today, amid the confusion of that disruption, it's tough to untangle mission and revenue. It is, however, a necessary task, for while we're trying to sustain our belief in our mission and the idea that advertisers ought to pay for it, the disruption has other ideas. And those ideas involve money.

180

As Hofstra University's Bob Papper said, "Television didn't hurt magazines by taking away their readers; television hurt magazines by taking away their revenue."

Two years ago, I first published this image of the iceberg that threatens local media. The Real Threat to Local Broadcasters has actually gotten worse, and it's mostly because we can't seem to see what's beneath the surface, choosing instead to play a game of multi-platform distribution.

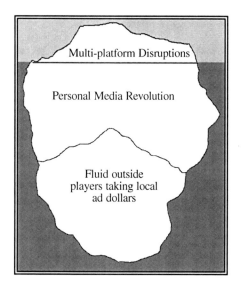

We dare not peek beneath the surface, but we must. As Upton Sinclair wrote long ago, "It's hard to get a man to understand something, when his salary depends on his not understanding it." This is our problem. This is our sin, one for which we can only assign blame to the mirror. Some local media companies are about to die — as in, go away permanently — if we don't do something about it.

J. D. Lasica first coined the term "Personal Media Revolution" in his seminal book, *Darknet, Hollywood's War Against The Digital Generation*, and it is complex and profound. However, most people in media think of it as just bloggers and YouTube and Facebook and such. The demagoguery of Andrew Keen in his book, *Cult of the Amateur* has done considerable harm to media company thinking, because it badly misses what's really taking place and instead offers a "professionals versus amateurs" theme. (1)

The problem is that the rise of personal media includes the use of its technology by businesses, and this is the ultimate disruptor for professional media and the advertising industry that supports it. When a business creates a dynamic website, it becomes a media company, and nobody knows this better than our friends at Google. Go back and look at the iceberg, for the rise of personal media is supported by the internet pureplay companies, who view the Web itself as their business platform.

When Google launched its money machine — an advertising system called AdSense — it allowed anybody with a web presence to earn money by placing simple text ads on their sites. The volume of its distribution is so staggering that Google can charge the advertisers based solely on the number of people who actually engage with the ads by clicking. A quiet industry built around this has bubbled up, and AdSense is just the beginning.

Now Google has announced free ad management software for websites, which will introduce all kinds of display ads to this same world. Anybody — read that anybody — can now sell advertising and run a complex rotating and targeting ad campaign on their website. Once again, Google is by-passing Madison Avenue in building an extraordinary machine to help the process of buying and selling in our culture.

The Personal Media Revolution gets stronger as the traditional media/advertising hegemony gets weaker.

Institutional advertising is saying, "Just show us the new formula (so that we can figure out how to game it on behalf of our clients)," while the new enterprise is gathering steam without them. It's all about by-passing the existing mechanisms, which is what textbook business disruptions do.

Internet visionary and pioneer Jeff Jarvis has been calling for an open source, open ad network for several years. He was prescient then, and his words in the wake of Google's announcement offer fair warning to traditional advertising:

> Google Ad Manager is one critical piece in creating the open network of networks where any site can take any ad and any marketer can advertise on any site. When that day arrives, we all become atoms that can attract to one molecule or another, no longer locked into one network. We start to see a truer marketplace for online advertising. We also get to see small sites gather together in large, ad hoc networks to compete with big sites — and this, I believe, will encourage and support the creation of more small sites. God's work. Or now Google's...
>
> ...There's just one issue: It's not open-source. And it's Google's.
>
> Google's benefits are clear: By offering free ad-serving to sites, it has an opening to be on many more sites, and when they don't have ads of their own to serve, Google can serve AdSense and make some more money. Google also gathers incredible data about ad performance and pricing and about the sites themselves. One big problem with its program is that it doesn't share that data with the publishers and let them use it to more efficiently serve its ads. It also doesn't share it with advertisers and let them take advantage of a more transparent marketplace.
>
> No, Google's holding onto that information itself and, once again, becoming smarter than all of us. And I say that's our own damned fault for not building our truly open ad marketplace. It's not too late, but it soon will be. (2)

Google's ad manager is also going to upset the Madison Avenue side of the media/advertiser hegemony, because it lowers the price of serving online ads to zero. In so doing, it calls into question the value proposition of online ad networks that require compensation of some form — beyond the revenue share — for the serving of ads.

But the biggest changes to come will be brought about by small entrepreneurs who are now able to serve any kind of advertising anywhere. Madison Avenue hasn't been willing to change, because there's too much at stake. So, once again, change will come from the bottom.

New forms of ad networks and ad agencies will spring up to connect advertisers with those willing to run ads on their sites. We can be the ones who do this, or we can continue to sit back and let it happen around us.

We need to build these networks, and they don't need to involve massive audiences. The most frustrating comments I hear from media companies in trying to help them build a network are complaints about the size of the audience in a niche. The old media mind thinks only in terms of mass and sets about a course to get from nothing to mass in a hurry. It's not about mass; it's about aggregating mass.

Media companies cling to their portal websites as if their place in the digital future is certain. It's not — and this is especially true at the local level — because commerce can and will be conducted without them. It's no longer (it hasn't been for awhile) about who has the biggest mass audience. Mass can be created through gathering lots of little pixels from the overall picture that is the World Wide Web.

Advertisers big and small will increasingly have marvelous tools at their fingertips that will allow them to talk to people in the community without going through traditional media audiences, and that will be the end.

After all, it's just business, and it's always about the money.

FAILURE AT THE TOP

In his famous 1960 paper for the *Harvard Business Review*, Marketing Myopia, Theodore Levitt first articulated the idea that many business failures stem from an inability to recognize what business they're actually in. The paper first articulated the oft-repeated claim that if railroads had understood what business they were in, they would have thrived in the new world of buses, trucks and air travel. This is what Levitt calls "failure...at the top."

The railroads did not stop growing because the need for passenger and freight transportation declined. That grew. The railroads are in trouble today not because that need was filled by others (cars, trucks, airplanes, and even telephones) but because it was not filled by the railroads themselves. They let others take customers away from them because they assumed themselves to be in the railroad business rather than in the transportation business. The reason they defined their industry incorrectly was that they were railroad oriented instead of transportation oriented; they were product oriented instead of customer oriented.

Levitt also wrote about Hollywood's failure at the top when television came along. Hollywood saw itself as in the movie business, not the entertainment business, and so it went through a painful reorganization during which many companies didn't survive.

Clayton Christensen advanced Levitt's beliefs in his seminal work *The Innovator's Dilemma*, because it is so fundamental to a correct response in the face of disruptive innovations. References to the concept are made in boardrooms, conferences and business schools worldwide, and yet, in today's revolutionary media world, it is amazing how many media executives seem unable to completely understand their business. This is a classic failure at the top, and it continues to lead company after company down roads that dead-end in crisis after fiscal crisis. As Thomas J. Wallace, editorial director at Condé Nast, recently joked, "Flat is the new up." (1)

A desperate search for some new, scalable revenue model for traditional media occupies the thoughts of every top level media company executive, but an inability to correctly understand the business itself gets in the way of seeing the solution.

It would be easy to follow the railroad metaphor and state that individual forms of traditional media — newspapers, radio and television — each think of themselves as in the "business" of their namesakes. Radio is the radio business. Television is the television business, and so forth. It's also correct to take a step back — as I've heard expressed at many conferences — and make the claim that these are all in the "information business" and leave it at that. It's certainly true, and it allows each to compete with the other. And where better to do that, the thinking goes, than on the World Wide Web?

But this is also a failure at the top, for information is not only being commodified at every level, there is also an inherent consumer demand that it be free. And where any "business" is free, there is no business.

So if the business of media isn't the medium itself or the information (and entertainment) it provides, what is its real business?

Media makes its money through advertising, and this is the only disruption that matters for traditional media companies, for new forms of media aren't taking readers, listeners or viewers away, they're taking advertising away, and this should be the principal focus at the top of all media companies, especially local media companies. Amazingly, it is not.

The Web attacks middlemen in any information value chain by rendering them unnecessary or irrelevant. This is true on the content side of traditional media, but it's also true on the revenue side, for advertisers simply don't need traditional media anymore to accomplish their goals. Advertisers are increasingly becoming media companies themselves, thanks to the tools of the personal media revolution, and this is a much bigger threat to media companies than fragmentation, consumer choice or any form of new platform. Advertising is the business of media, and it's here where our energy must be directed.

Automobile dealers, for example, are moving money that formerly went to local media companies to their own web properties and the known online stream that buyers follow when searching for a new vehicle (hint: they don't start at media company websites). Auto dealers have discovered that the brand advertising offered by mass media isn't as important as it used to be in reaching consumers, and that spending money online is a very efficient way to influence the bottom line.

With limited success, media companies have responded by trying to insert themselves into the online stream or using the reach of their brand extension websites to drive traffic to dealers' websites, but nobody has found the formula for getting back into the *deep* advertising pockets of auto dealers. The reality is there will be no formula as long as media companies insist that their own brands offer competitive solutions for dealers. This is a failure at the top.

Nobody understands this better than local online advertising guru Gordon Borrell. His company tracks the money being spent in every market, and their data (What Local Media Websites Earn May 2008) offers evidence that is hard for local media companies to swallow: outside internet pureplay companies like Google, Yahoo!, AOL and MSN now take 60-cents out of every dollar spent in a typical market for advertising online. The growth of this piece of the local ad pie is staggering, and it should be the main concern of those at the top of media companies everywhere. It's not, and even if it was, most wouldn't have a clue as to what to do about it. (2)

Borrell defines "pureplay" as "an organization that does business purely through the Internet." In the months to come, the pureplay piece of the pie is going to resemble Pacman devouring everything else, and this is the real business problem for all of traditional media. At the very top of media companies, it must be seen that the overall market is the target, not just the corner reserved for brand-extension online plays.

In many ways, it's almost too late to be saying this, but if you run a television station, a radio station, a newspaper or any other form of local media company, your online competition is Google, not the guys you've been competing against all these years. That is a simple fact. We may not like it, but to deny it is to ignore the heavily-armed battalions slowly surrounding your position.

And that position is indefensible, because to defend it is to cease to grow. This, too, is a failure at the top.

Google thinks of itself first as an advertising system, one that serves the entire Web. We also have an advertising system, but it can only serve that which we manage, and that's not much. We're thinking like traditional media — that the distribution of scarce information can scale in an environment like the Web. It can't, and it won't. The more people find other ways of informing themselves, the less they need our walled gardens. So our advertising systems decline in relevance, when the task is to get them to grow. Again, this is a failure at the top.

Current thinking in some media circles is that the creation of community information portals will do the trick in terms of increasing the advertising system of local media. These already exist or are under construction in some markets, and their creators deserve kudos. They are excellent sources of information, and a ton of work has gone into creating them, but they still function with a limited advertising system inside the market. Moreover, the way local media companies think is that if one does something, everybody has to do it, so eventually we'll have, let's see, at least four of those in every market. And each will feature the content from its offline brand, so the idea can easily become just a news portal site in new clothes. Google would love that.

Of course, we could always include links to the other guys' content, but we'd still feature our own.

In order to compete with the likes of Google, we must offer a better local advertising system than they provide. This can be done, because local media companies already have feet-on-the-street, whereas Google is moving from an outside-to-in position. Google also has limited access to local information (it can only scrape that which is on the Web), but these are things that we can easily gather to build a better database. There is still time, but the window is closing.

Local media companies can do two things. Both require hard work, and one is definitely outside the media company comfort zone. The first is to create a horizontal local ad network, one that serves all websites within the market and about which I have written extensively. This is the holy grail that the pureplays seek (and are well on their way to creating), but it's one that we are already equipped to create and manage. Who will do it?

The second option is to combine resources to create a single local information portal and to compete within that instead of standing alone on the Web — where we are divided — and offering to our communities fragmented local news and information. This may seem idiotic at first brush, but a successful example of it is already growing rapidly. It's called hulu, and one day all networks will offer their programming through its doorway. What began with NBCU and NewsCorp (Fox) has already grown to include Viacom and PBS. It works so well, because it is so customer-friendly, not only for viewers but also eventually for advertisers.

As Levitt noted, the most important duty for those at the top is to think about their business from a consumer's perspective.

When faced with criticism for offering a phone-less version of the iPhone, Apple's Steve Jobs made a remarkable statement that all media company executives would do well to hear. "If anybody's going to cannibalize us, it's going to be us." With this perspective in mind, creating a single local information portal with all local media companies participating becomes a logical business initiative. Moreover, if we don't do this, one of these pureplays will do it for us, and we'll just be the content providers, not the owners of the advertising system within.

This is not to say that local media companies should give up on their own brand-extension sites, but there are significant advantages to working together on such an advertising system. Here are just eleven:

1. It is extremely pro-consumer, in an age when that is an operational mandate.

2. It creates new value within the community for consumers.

3. It provides an advertising platform that goes beyond the walls of our branded sites.

4. With everybody on the same software platform, content specific RSS feeds can include multiple original sources.

5. As its popularity grows, so does its ability to create maximum "Google Juice" benefits for advertisers in their SEO strategies.

6. Revenue algorithms can be constructed so as to benefit the creator of the content being consumed.

7. In aggregating content that's not actually created by the partners, revenue can be split between all players. Half a loaf is better than none. The mission is to dominate the local information landscape, not hand it over by default to an outsider, because we're too busy trying to protect our own brands.

8. All participants can sell ads anywhere. Again, revenue algorithms can be created, so that the bulk of the revenue goes to the owner of the content adjacent to the ads. This gives

everybody an incentive to sell and greatly expands the reach of any individual contributor's branded advertising system.

9. Cookie data is shared with all participants, thus enabling contextual or even behavioral advertising — within or without the information portal.

10. Self-serve advertising revenues can be split evenly, assuming such an application is created.

11. All local media companies would be working to overcome the common enemy presented by the pureplays. As the ancient proverb says, "The enemy of my enemy is my friend."

To be sure, such a concept is fraught with issues and problems, not the least of which is overcoming traditional competitive thinking. But today's environment demands the willingness to be different and do different things, and the barriers standing in the way of a shared portal are merely process and procedural issues that don't have to block the end game. The point that really matters here is that, whether it's the creation of a local ad network or the building of a joint information portal, media companies MUST do something to expand the advertising systems within which they do business. To do otherwise (or nothing) is a textbook failure at the top, which future business school gurus will write about one day.

As Levitt wrote about the railroads, "they were product oriented instead of consumer oriented." This is our blind spot, that which makes us cling to our content and the ads that support it as our core business.

To be sure, the paradigm of ad-supported content isn't going to go away. Media companies will continue to make good money from their own content, but it will never be the growth engine it once was. We simply must find another way, because the more advertising evolves without us, the harder it will be for anybody to sustain the kind of business we've known in the past, much less make it grow.

These are challenging times for those at the top of media companies big and small, and while we can easily point fingers of blame at culture, technology or a hundred other things, it's the responsibility of our leaders to rise to meet business challenges. The only failures that matter, therefore, are those at the top.

And just as it was during the time of those early business challenges to railroads, the demand for what we do has never been greater. More people are watching television and consuming media than ever before, and that affords business opportunities for those who can rise above the fear, the noise, and the tyranny of the quarterly reports.

THE FIRST LAW OF SOCIAL MEDIA

In the new HBO hit series *True Blood*, we're introduced into the fantasy world of vampires in Louisiana. It's a fun series, because the books upon which it is based give us a world where vampires have just won civil rights. Conflict is everywhere, and author Charlaine Harris's vampires are not like those of Transylvania and the literature of yesterday. They're much more socially acceptable, and the world of their supernatural rules is what I find most fascinating.

In the series, John Compton, a vampire, is in love with Sookie Stackhouse, a human, and it is through their relationship that we learn most of these rules. One of them is that John must be invited or "welcomed" into Sookie's home, and if that welcome is ever rescinded, he is "expelled."

True Blood is, of course, true fiction, but this rule is most definitely not, especially in the invitation-only world of social media. It is so significant that I call it the First Law, because the entire paradigm of social media is based on it. I am in charge of my personal walled garden, and I decide who's welcome and who isn't. And the thing about rescinding my welcome is that it's very unlikely I'll ever invite you back.

This has profound significance for media companies — and others — who see advertising gold in the hills of social media. A recent report from IDC found strong growth in social networking services (SNS), but that salivating advertisers have yet to realize its potential for advertising.

IDC expects that lower-than-average ad effectiveness on SNS will continue to contribute to slow ad sales unless publishers get users to do something beyond just communicating with others. If the major services succeed in doing so, they will become more like portals, such as Yahoo! or MSN, and they will come closer to the audience reach of the top services. If that happened, publishers would be better able to monetize their SNS.

Notice the phrase "get users to do something." This is the essential problem that Madison Avenue has with social media, and that's because it refuses to acknowledge that these are personal pages and that advertiser (or media company) presence comes by invitation.

This problem was noted in an AdAge article (P&G Digital Guru Not Sure Marketers Belong on Facebook) that quoted Ted Mc-Connell, Manager of Digital Marketing Innovation at P&G in Cincinnati, as saying, "What in heaven's name made you think you could monetize the real estate in which somebody is breaking up with their girlfriend?" Social media guru John Battelle took on AdAge:

> "'Social networks may never find the ad dollars they're hunting for because they don't really have a right to them,' said Ted McConnell," the article begins. It then goes on to lay out the reasoning behind such an assumptive lead: McConnell doesn't like random banner ads, and Facebook's targeting, which purportedly solves the issue of randomness, leaves him cold. Given those two things, AdAge drew what I must say is an extremely lazy conclusion: Advertising on social networks doesn't work — look, a senior guy from Procter says so!
> Well, I'm here to call bull on this myth. And I'm pretty sure McConnell would agree with me.
> Let's break it down. To begin with, the article makes this easy assumption: Social networks are "hunting for ad dollars." That presumes a very traditional approach to media — that social networks have traditional packaged goods media assets (like, say, a television

show or a magazine), and are out "big game hunting" — IE, trying to sell proximity to those assets to "big game" like P&G.

But as I've argued (over and over and over) social media "assets" don't look like packaged goods assets, and neither should social media marketing. As McConnell rightly pointed out, you can't barge into the middle of an intimate social situation, yell "buy my stuff!" and then leave. A brand that does that will certainly be remembered — as a clod. (1)

Being a clod is certainly the way to get kicked out of the social media party, but the decline of every form of media begins with the rescinding of a welcome. Media companies don't see this, so we don't believe it. We believe our own hyperbole, and can't imagine that we're actually doing things to make ourselves less welcome in the lives of consumers.

Radio abandoned the world of local personalities and events in favor of more profitable, remotely-served and carefully researched "formats." The only thing local is the ads.

Magazines lost their essence in the quest for revenue by cramming content in between all the ads.

Newspapers lost classifieds by charging exorbitant rates, because they could. Newspapers also suffer from relevance decay in the pursuit of the Woodward and Burnstein model of journalism, but that's another story.

Television reduced the length of programs in the name of adding more spots. Ad pods of four and even five minutes in length — once thought absurd — are now finding their way into the mix.

Cable will be next (you find a lot of those lengthy pods there), and then will come the Web. It is our nature in media, it seems, to take advantage of our fans rather than putting them first. In fact, the web properties of most traditional media companies are already famous for dissing users in the name of revenue, and that, too, will have its consequences. "Driving traffic" within a site raises the price of interaction with that site, and nobody feels welcome in such a scenario.

I remember a conversation with a general manager once about the essence of the local television business. He came up through the sales side and got the GM job, because he correctly answered a question posed by the group vice president: "Are we in the business of serving the community, or are we in the business of making money?" You can guess which viewpoint got him the job.

And that's precisely the problem, for somewhere along the path to profitability, we crossed a line and entered into the assumption that, as the masters of our businesses, we could behave in any way we deemed appropriate, regardless of how inappropriate our customers felt we were behaving. In the final analysis, for example, television doesn't have a revenue problem nearly as much as it has an audience problem. Fix that problem, and the other goes away.

This inability to accept culpability in our current conundrum is one of the things that keeps us from doing anything about it. The old adage about digging yourself deeper into a hole is relevant, because you have to know you're doing the digging before you can stop. This is evident in the blame game currently underway involving Jeff Jarvis and traditional journalists. Jeff thinks journalists need to look in the mirror in assessing their current crisis, but that's offensive to those who believe they are victims.

As media companies, we must make the assumption that we have customers — our users, not our advertisers — only because they've invited us into their lives, whether it's a TV signal, a newspaper, the Web, or whatever. Our first responsibility, then, is to respect that invitation and not be rude or boorish or, worse yet, overstay our welcome. It's basic relationship stuff.

I'm often drawn back to simple words of Tim Berners-Lee, widely regarded as the creator of the World Wide Web. Early in its development, he said, "The Web is more a social tool than a technological one," so this idea of an invited guest is even more apropos here. The pros of tech media — and especially experienced bloggers — understand this well, because they know that only in serving and respecting their readers do they stand a chance of "influencing the influencers" of the new world.

New York venture capitalist Fred Wilson is one of these people. His company funds some of the top, cutting-edge start-ups, and Fred's been blogging for several years. You'd think a guy like him wouldn't have time to blog, but he considers it a valuable use of his time. In a recent post (Do you ever do any real work?), Fred revealed his understanding of the principle of the invited guest and of what that means in the long run.

He wrote of a new investment, Boxee, and how he'd spent time sending free invitations to the people who had left comments about the company on a blog post he'd written the day before. It took him an early morning hour to cull through the comments, find email addresses and send out about 100 invitations to the alpha release, a number that seems insignificant when compared with Boxee's already 50,000 registered users. But, as Fred pointed out, in the world of social media, it isn't the number that counts, it's the guests themselves.

> …the time and energy I've put into this blog for the past five years has built a unique and very sophisticated audience. You are connectors and hubs of influence.
>
> I know that one person out of the 100 I invited this morning will be incredibly impactful for boxee. It could be five people, it could be ten. Who knows?
>
> But in the world of social media, word of mouth and word of link marketing, it is connectors and influencers like all of you that make the difference.
>
> And that's one of the main reasons I keep writing, commenting, discussing, and participating in blogs, tumblr, twitter, disqus, and the social media world at large.
>
> It's about the "realest" work I do. (2)

Fred is an influencer, and he understands that building an expanding circle of other influencers is smart business. He treats them as he would want to be treated, knowing that they could just as easily find other sources of influence. He's leading a tribe, and while you'd be hard-pressed to find a smarter, more connected and powerful individual, his behavior towards his readers is humble, transparent, honest and authentic.

Fred Wilson is also keenly aware of the power of unbundling, for his blog is likely consumed via RSS far more than by people actually coming to his site. His use of social media evidences his clear understanding of the concept of rescinding the invitation, for when your thoughts and ideas exist on somebody else's personal web page, you're smart to respect the invitation.

Seth Godin, who wrote the book on Tribes, is another influential guy that really "gets" this concept. To Seth, the Web is all about connections, and it is in those connections that opportunities for business exist. The connections, however, follow the simple laws of human interaction, including the recognition that forcing a connection isn't really a connection.

Seth wrote that to make money on the Web, you only need connect the disconnected:

- Connect advertisers to people who want to be advertised to.
- Connect job hunters with jobs.
- Connect information seekers with information.
- Connect teams to each other.
- Connect those seeking similar.
- Connect to partners and those that can leverage your work.
- Connect people who are proximate geographically.
- Connect organizations spending money with ways to save money.
- Connect like-minded people into a movement.
- Connect people buying with people who are selling. (3)

There is no connection where one side is manipulating the other. There is no influence where it's forced. There is only diligence in serving the connection with others, and that means honoring the invitation that you've been given.

And here's the real problem for traditional media companies about all of this. The new media companies of today are the advertisers of yesterday, and they are learning the rules of social media. Why ride the back of a third-party — a traditional media company —

when you can work the invitations yourself? Advertisers are already experimenting with this through MySpace and Facebook pages, offering clever applications, building lists of "friends," and exploring how to connect directly with people who may be interested in their brands. In so doing, they're learning this first rule, and I guarantee you that they will be very careful in managing those relationships.

If advertising is the business of media, then what's left for us? As Seth Godin notes above, it's about helping advertisers make those connections, and that means we have to observe the rules of being social.

There's a lot of difference between being the person on the stage and being a part of the audience, but when nobody's looking at the stage, the audience is the only place to be. And down here, among the throngs, it's all about the invitation, for it may resemble the bar scene at times, but it functions more like a party at somebody's house. We can be an ass and never get invited back, or we can respect the invitation.

[*Author's note:* The reference to HBO's vampire saga is in no way intended to be a metaphor for traditional media companies and their customers.]

Embracing the Disruption

When Antonio Perez took over as CEO of Eastman Kodak in 2003, it must have been a little like taking the wheel on the bridge of the Titanic. What has happened since is a story that will be told in business schools for many years to come, because Perez did what many felt was impossible — he cleared the iceberg without sinking Kodak. The company has not only avoided collapse, but it is now prospering in the world of digital photography.

East Bay Business Times writer Connie Glaser visited Kodak late in the summer of 2008 and wrote of the remarkable reinvention of a company once thought dead.

> Kodak, which used to be called "The Great Yellow Father" because employees remained with the company their entire career, has dramatically changed. Sixty percent of the people at Kodak today weren't part of the company four years ago. Hayzlett (chief business development officer Jeff Hayzlett) calls the new focus "Kodak 2.0," and explains that within the past four years 70 percent of Kodak's "traditional business" (i.e., film) has been shifted to digital. This has led to the development of 19 products that now comprise 80 percent of revenue. (1)

Think about that for just a minute. 80 percent of Kodak's current revenue comes from products created within the last four years!

Let that sink in, because it reveals what can be done in the face of disruptive innovations.

There are many lessons to learn from the leadership of Perez, but for media companies deep in strategy decay, the most important takeaway is to become a part of the disruption — to be fearless in attacking yourself and even your core business. This is the key reinvention concept missing in media company digital efforts, and especially those of local television.

One of the most common questions I get from media companies involves confusion over using the legacy platform to market multiple web products. Conventional mass marketing wisdom says to use the TV station or newspaper to drive traffic to a single point of entry, usually a portal website. This cannot provide sustainable growth, because no matter how "big" the portal is, it will never be big enough to keep pace with the growth of the Local Web itself. The real problem is that this "one-stop" thinking is exactly the opposite of what's necessary, because the Web is the disruptor, and it's perfectly capable of promoting itself.

The early models of television station websites were mostly created and maintained by ad networks, who made their money through aggregating large audiences for national advertisers. These companies provided ways for local media companies to get their content online and make some cash through convergence advertising packages that used the TV station to drive eyeballs to the Web. In the minds of everybody involved, the TV station was where the real money was, and offering special web promotions was just a way to make extra dollars for broadcast advertising.

The same concept for newspapers is called "bundling," and it's one of the problems leading to the online inventory squeeze being felt by many newspaper companies. If the inventory is given away in the name of newspaper ads, what's left to sell?

No one ever considered that the Web itself was capable of sustaining a business without the "help" of the mothership, and the extent to which this attitude exists today is a key factor in why the disruption continues to advance without traditional media at the helm. Like Kodak, we must be willing to give the disruption its due — to embrace it fully as THE way of doing business downstream.

So the idea that owning a local television station in a market is an online competitive advantage needs to be re-examined, because we're looking at it backwards.

When the question of multiple products comes up — and the marketing person starts talking about how it's better to just point viewers in one direction — I ask this question: what would an internet company do to grow and expand in this market absent a television station? While the truth is it would be an uphill battle, the Web is perfectly capable of providing the growth necessary to sustain an online business. In fact, that growth and business has a lot better chance in the long run. because it has played by the rules of the Web, without the artificial advantage of an outside driver of traffic.

Witness what's happening in the world of neighborhood sites, like Cory Bergman's neighborhood blogs in Seattle, hyperlocal sites, like Lisa Williams' h2otown.com, and online-only newspaper sites like The Batavian and Bluffton Today. There are untold thousands of others, each competing with the portals of the traditional media companies and using the method of serving the information needs of a niche audience to draw the eyeballs that advertisers seek.

The Batavian is "published" by Howard Owens, director of digital publishing for a northeast media company. Widely regarded in the newspaper industry as one of its most astute observers and digital innovators, Owens launched the site on May 1, 2008 using the open source software Drupal for content management. It's delivered in a basic blog format and is the first local, online-only news source for Batavia and Genesee County in New York.

"The Batavian began as an internal discussion," Owens wrote in an email, "about what we might try online in the local news space without involving directly a newspaper. It was kind of an evolutionary process of discussing and thinking through ideas before we decided to go the direction we did."

"A good many local newspapers now get 8, 10 even 15 percent of their revenue from online now. And the criticism of this gross amount of revenue is that it isn't enough to sustain a typical daily newsroom. There is also an assumption that because most of this revenue is derived from up sells, that you can only get to that amount when attached to a newspaper. We decided to turn both of those ideas on their head. What if we could achieve nearly the same amount of revenue without a newspaper? Then, what sort of news operation could that amount of revenue support. The experiment here, if you want to call it an experiment, is that we first build the news operation we believe the local market can support, get the audience, then try to fund it to the levels we believe achievable." (2)

Without revealing numbers, Owens says he's happy with the results so far, although he plans advertising modifications to do better. The Batavian is an interesting concept on many levels, not the least of which is it doesn't have to deal with the reticence of traditional newspaper sales account executives to sell against themselves with their online products.

Note especially Owens' reference to the "up sells" dilemma of newspapers. This is exactly the problem with the convergence advertising packages that came from the old ad network model for TV websites in the 1990s. As long as media companies continue to use the Web to create legacy advertising packages, they will undervalue their web properties. And while local stations are busy stunting with convergence, the ad networks are making money from the traffic driven to those sites by the very nature of the convergence deals. This is good for the ad networks, but its value to local media companies is problematic.

Mike Orren has been running Dallas-based hyperlocal site Pegasus News for several years and has mixed feelings about going it alone or being a part of an incumbent media company's brand. "The upside to going solo," he wrote in an email, "is that you don't have all the baggage of the incumbent operation: Fear of user-gen content in the same environment with professional; resistance to linkouts; aversion to YouTube and Flickr as content; and the conversational tone and community ethos that I've yet to see a traditional outfit pull off successfully."

The advantage of being with a known brand, Orren notes, is in sales. "It took us a year and a half to get over the 'who are you' problem," he wrote. This extends the sales cycle for Pegasus, but he still believes the advantage of being able to use all of the tools available in the online media space is worth the extra sales effort. "Traditional media (YP, TV, radio, newspaper) have the feet on the street to do it," he added, "but first, they'll need to lose some baggage before a pure-play like us with deeper engagement and harder-won relationships beats them to it."

Operating an incumbent media business in the same community with local web initiatives will always be a competitive advantage, as long as the legacy platform can be used to market the web properties. But there are bigger advantages to consider. One, the web products can use the legacy platform for "reverse" bundling or convergence, where air time or print ads are used to add value to online advertising. This may be the biggest value of operating an incumbent local media brand struggling to boost its online budget, and in a down time of mainstream advertising, the inventory is certainly there. Two, the Web can be used to boost "traffic" to the legacy platform, and this the opposite of what most marketers see. Rather than building something to extend the brand of our legacy businesses, perhaps we should be thinking of building things that will enhance that brand from the bottom up.

If the Web is growing, then it should be our primary focus, using everything we have at our disposal to reach revenue levels that will sustain both. Moreover, if we only use the legacy platform to drive traffic to the Web, that effort is limited to the reach of the legacy platform. In the TV business, this is especially foolish, for the eyeballs in the community are split four and sometimes more ways in following the "favorite" stations of viewers. Competing on the Local Web can reach much larger shares of the community, which is another reason not to limit our web efforts to only a single point of contact.

We simply must remember that our competition online is not the other legacy media outlets in town, no matter how hard third-party ad networks try and force it to be otherwise. Third-party networks make their money by providing reach for their clients using as few outlets as possible. It's more cost-effective for their business to handle national clients this way. They could care less about the structure of the Local Web and the enabling of commerce therein, and the extent to which we've allowed ourselves to serve them and not the local advertising community is the shame of local media companies everywhere.

We're in a fight for our lives, and we'd be foolish to reject any revenue we can obtain, but we must start thinking strategically about the nature of the Web and what's really taking place around us. Reach Local, for example, is a company using non-legacy media web advertising tools to assist local businesses in reaching customers. The company resells Google AdSense ads, among other tools, and teaches local advertisers the value of how the Web works. The Newspaper Next project is now suggesting that local newspapers provide the same kind of service, becoming ad brokers for local advertisers. This may be a case of too little, too late, because Reach Local is well-established and growing every day, but the idea is certainly worth exploring.

Traditional media has a history of waiting for innovations from others and then copying them for success. We're happy to "lift" an idea from another community and make it our own, but this habit is deadly in the online world. That's because the innovations are coming from outsiders with their hands in our formerly stuffed pockets. They're omnipresent, and they have no intention of succumbing to our vaunted brands. To the users of the Web, MySpace, Facebook and thousands of others are local sites. They don't have to be geographically-based to have a geographical influence, and those hip to the ways of the Web know this, including a growing number of local advertisers.

Kodak embraced the disruption that was decimating its film business. The company is riding the disruption into the future by never looking back at the "good old days." It did not come without real pain, however, for reinvention has no respect for those who fight or otherwise refuse the future it offers, nor does it — or can it — concern itself with the unfortunate souls who are, through no fault of their own, caught in its need to save the many at the expense of the few. Note that 60 percent of Kodak's workforce wasn't there four years ago.

It's like that when customers demand something other than what they've been getting.

USING FREE TO SELL PAID

There is a misconception in the world of journalism that news has only one definition — one set of rules and guidelines — and that the demand for news, therefore, is limited to what those rules and guidelines can produce. Moreover, there exists an ancillary misconception that the output of a news organization must always be monetized. In the world of Media 1.0, these beliefs are connected. In the Media 2.0 world, however, neither is correct, and the combination places a major structural barrier in the path of reinvention.

For media companies, this is fatal, because the "all eggs in one basket" approach — where every feature, event or investigation is a "story" with ads attached — leaves us helpless in the face of disruptive influences to the model that supports this practice — mass marketing. We can be excused for this approach to the news, for that's what we know and have practiced for at least the past century.

But for a minute, let's leave the comfortable confines of this nest and venture out into the seemingly chaotic void of the Internet Superhighway. But wait! We can't do that, because there is no highway, only the illusion of one. There is no void. There are no roads, no maps, no dwellings, no trips, no visits, no point-A or point-B. There are only databases and documents with sophisticated code that come alive when your browser tells them to do so, right there in front of you.

This simple reality is the most important piece of knowledge we need to move forward, because nobody comes to our stage in the World Wide Web. We go to them, individually. As such, it's a world of direct marketing. The Web doesn't exist for you, absent your browser, and that browser window of yours is unique. This is the great disruptor and yet the great hope for all of us, especially the people formerly known as the advertisers.

In the news business, revenue is derived from our stage, either through ticket prices or dancing advertisements. We can and probably always will make this kind of money from browser windows, too, but that will never take the place of money from the stage, because the browser window is too precise. The stage allows for a degree of opaqueness. Value is determined, not by the individuals present, but the audience as a whole, and that puts us in a command position. We call this "reach," and it's what we know well. Online, however, advertisers don't need our reach, so our branded stages don't have the same value proposition, and this shoots a big hole in the "all eggs in one basket" formula for news.

To fully understand business strategy for news organizations involving the Web, we must go back to that single browser window, whether portable or not, and consider what we know from existing research. The top two reasons people use the Web for news are for breaking news and the weather, and yet we use the Web as a "platform" for our "all eggs in one basket" approach. That which we produce for the stage is that which we produce for the Web, because our ability to do business is tied to the content we create. This thinking must be exorcised from our minds, if we are to find a place in the world of Media 2.0.

If people use the "news web" primarily for breaking news and the weather, we ought to be able to meet those demands and, in so doing, drive traffic to our stage. So the value of online news to the news organization is almost entirely marketing, and in chasing revenue the old-fashioned way online, we're actually helping to devalue our stage. Pause here, and think about that for a minute.

Chris Anderson, the *Wired* editor who authored the "Long Tail" theory of web economics, has a new book coming out this summer on the economics of free, called "Free. The future of a radical price." Free is not a business model, but it is a smart strategy, according to Anderson. Google, for example, doesn't charge people to search. That's "free," and they make their money — lots of it — by putting ads on everything in those "free" search results. In an email, Anderson told me that "free is the best form of marketing."

> That's true for software (freemium), books (my book will be free in digital form), music (recording music is marketing for the concerts), games, etc. Indeed, wired.com is in some sense free marketing for *Wired Magazine* (like most of our titles, the website's business function is in part to sell subs).

From an advance copy of Anderson's book:

> (Information wants to be free) is misunderstood because it is only half-remembered. Brand's (Stewart Brand, creator of the *Whole Earth Catalog* and regarded as the author of the phrase) other half — "information wants to be expensive, because it's so valuable" — is ignored, perhaps because it seems both paradoxical and tautological. Perhaps a better way to understand it is this:
>
>> Commodity information (everybody gets the same version) wants to be free. Customized information (you get something unique and meaningful to you) wants to be expensive.
>
> But even that's not quite right. After all, what is a Google search if not a unique and customized sort of the Web, tailored just for you to be a meaningful response to your query? So let's try again:
>
>> Abundant information wants to be free. Scarce information wants to be expensive. (1)
>
> In this case, we're using the marginal cost construction of "abundant" and "scarce:" Information that can be replicated and distributed at low marginal cost wants to be free; information with high marginal costs wants to be expensive."

The concept of "free" shoots a big hole in the "all eggs in one basket" paradigm for news, because it suggests a new role in the dissemination of news content — a vehicle to move people to other, more monetizeable forms of media, including advertising. But Anderson is not speaking of the "tease" strategy employed by contemporary media online. "Free" as a tease is not really free, so we're talking about a new form of free information.

So let's assume that a free form of news is strategically smart to use as a marketing tool for forms of news delivered from our monetiziable stages. This frees our minds to think differently about that browser window, for rather than seeking to build our service around revenue, we can now build a service that is largely promotional, and we can target that service to individuals, based on behavior or preselected interests. This also means we don't care where or how this service is consumed, because its value proposition to us is not as a direct revenue-generator. We can freely unbundle (as in RSS 2.0, full feeds) this kind of content, because its purpose is other than the "all eggs in one basket" approach.

This also helps us overcome the speed versus depth argument for news. A service that meets the breaking news and weather needs of consumers needs to be delivered in many fast and short bursts. It's easy to consume that way, and it works across many platforms. The "all eggs in one basket" approach doesn't permit us to do this, because we want everybody to experience the depth of our work. However, it is foolish to assume that an appetite for speed equals no appetite for depth, and driving people to that depth is the central, strategic mission of the continuous news model.

Media companies may think they already practice this with RSS, but using RSS to drive people to brand-extension content with advertising is a lame and irritating substitute for a bonafide continuous news model. It insults the user, when the user is who we are trying to attract. RSS wasn't created to tease; it was created as a way for people to pull content that they want to their browsers. We can do better than teasing, and we need to, because our legacy platforms are where the real money is. By assuming that our future was in shifting our "all eggs in one basket" model to the Web, we have participated in the dismantling of those legacy platforms, rather than using the Web to strategically build them up.

This is because we believe in our legacy platforms, but we don't believe in the Web.

According to February Nielsen numbers, the syndicated program "TMZ" is the #2 entertainment news program season-to-date in syndication among Adults 18–49, Women 18–49 and Adults 25–54, and #1 among Adults 18–34. This achievement is remarkable for two reasons: one, the program launched in the fall of 2007, and, two, it is the fruit of the entertainment website TMZ.com. The website promotes the TV show, and it does it throughout the day and in the right column content of the site. The important thing to understand here is that the site was built to communicate a continuous stream of "news" to its users, and while it is profitable on its own, the real moneymaker is the TV show.

From a TMZ press release:

> Since its launch in November 2005, TMZ.com a joint venture between Telepictures Productions and AOL has become the Internet's number one entertainment news destination. TMZ.com is consistently credited with breaking stories dominating the entertainment news landscape and is one of the most cited entertainment news sources in the world. (2)

The point is that, by using the Web as it was created to be used, a concept that began three and a half years ago now produces one of the top syndicated programs in television. How exactly did this happen?

The Web is marvelous marketing tool, and those who view it as such do a remarkable job of spreading themselves and their products around. But they begin with that single browser and create a rich experience for the eyeballs that are viewing it, while at the same time exploiting how the back end works to build their own (free) brands. Media companies do it backwards. We begin with our "all eggs in one basket" formats and try to use the Web as just another distribution channel. The Web can do that, but it is also so very much more.

Twitter, for example, is an outstanding marketing tool for media companies, because is uses the free model to accomplish four things. One, it's a brand-extension marketing play, and it we wish to stay relevant in the world of news and information, we'll need these kinds of marketing options. Two, it can move people to stories on the Web that are attached to ads. Twitter is a growing inbound reference to media company websites, assuming the company plays in the Twitter sandbox in the first place. Three, in cases of very big stories — or certain highly attractive franchises — it can drive traffic to our television audience. Four, it's our entryway into the online discussion that is news. Twitter isn't just a distribution platform; it's also a listening post.

While many media company people can understand this about Twitter, they seem unable to see it relating to their entire web strategy, and choose instead to use, for example, their TV station to "drive traffic to the Web." That's an archaic model, albeit one that was important to the third-party ad networks that used to host those websites. Thankfully, media companies are beginning to wake up to the reality that they'll never develop the concepts and revenues they need, if their software is driven by a third-party ad network. The model of driving traffic to a station's website has been a net liability to local media, for all it does is devalue our core business.

Instead, we need to see the wisdom of using the Web to drive traffic to our legacy platforms, and if we could just BEGIN with that assumption, we'd do things a whole lot differently online. The starting point for all of it is that browser.

So here are five tactical recommendations that any local media company can do to almost immediately.

> **Create a news product for the Web that doesn't involve repurposing content from the "all eggs in one basket" paradigm.** Think differently. If you had no TV station or no newspaper, what would you do to meet the online news and information needs of the community? We think that's some form of a Monday–Friday, 8 a.m. to 5 p.m. continuous news stream, and it doesn't take tons of resources to accomplish this.
>
> **This product should be unbundled for place-based distribution,** including mobile, RSS, widgets, SMS subscriptions, or any other method of pushing this free product to

those who are interested. We don't care how or where it's consumed, because its principal purpose is marketing.

Build from that product back towards the TV station or newspaper. Use its marvelous marketing opportunities to set and maintain the information agenda throughout the day, and in the process, steer people to various platforms you have for making money from your content, whether online or off.

Get out of the mindset that everything you do has to carry with it a balance sheet. This has been the great failure of the Newspaper Next project, because it considers the needs of the media company over the needs of the people formerly known as the audience. As I have been saying for years, we don't have a revenue problem as much as we do an audience problem, and absent efforts to fix that, we'll never solve the revenue issues. Free is the strategy we must be prepared to embrace, but that doesn't mean giving away that for which we get paid.

Use your clout and your sales feet-on-the-street to enable commerce for businesses in your community by connecting them with those browsers who pull you to them. This is not "advertising," in the traditional sense; it's using advertising as content in stand-alone revenue plays to help people connect with businesses. And here's where your legacy platform can help you.

The Web may appear chaotic to the logical mind, but it's actually a highly sophisticated, organized, and living machine. To thrive in tomorrow's multimedia world, we need to start paying less attention to our stage and more attention to how the life form functions. If a car dealer, for example, can use the Web to sell cars, why can't we use the Web to sell ourselves? To the dealer, the automobile hasn't changed and neither has the demand, only the mechanism by which he or she reveals inventory to consumers. The news is still the news and the demand is still there, but we're stuck in the past in terms of how we move our own inventory.

Is the Mainstream Winning?

In the Marketing Warfare world of Ries and Trout, there is a "rule" that the market leader can crush the efforts of all others, if it is paying attention and chooses to do so. So powerful is this concept that, in a period of challenge, market observers will point to the leader and simply say, "Just wait."

In the "market" of communications — especially the world of news and information "content" — traditional media companies have been taking a beating from web-based disruptions since the beginning, but there's evidence today that the giant has awakened, and people are beginning to say, "Just wait." It is a dangerous belief, however, that traditional media can overwhelm the Web and tame it in such a way as to make it its own, because there are actually two markets at play: news and information and the revenue gained from attaching ads to that news and information. Traditional media may, in fact, win the battle of the former but lose the war of the latter.

When Yahoo! announced it was shutting down GeoCities last week, it set in motion a series of nostalgic wanderings throughout tech media, including a fascinating piece by Harry McCracken at Technologizer called Whatever Happened to the Top 15 Web Properties of April, 1999? McCracken observed that in April of 1999, GeoCities was one of the top ten internet properties (#6), so he compared the list back then to the list today. It's an interesting piece of evidence in the view that traditional media is increasingly seizing the Web.

214

Rank	April 1999	April 2009
1	AOL	Google
2	Microsoft	Yahoo!
3	Yahoo	Microsoft
4	Lycos	AOL
5	Go Network	Fox Interactive (+MySpace)
6	GeoCities	Ask Network
7	The Excite Network	eBay
8	Time Warner Online	Wikimedia Foundation
9	Blue Mountain Arts	Amazon.com
10	AltaVista	Facebook
11	Amazon.com	Glam Media
12	Xoom.com	Apple
13	Snap	Turner Network
14	Real Networks	CBS Interactive
15	Cnet	New York Times digital

Traditional media companies have cracked the top 15 and the others aren't far behind. Viacom Digital, The Weather Channel, Comcast, Verizon, and Disney are all in the top 25 in 2009. (1)

In its March 2005 "State of the Blogosphere" report, blog search company Technorati tracked inbound links (a measure of influence) and found blogs and traditional media companies sharing the top-50 list.

Just two years later, measurements of the mainstream had shoved aside nearly every blog.

Clearly, traditional media companies have been upping the ante on their use of the Web in the last decade. For legacy media, it's all about brand extension — a way to move their existing mass to the Web and creating another form of that mass.

Sensing this slow evolution, Richard Ziade of Basement.org penned a recent lament over the fading dream of the Web: the democratization of media. Called Big Media's Head Start, Ziade wrote of how easy it is for any *New York Times* reporter to generate hundreds of story comments, or how Twittering during a cooking segment on Good Morning America can produce hundreds of thousands of followers.

> As for little ol' me. Well, I enjoy a modest existence on this blog and I've just broken 100 followers on Twitter. Let me pitch my credentials on Larry King, and you've got a very different story.
> New media has tried to create its own megaphones based on mass validation. Delicious, Digg and the like. But it doesn't really work. The celebrities (and yes, a link has its 15 minutes of fame too) come and go very quickly. It's a transient existence. There have been a few bona fide new media franchises — Perez Hilton and Boing Boing come to mind — but they're very few and far between. (2)

In his lament, Ziade — mistakenly, I believe — views success as the creation of mass, and to this end, he and every other blogger faces an impossible task, compared to the power of mass media to influence their own users. With the Web, however, it's not so much about how many you influence as who you influence, their connections, and so forth.

And then there's the new data from Borrell Associates showing that online revenue growth at those traditional local media companies that are approaching the Web as a separate business is outpacing that of the pureplay companies in the same markets. That is a first, and it could signal a sea change in the fight for dominance in the Local Web.

Or it could not.

The tendency here is to look at all of this information and conclude that traditional media companies are executing market leadership practices, a la Ries and Trout. I've long written that the big advantage traditional media has over the pureplays is the megaphone of their legacy properties, and it's pretty clear we're using those megaphones today. The size and volume of the megaphone can move people to digital applications that people otherwise might not find, so what we're seeing here is explosive growth on the Web side driven by the mainstream, a mainstream, however, that assumes the Web is another form of mass marketing.

This is why traditional media likes Facebook and Twitter — they're ways to move a message from point A to the masses. CNN, for example, has no intention of following the one million people that follow it via Twitter. To them, Twitter is a way to market themselves to the masses and to receive user-generated news when it needs it. But Twitter is about conversation, not mass media, so is CNN participating in Twitter or bolting it on to its existing business? To those who've used Twitter since it first came along, it is a much different tool than what is being taught to the public via traditional media companies, who see it as a tool for them.

Which is more real? Good question.

Likewise, Facebook is a tool for people to keep in touch with their social network, friends, family and acquaintances. You tell me what's happening in your life, and I tell you what's happening in mine. I share my thoughts, preferences and even my recommendations. It's, like, social, dude.

But to media companies, it's another way to move the message, to promote and tease, to drive traffic. When media companies talk about Facebook through their legacy megaphones, are they being social or distributing content (or content links)?

And which is more real? Good question.

Perhaps the best answer is that the Web can be both, but here's the real rub: the Web can extend brands, but it is at its best when it's just the Web, when it's being social, when it's connecting various people with each other and the products and services they choose. And this is the danger of treating it only as a way to move messages to the masses.

For what is the assumption of media companies creating mass if not to serve unwanted, albeit paid messages to that mass? But the central assumption of the Web is it disintermediates all that and empowers people to flee from those same unwanted messages. The people formerly known as the advertisers are increasingly aware of this, and big gobs of their money aimed at that mass is neither a guarantee nor an inalienable right for media companies.

Moreover, when Good Morning America moves people to Twitter, it is moving an audience it already "owns" and monetizes. This is not how the Web can best serve the wants and needs of contemporary professional media.

It's why those media companies who are successfully competing with the pureplays locally are doing so with products and applications that connect people wishing to buy with people wishing to sell and not relying on mass marketing as the primary way to do that. These companies have discovered the secret of the Web, that advertising itself is a valuable form of content.

Every advertiser today can have a website, a Facebook page and a Twitter account. They may not reach the audiences of the mass (yet), but they're growing, and the reach they do have is with people predisposed to their products and services. In addition, advertisers are increasingly exploring ways to reach consumers outside the mass (and its accompanying rates), and this is the real danger for media companies who only view the Web only as a way to extend their brands.

There are examples of how media companies — and especially certain members of the organizations (such as Amy Wood of WSPA-TV) — have embraced the Web and use it to *move people to their legacy media properties* instead of the other way around. This is the right use of the Web for traditional media, but in order to do that, we must believe in the Web, and clearly most of us don't.

We cling to the power of our brands. It's what we know, and what appears to be traditional media swarming all over this thing called "the Web" is mostly just the tactical efforts of a market leader, whose only solution to an attack is to co-opt, to overwhelm. While the Web certainly can be used to extend brands, we must eventually come to the realization that all we're doing is driving, to paraphrase NBCU's Jeff Zucker, our own analog dollars to digital pennies.

THE FOUR OPPORTUNITIES OF 2010

Everybody goes though it, the process of grieving. My most recent experience was the death of Allie, and while I don't look forward to the next time I must grieve, at least I know I can get through it. Grieving is a process, I learned. There's no way to shortcut it. You can't go around it, above it, or below it; you must go "through" it, and that means surrendering to the process.

Modernist media institutions are grieving, and in my discussions with leaders and groups, I think we've advanced up the ladder created by Elisabeth Kubler-Ross (Denial, Anger, Bargaining, Depression, Acceptance) (1) and are now in a position to do something about it. Acceptance is the final stage of grieving, and I think we've arrived. Oh there's still a lot of bargaining going on — case in point: Rupert's war of words with Google — but the people I regularly hang with seem to have gotten past that.

So what's ahead? What will 2010 bring?

Firstly, I think we'll climb out of this nonsense of calling the year by its numerical name and finally usher in the millennium of the Twenties. It'll be "Twenty-Ten," not "Two-Thousand and Ten." But I digress.

Seriously, though, four themes will dominate media growth and development for those in the know in 2010:

- The news becomes Web-Centric
- Data is our business
- Personal branding is our urgent task
- Mobile opportunities lie beyond our content

We simply must understand that advertising is the real disruption that media companies must study. Nearly everything written about disruptions to media is about content, but content is not our business — advertising is our business, and in 2010, that's never been more important to understand.

THE NEWS BECOMES WEB-CENTRIC

After years of playing around with the Web, local media companies will finally shift enough resources and attention to the Web for it to become the central focus of smart newsrooms in 2010. As more and more attention shifts to the Web, we have no choice but to respond or risk downstream irrelevancy.

One of the central tenets of a Web-centric newsroom is that we use the Web to drive traffic to our legacy or "finished" products, whether those are in print, on TV or even on the Web. The Web is one of the most marvelous marketing tools ever created, and its strength is not branding — it's the "call to action" messaging of direct marketing. Once those who run the promotion side of any media company have this revelation, the opportunities will explode.

For example, we know that one of the online traffic spikes for media company properties is late in the afternoon. People are checking in to get caught up on the news before heading home. For TV stations in the past, this has been problematic, for who needs to watch a newscast when you already know what's going on? In a Web-centric news world, however, we use that daypart to give people reasons to tune in when they get home. We never "tease" people online, but we can say things like this:

"When you get home tonight, turn on your TV, because you won't want to miss Jim's interview with Coach Phillips and catch the facial expression when he asks him about T.O."

The whining about "giving away stories to the competition" will give way to excitement coming from the instant feedback of breaking stories online. Good grief, we're "news" organizations, aren't we? We break stories when we have them. It's the only way we can ever be expected to be taken seriously in the only place where it matters, on the Web.

The online audience for news is Monday through Friday, 8:00 a.m. to 5:00 p.m. We know this from studying server logs of media companies. It's so important that we've labeled it "the new prime time," and our best effort to meet the needs of this group is to create an ongoing service instead of a finished product. This is the Continuous News model, and it's one that will blossom in 2010.

DATA IS OUR BUSINESS

In the old days of media, advertising was about the mass attention that we could bring to the table. "Attention" is defined by Wikipedia as "the cognitive process of selectively concentrating on one aspect of the environment while ignoring other things." Advertisers seek attention, whether it's some form of showing off, as a man often does with a woman; shouting from a stage to a gathered audience; or a big picture of a piece of pie on a restaurant's menu. Our culture is awash in efforts to get attention, so the prize "back in the day" went to who could provide the most attention. For that, people would pay healthy sums, and so mass media prospered.

To control attention, one must control the environment, and that's become a nearly impossible task online. Moreover, technology itself has shifted this control to the user. The pyramid is inverted with the consumer able to decide which messages deserve his or her attention and under what circumstances.

To content-minded media companies, this is a disaster, for the very foundation of our business model is crumbling.

But the biggest, most uncrossable chasm for media companies to overcome is the way technology is able to "steal" whatever captive attention is left. It is theft indeed, and here's how it works:

ESPN, which last year led a small publisher's revolt against third-party ad networks, caters to a sports-minded audience, the kind of which certain advertisers wish to reach. In the old model, such advertisers would have to buy space on ESPN.com in order to sneak into the attention range of its audience. Online advertising, however, is a two-way street, with data about users being captured while an ad sits on a page. This is the way third-party ad networks make money, and it's why ESPN no longer wants anything to do with them. How do they make money? Pay attention.

Let's say you visit the sports page of WWWW.com, which includes an ad from AnyAdServerUSA, what we'll call one of the world's largest third-party ad networks. The ad places a cookie on your computer. Even if you clear cookies every day, they sill have your IP address, because as the ad is being served, information about you is being sent back to the ad server.

Despite what you might think, at core, the Web is a database, and data is the Holy Grail for advertisers. Why? Because advertising is shifting from the mass to the direct. Ad-serving is a two-way street, and that which "comes back" to the ad server has real, tangible value.

Now let's say you're an advertiser who wants to reach people who visit the sports page of WWWW.com. You can either pay for expensive ads with WWWW-TV, or you can go to AnyAdServerUSA and pay pennies for remnant ads anywhere else on their network where people who have previously visited WWWW.com's sports page might appear.

So the property on which the ad is being served is irrelevant; the only thing that matters is the eyeballs viewing it.

In other words, AnyAdServerUSA is serving ads to individuals, based on their behavior, while WWWW-TV is serving ads in context. In this way, AnyAdServerUSA can "steal" WWWW.com's audience, and advertisers don't need to pay a premium to get within the attention range of those who are predisposed to the types of content WWWW-TV creates and serves.

This is one of the reasons CBS Interactive decided this month to join ESPN and others in refusing to accept "most" third-party ad network money. They've admitted it'll cost them in the short term, but they feel they'll benefit in the long run by being able to control rates and by exclusive ownership of the data from their own ad network.

Think other media companies aren't aware of this? Ad agencies and the Interactive Advertising Bureau (IAB) last week announced new voluntary guidelines that restrict, up to a point, what ad agencies and publishers can do with data involving third-party ad networks. Advertisers — and, I assume, ad networks — can't simply repurpose or retarget ads to users of media company sites without negotiating a separate deal with the media company for use of that data. This would seem to be good news for publishers, although I'm not sure how such an arrangement would be policed. Moreover, a publisher's ability to use data gathered through an agency's serving of ads is also restricted, but, again, policing such is problematic. Neither group has any enforcement power anyway, so these "guidelines" are merely that.

It's in Madison Avenue's best interest to keep the ad impressions mill going, because the more uniformity is maintained, the easier it is to make money from afar. Publishers are just beginning to wake up to the realities of what's been going on, and 2010 will be a year when more and more get into the ad-serving business.

Enabling commerce is the real mission of local media these days. In some ways, it's always been that way, but the stakes get higher every day. As the year draws to a close, there's talk of Google acquiring Yelp, the local business review site. This would be in keeping with Google's plans for local revenue, and that's not good for local media. Every dollar a merchant spends on Yelp is a dollar that used to be (and will likely never again) spent with us.

PERSONAL BRANDING IS OUR URGENT TASK

Attention is also shifting away from media brands and to the individual people who are employed there. The Web easily facilitates "following" someone, and chances are that such a someone has a Twitter feed and a Facebook account. If you like their work — or simply like them — and it's easy to keep up with their work.

This attention is a two-way street. Individuals must make a case that their friendship or loyalty is worth pursuing before the attention they gather can be monetized in one form or another.

But employees of media companies aren't the only ones who are seeking this kind of attention. Every day, new media stars are being discovered among the vast and flourishing fields of grassroots purveyors of news and information. They can be individuals or teams of people together to "cover" a neighborhood or small community. Make no mistake; these people are known by name, not by their media brand or clever blog title.

I always point to The Huffington Post as the model of personal brands loosely organized. While people may recognize the brand of the group, each writer has his or her own RSS feed. Why? Because Arianna Huffington is a smart cookie and realizes that what's good for the personal brands of those who write for her is good for her as well. And now she's going local, duplicating the model at the local level in select communities.

Personal branding is the "must-do" quest of traditional media in the year 2010. People follow people, as I've often written, and this is especially true in the world of social networking, where each gets to decide who influences them and how.

We create Facebook pages and Twitter feeds for our media companies, and we're pretty good at building a following of fans. But people who "follow" media companies have a different expectation than those who follow individuals, and what do you do if some people like your people but don't like your brand?

We simply must recognize that to really compete in the social space, we must do so at the individual level, and that means growing and nurturing the personal brands of our employers. Go ahead and promote your Facebook page, but spend more time promoting those of your anchors or your writers. Encourage your employees to blog, to define their own brands, and then use the traditional media company to give them a boost.

MOBILE OPPORTUNITIES LIE BEYOND OUR CONTENT

Most observers in the technical world, including the online publications that serve it, suggest that "Mobile" is where "the Web" was ten years ago. Local media companies are acting with it just like we did with the Web back then, and that's Einstein's definition of insanity. Otherwise-smart people are advising media companies to dip our toes in Mobile's water but not to contribute a lot of resources to the effort, because it will take awhile for advertising to catch up.

Normally, I would think that's good advice, but not when you consider that Mobile is "like the Web was ten years ago."

Play this game: Think back ten years and ask yourself which local business you'd get into based on what you know now? Would you play only the media content game, or would you branch off to some of the services that are really making money today?

> That's exactly the choice we have today with Mobile, so why wait for another ten years to pass without moving forward aggressively to pursue enabling commerce on Mobile devices? These are the kinds of investments we need to be making today, not a year from now. Let me repeat: Advertising is our business, not content, and to those who see that, Mobile is at the land grab stage.

I love local search, but I love it even more with the geolocation aspects of Mobile. Let's help people looking to buy connect with people looking to sell, not wait until somebody figures out how to do brand messaging adjacent to our Mobile content (I have ideas about that, but let's stay on point). Separating revenue creation from our ability to make content is the most important change we would make, if we could go back ten years and start anew with the Web, and that's precisely what we need to be doing in 2010 with Mobile.

The new world really isn't as complicated as it seems, but it does require us to think and act counterintuitively from time to time. That will be the real challenge for managers of media properties in 2010. Will we have the courage to be leaders and move our companies boldly forward, or will we continue to wait and see if somebody else figures it out for us?

Your answer to that question will determine your success in 2010.

PUREPLAYS AND THE 50% THRESHOLD

I was first introduced to the 50 percent threshold concept in the early 1980s. The product at the time was VCRs, and the issue was what would happen to television when over half of the homes with TV sets in the U.S. had VCRs attached? The forecast wasn't good for broadcasting, and that was just the beginning. About the same time came the remote control, and the die was cast for serious technological disruption.

There's something magical about the 50 percent threshold. It's almost like nobody takes any threat seriously until it impacts half of the marketplace. By that time, though, reactions to it are always defensive. Before? Well, it's just an upstart with big ambitions. Who cares?

The axiom, however, seems to govern business, and that's why we need to see a piece of recent research from Borrell Associates in a different light.

Each year, Borrell publishes a pie chart showing the shifts in the local online advertising marketplace. (1) Which type of media gets what kind of share of the local ad pie, and so forth? I've added and recolored the image from 2004, so that we can compare the market five years ago to the market today. The pie itself has been growing, and for 2010, Borrell is projecting it'll be $14.2 billion. It's a big pie.

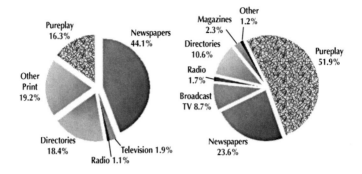

Notice the shift in the textured slice. Pureplay Web companies — those businesses without a brick and mortar connection — now get 51.2 cents of every dollar in the world of *local* online advertising. In 2004, that number was just 15%, and this latest report represents the first time pureplays have crossed the 50% threshold for local advertising. By "local" here, I mean money that originates in the market, including franchises, whether controlled locally, regionally or nationally. Over half of this money is now flowing elsewhere, and the point is it didn't used to be that way.

The pureplay category includes players like Google, Yahoo!, MSN, various other content portals, social sites like Facebook and My-Space, and hundreds of smaller companies with software that helps enable commerce like Yodle, Reach Local, Yelp, Groupon and many, many others. One thing they generally have in common is that whatever they're offering to local businesses and merchants, it works, and in many, if not most cases, it's measurable and better than what local traditional media companies have to offer.

Not only has the share of the pureplays been growing, it has been doing so against a backdrop of dramatically increased online spending. Regardless of how you slice it or define it, this is money that used to go primarily to local media companies. Notice, for example, the dramatic loss of share for local newspapers.

The significance of this is completely lost on the local merchants who are unaware they're sending their money outside the market.

After all, they assume, "My nickels and dimes don't mean much," but it adds up quickly.

Think about this for a minute. In a market like, say, Louisville, Kentucky, where Borrell projects 83 million local dollars will be spent for online advertising this year, 51.2 percent — or $41.5 million — will leave the market to line the pockets of companies who have absolutely no stake in the Louisville community whatsoever. They don't pay taxes. They have no employees. They don't donate to the local United Way. To paraphrase Perot, all Louisville gets is just a great sucking sound, and it's damaging the very economy from which local businesses draw their sustenance.

This is a serious, serious matter for local economies, and when businesses find out about it, they are not happy. I know, because I'm sharing the message in various places as I talk to people about the value proposition of local ad networks.

PARTNERSHIPS

Gordon Borrell thinks that the pureplays will continue to take money from local markets. Pureplays are generally well-funded and all share the knowledge that "local" is where online revenue growth is. It's no surprise they all want an increasingly bigger piece of the pie. Borrell told me that the share will taper off, however, as the pureplays realize they can only go so far without sales feet on-the-street. This will force them into partnerships with local media companies who have such sales teams.

This is reflected in an interview I did with Fred Wilson two years ago. Wilson is one of the top VCs in the new media space, his Union Squares Ventures having funded, in part, such well known companies as Del.icio.us, Feedburner, Boxee, Clickable, Disqus, Foursquare, Meetup, Outside.in, Tumblr, and, oh yeah, Twitter. Noting that venture-funded companies are taking money out of local markets, I asked if he felt like a competitor to local media.

"I'd rather be a partner with local media companies," he replied. "We don't want to build the sales organizations. We don't want to go into each individual city or town and start to develop the relationships with local merchants. What we can bring to the table are new technologies and new business models, and I think we can partner with the local media companies to help with sales."

Media companies are catching on. Jay Small, president of Cordillera Interactive, is into the idea of partnerships and makes a strong argument for strategic arrangements:

> Almost every company that represents the pure-play revenue in Borrell's data will, or would, entertain reseller partnerships with incumbent local media, as an alternative to building its own sales forces especially in markets smaller than the top 25. Incumbent media can resell best-of-breed interactive and mobile marketing solutions profitably. Plus, the incumbents do still have significant distribution clout via their legacy, offline operations, and will for many years to come...
>
> ...If a local media operator can claim to sell products on par with best-of-breed marketing platforms, online and offline, then we shift the game back to differentiators that actually matter: our people, our relationships, our client service, our commitments to the communities in which we operate. (2)

Small argues rightly that the sales teams attached to legacy media are not necessarily the feet-on-the-street sought by these pureplays, however, because, among other things, "legacy products remain easier to sell to existing customers, at higher gross dollar amounts and much higher margins than anything the 'interactive department' can show." Like Borrell, Small believes that separate sales staffs will ultimately be needed to handle these kinds of arrangements.

And so begins a season of local media companies partnering with pureplays to solve commerce issues within the community. This is logical and smart, but it comes with a caveat: the 50-percent threshold is guaranteed in any arrangement where local employers send half of partnership revenue elsewhere. We can argue the inevitability of this, but that doesn't make amends for the outcome.

The first such partnership was the Yahoo Newspaper Consortium, the network of 800 newspapers who "sell into" Yahoo! properties as a way of gaining market share. The Yahoo! technology also brings newspapers into the world of selling behavior. The revenue split is 50:50, with Yahoo! providing the technology and the newspapers providing all the expense of maintaining the sales arm. The newspaper consortium began in November of 2006. It has not stopped the shrinking of market share for newspapers, nor has it slowed down the growth of share for the pureplays. That was apparently never the point, however, because Yahoo! was considered a friend, not a competitor.

THE ONLINE MARKETPLACE

One of the problems here is that we in media still don't view the whole local online marketplace as ours. We behave as though we're competing only with other traditional advertising companies online. We watch what "they" do. We imitate what "they" do. If that station does hyperlocal, I've got to do hyperlocal. If "they" run rich media ads, by God, we've got to run rich media ads. We compete to see whose practices can win accolades against other media companies, and we judge our success based on "their" success. We look around the industry to find those who are doing it "right," whatever that means. Apples to apples, we think. This is understandable, given our history, but it plays right into the hands of those same pureplay companies.

Besides, there's a new history being written, and here are ten facts that reveal a much different marketplace.

1. The very essence of advertising is in full-blown disruption. Rather than immerse ourselves in this disruption, we've chosen to let others innovate while we invest in seeing how best we can make the disruption conform to our beliefs and practices.
2. Advertisers themselves are now a form of media companies, able to connect with customers outside our walls. The inexpensive tools of personal media have opened doors nobody even considered just ten years ago.
3. The legacy brands that sustain us are of declining value, because people under 25 generally don't even know who or

what they are. Those people will run the businesses of to-morrow, so even if those brands open doors today, we cannot believe that it will always be the case.

4. For local television, people are now being conditioned by technology that programs are separate from sources, and innovations like GoogleTV will continue this reality. Programs separate from sources pose significant problems for those of us who monetize such sources.

5. Hyperconnectivity impacts marketing more than anybody cares to admit. We're no longer just connected "up" to brands; we're connected horizontally, and this undercuts the strategies and tactics of traditional advertising. We dare not underestimate empowered consumers.

6. To consumers, advertising has always been an annoyance, but technology now enables them to ignore it. For every new method to "reach" people, those who don't wish to be "reached" find a new way to block it. Madison Avenue's grip on the institution, however, cannot allow honest acceptance of this, and so — like newspapers 15 years ago — the advertising industry is involved only in how the Web can serve its interests, consumers be damned.

7. Consequently, industrial age, top-down marketing — every bit of it, including its language — is fast becoming an archaic relic of a former age. MBA programs that are built on the old will have to change, 'lest their offspring be ill-equipped to run the businesses of the twenty-first century.

8. The paradigm of mass marketing is giving way to the direct marketing tilt of the Web. As more and more local businesses learn that they can access customers or potential customers directly through the above hyperconnectivity, the less they need any — yes, ANY — old-school marketing.

9. Core strategies are giving way to edge strategies, a whole new academic and practical discipline being written right before our eyes. Headed by Deloitte & Touche's think tank, under the guidance and leadership of John Hagel, moving business resources away from core competencies and to edge competencies is the model of the twenty-first century.

10. Finally, the very definition of local is changing, because local isn't defined simply by location anymore. Jeff Jarvis has a phrase that articulates this: "Local = Mobile = Me." When Amazon will sell you a vacuum cleaner cheaper than Sears and deliver it to your doorstep for free the next day, what is the value of the local store, except for returns? This redefining is a part of the bigger picture, but it puts yet another strain on our need to think strategically about all of this.

So partnership deals with pureplays may shift a little of today's money around, but they ultimately position us at the wrong end of the value chain: we handle all the expense of sales and reselling, while the pureplays provide only technology and the business model.

The revenue available to media companies behaving as media companies — that is to say using ads adjacent to scarce content — is insufficient to make a dent in the now-52 cents of every dollar that goes to pureplays. Moreover, partnering with them guarantees the 50 percent threshold remains. We're doing their work for them.

When McClatchy inked a deal with Groupon to bring the "deals" giant to its newspaper chain, local media consultant and former Kelsey Group Web guru Greg Sterling wrote that the deal made sense for both companies, although he likened it to the old "keep your friends close and your enemies closer" adage.

> In the relationship Groupon will apparently "own" the advertiser, while McClatchy will have the relationship with the reader-consumer. Collectively US newspaper sites reach almost 60% of the online audience according to comScore. Groupon will get additional reach in McClatchy markets and presumably some additional branding and visibility. In a short period of time, however, Groupon won't need newspapers…
>
> …In my mind it's a kind of a smart "stop-gap" in the near term. However it's doubtful that McClatchy is building any long-term value here for itself. (3)

I couldn't agree more.

These pureplay companies are not our friends; they're our real competition, and we get in bed with them at some risk. What I like least about these arrangements is how accepting we are of the new status quo. Rather than actually compete, we're capitulating in the name of an easy buck. Every time a media company "partners" with a pureplay company, we affirm and strengthen the pureplays' grip on local advertising. Remember, these people don't employ anybody in our markets. They don't pay taxes and they certainly don't support local charitable giving. To them, we're willing participants in our own demise.

As Jay Small notes, none of these companies have relationships in the marketplace, but we do. They're willing to share their better mousetraps with us for, in most cases, a 50:50 revenue share. Sure, we get 50 percent, but the other half leaves the market, guaranteeing growth beyond the 50 percent threshold. There is no future in this for us, and especially for the local economy. And 50:50 is such an arbitrary ratio anyway. Shouldn't the "partner" who carries the biggest expense get the biggest share in any such arrangement?

Every dollar originating in the marketplace that goes elsewhere is multiplied many fold in its negative impact on the local economy, increasing the demand on the community itself to make up the difference. Let me repeat: when the business community learns of this, it is not happy, and we can use that energy to our advantage.

Jay is absolutely right in that building "me-too" projects is very bad strategy, but what about something completely different? It may come to the point where we need to work together at the local level to build a better mousetrap. As long as we keep fighting each other, we're handing victory to outsiders. It's that serious, and it will take a tremendous amount of courage for anything to really change.

We can also launch a year-long campaign to inform local businesses about what's really happening. Use Borrell's local data to tell the story. These companies, regardless of how tempting their applications seem, are not the friend of local markets.

In the interim, the best advice is Sterling's. Let these arrangements be short-term only. Recognize these people as what they are: enemies who must be kept close.

The Web is not newspapers.
The Web is not television.
The Web is the Web.

Media 2.0 101

by Terry Heaton

Media 2.0 is the umbrella term we use at AR&D to define and strategize those elements of technology that are disrupting and disintermediating traditional local media. Media 1.0 is mass media, but Media 2.0 is everything but mass. This is why we advise clients that they need both Media 1.0 and Media 2.0 strategies going forward and that it is not only possible but necessary to separate them.

The business model is the thing. Media 1.0 is driven by the mass, but Media 2.0 is more direct. The Media 1.0 world is top-down, while the Media 2.0 world is connected horizontally.

I first began using this concept in 2004 and brought it with me to AR&D, where it found its way into our weekly newsletter, AR&D's Media 2.0 Intel. Since the newsletter could be used, in part, to instruct, we felt that a useful franchise would be one that defines the term on an ongoing basis. Hence, "Media 2.0 101" was born.

What follows is four years worth of these little essays, and if you'll take the time to read and understand them, you'll be much farther down the new media path than your competitors.

TECHNOLOGY'S BIGGEST CULTURAL DISRUPTION

From his office at Harvard, Doc Searls is working on tools and systems that he and his co-workers hope will help further enable and empower everyday people. He wants nothing less than to turn the whole relationship between business and customer on its head. Instead of businesses sending signals to customers about what they're selling (a.k.a. advertising), Searls envisions a vast system where customers can send signals to businesses about what they wish to buy. Instead of customers responding, therefore, businesses would respond. It's nothing short of revolutionary.

What makes something like this possible is horizontal connectivity among human beings, which is the most disruptive element of the age we're entering. What does it disrupt? Anything and everything that counted on top-down connectivity to sustain the value of scarcity. The fact that we're connected both ways by technology is what makes all of this so incredibly dangerous to the status quo of the age before it existed. A lot of people are going to lose everything as this plays out, and it's really just beginning.

If Doc Searls is successful, for example, it'll mean a major cultural shift away from advertising, something Doc has dreamed about for many years. His disdain for traditional marketing is well-documented. It's one of the forces that led to the publication of *The Cluetrain Manifesto*, the seminal document for the new age of media. Searls is one of its authors, and long after we're all gone, historians will point back to *Cluetrain* as the thought piece that jump-started the Internet revolution.

Cluetrain's prime clue is this: "We are not seats or eyeballs or end users or consumers. We are human beings, and our reach exceeds your grasp. Deal with it!"

Doc Searls thinks the word "consumer" is a demeaning insult, and I referenced his negative description of "passive opens mouths crapping cash" in my 2005 essay, "The Economy of Unbundled Advertising:"

> The language of mass marketing is all about warfare. We "target" this; we "launch" a thrust here; we "attack" and "saturate." It's all so exciting. Ries and Trout called their seminal book, *Positioning: The Battle for Your Mind* — a battle with victory being sales.

But the advertising industry forgot to ask people for permission to play war games in their minds, and now things like DVRs and the Internet are enabling people to simply shut the door. Nobody wants to be targeted. Nobody wants to be positioned. Nobody wants to be manipulated. The consumer is now the one with the power, and people with goods and services to sell need to start thinking of them again as customers.

Doc Searls' latest venture is *Project VRM*, which stands for "Vendor Relationship Management." While vendors have lots of tools to help them "manage" customers, who speaks for the customers? This is what Project VRM is all about.

VRM tools provide customers with both independence from vendors and better ways of engaging with vendors. The same tools can also support individuals' relations with schools, churches, government entities and other kinds of organizations.

> …VRM development work is based on the belief that free customers are more valuable than captive ones — to themselves, to vendors, and to the larger economy. To be free —

- Relationships must be voluntary.
- Customers must enter relationships with vendors as independent actors.
- Customers must be the points of integration for their own data.
- Customers must have control of data they generate and gather. They must be able to share data selectively, voluntarily, and control the terms of its use.

- Customers must be able to assert their own terms of engagement and service.
- Customers must be free to express their demands and intentions outside of any one company's control.

VRM research work probes the willingness and ability of customers to assert and enjoy independence from vendors — and of vendors' willingness and ability to value and engage with independent customers. It also follows changes in the marketplace as VRM tools come into use.

It is this desire for customers to own and manage their own data that led Searls to inform his followers that *"the tide turned today"* on July 31, 2010, when the *Wall St. Journal* published a *series of articles* about the depth and breadth of the online data tracking business. Stating that there is no demand for tracking data from customers, only from advertisers or people selling to advertisers, Searls wrote that customers aren't going to stand for it much longer.

Here is the difference between an advertiser and an ordinary company just trying to sell stuff to customers: nothing. If a better way to sell stuff comes along — especially if customers like it better than this crap the Journal is reporting on — advertising is in trouble.

Here is the difference between an active customer who wants to buy stuff and a consumer targeted by secretive tracking bullshit: everything.

Two things are going to happen here. One is that we'll stop putting up with it. The other is that we'll find better ways for demand and supply to meet — ways that don't involve tracking or the guesswork called advertising.

I've said it before: Improving a pain in the ass doesn't make it a kiss.

While all of this anti-advertising talk may seem like a doomsday scenario for media companies, I view the insight as an opportunity. And so potentially vast is this opportunity that it could become, in fact, the new "business" of media. We've always viewed ourselves as a portal for all sorts of messages — or signals — *to* the public. Those with the most cash could obtain the most messages, while we practiced journalism as the lure.

But what if we could do it backwards? Would the people formerly known as the advertisers pay to have their products and services respond to the signals from customers? Of course they would. Isn't search, after all, such a signal of desire?

The money exchange would be the same, but the flow of the signals would be both horizontal and vertical.

Seem far fetched? You bet, but unless media companies get busy creating value independent of the old one-to-many, top-down advertising paradigm, we're going to be forever fighting the real disruption of technology. Advertising is changing before our eyes, and while it may not go entirely the way that people like Doc Searls would like to see it go, the changes will be radical enough to impact everything that the current model touches. And that's especially true for those, like us, whose entire business model is based on the assumptions that advertising brings along with it.

THE FUTURE IS ABOUT
UNBUNDLED DISTRIBUTION

One of the things that keeps media companies from realizing the potential of the Web is an instinct that says, "I must control my distribution." In the world of scarcity from which traditional media comes, this is an understandable and necessary thought, but online, it's ultimately suicidal, because the world of the Web is one of abundance. The issue then becomes one of "how do I get my content to stand out in a world of abundance," not how do I limit its distribution to create scarcity.

This was played out last week in Knoxville, when veteran radio newsman Dave Foulk was forced to remove a news and traffic report service he had created on his Facebook page, because his employer wanted those people to come to its website only for such information. The 42-hundred plus "fans" he was serving are upset, because they'd come to know Dave as a trusted source. They will not go to the station's website, no matter what the station does, so the end result is just 42-hundred pissed off fans.

In a world of scarcity, restricting access creates value, but in a world of abundance, it does the opposite. People didn't need to chase Dave Foulk; they read him, because he made it convenient for them. Can they live without that information service? Of course, and they will. We've got this idea in our heads that we can "force" behavior, to which empowered consumers now respond, "Screw you!"

(This decision by Foulk's employer also conflicts with our beliefs about the value of personal branding, but that's another entry altogether.)

Scarcity and abundance are diametrically opposed concepts. The dos for one are the don'ts for the other, It's the central explanation for the bruising on my head from bashing it against the wall when well-intentioned news people argue with me about things like, for example, website design. We think design is the top priority, because we think the home page is where people interact with us. It's our doorway, we think, the place where interested people judge our skill in keeping them informed. The truth, however, is it's just another URL in a literal sea of others. Do we honestly think ours is "special?"

"Well, Terry, if it's the only choice they have about getting our content, then they'll HAVE to come."

No they won't. And those who do will, at best, be your most loyal viewers, so what have you gained?

In a world of abundance — where aggregation is king — website design matters nil, because for all media today, it's what you send into the real-time stream that counts and that can be "received" lots of different ways. We keep wanting to create a nice user experience that assumes people come to our websites for a visit, when the Web itself — and especially those who are designing and building its applications — cares ONLY about what's in the wild that it can use. In this context, "the Web" refers to the multiplied thousands of people who are constantly working to evolve the tubes and pipes into the real time experience it was built to become. If the Web was just the infrastructure, media companies might have a case for strategies that smack of scarcity, but it's not.

Facebook isn't so much a destination as it is a precursor of the Web itself.

I don't want this to be a rant or to sound critical, but our obsession with developing revenue instead of making money prevents us from working with the Web itself. Rather than try and go WITH the flow, we foolishly try to force the Web into our own wants and needs, and in the end, this will hasten our demise.

So let me repeat something I've said often in the past: your RSS feeds are vastly more important than your website.

What you release into the wild for others to use — as they see fit — will determine your health as a business in the years to come. We should be designing for our feeds, not using them to drive people back to our websites. This is contrary to what the industry believes is best practices, but it is the truth.

I first began exploring the concepts of unbundled media in late 2004 and published *The Remarkable Opportunities of Unbundled Media* one year later. People were already using the Web to unbundled things that others wanted kept bundled, such as, oh, music cuts. There was an extremely powerful consumer message in this action, and one that, frankly, most media company people ignored entirely. Then came YouTube, and again, people unbundled — made into clips — that which traditional media wanted kept bundled.

Never underestimate empowered consumers.

Also never underestimate the smart people trying to meet empowered consumers' demand. Whole new business concepts have been developed — funded primarily by venture capital — that help people unbundle and rebundle to fit their needs (and their busy schedules). Can you say "TiVo"? If there is one truth that you can take to the bank in looking towards tomorrow, it is that content will be separated from its source. Fight it at your own risk. Explore it, and you'll find opportunity.

For example, GoogleTV is almost upon us. By this time next year, many people will have TV sets or set-top boxes that allow them to find programming through Google's TV search engine. What will you put into the stream that will "help" Google find it? How will you monetize that? These are incredibly important questions, because Google's intention is to, again, assist in separating content from its sources.

Another example is the application Ken featured above, Flipboard. Flipboard is controversial, because rather than take RSS feeds, it scrapes content and images from media websites (with appropriate links back to the original source). It does so, because a) it can, and b) the RSS feeds of most media companies are crap. Flipboard rightly wants to create a great user experience, and I expect there will be some sort of legal fight downstream over this. If media companies "win," they'll actually lose, because, once again, we live in a world of content abundance, not scarcity. The right response would be to pay attention to what we're distributing in the wild.

We've developed the concept of Continuous News and are currently helping media companies reengineer their news departments to better serve the genre. It is quite an undertaking, but the results are magnificent, and these companies are much better positioned to meet the demands of tomorrow than those who cling to old ways of operating.

In the Continuous News environment, the output of the stream — and that includes the Web, Twitter, Facebook and any other application that will come along — is the reason these news departments come to work. We're continuing to define and redefine that output, but at least we're working on it, because we recognize that developers working on Web applications outnumber us and outgun us, so our only choice is to "give" them better content to work with. That begins with designing it for unbundled distribution and trusting that we will benefit in the end.

As I wrote in *The Economy of Unbundled Advertising*, ad snippets that are released into the stream can be reassembled to produce the sale paper of tomorrow:

If unbundled media is where we're headed, then unbundled advertising must necessarily follow. This is a scary concept, however, for there is no command and control mechanism or manipulable infrastructure in the unbundled world. The upside, though, is that it costs very little to participate. All that's necessary is the release what I call "ad pieces" into the seeming chaos of the Internet, where other businesses will take those pieces and reassemble them when summoned by customers who are trading their scarcity for information they actually want.

This is already taking place on a small scale with Twitter, but I suspect it will be the source of whole new business models downstream. We simply live in an unbundled world, although most of us don't realize it yet.

Here are five things you can do today to get you moving down this path:

1. Establish in your thinking that the Web is about abundance, and that your mission is to stand out, not control. Attraction always works better online than promotion, because consumers are in charge.
2. Bring your RSS feeds to the top of your priority list and keep them there. Make them full feed. Refine them. Hone them. Put ads in them. This will be the content that you make available to "the Web" to distribute as it sees best, including GoogleTV.

3. Build any unbundled content "apps" around your RSS feeds. Got an iPhone app? Is your RSS output its main content source? Work *with* apps like Flipboard to let them know YOUR content is available to them for distribution beyond your ability.

4. Experiment with measurable ways to monetize unbundled content. Don't know how? Read my 5-year-old essay and then talk to me.

5. Establish in your revenue thinking that the creation of new value — i.e., "making money" — is at least as important as growing revenue.

Above all, get it in your head that unbundled output is where you HAVE to be, no matter how that conflicts with your traditional instincts and training. We are just beginning to realize the reality of content separated from source, and it will dominate the media landscape in the years to come.

THE INBRED RESULTS OF COPYCATS

Traditional media companies specialize in copying. I'm not talking about plagiarism — although some would say that's a big issue, too — but rather copying of the business model variety. After all, we're an "industry," so we should all behave the same, right? Strategies or tactics not currently in practice somewhere stand little chance of implementation anywhere until somebody takes the leap and dives in. This is true in content, and this is true in sales.

This means we're stuck in a descending spiral, because now is the time for innovation, not copying, and yet we can't seem to bring ourselves to try anything unless it's first proven by somebody else. I encounter this everywhere I go and with any group I address. "So, Terry, can you point us to somebody out there who's really doing this right?" The answer, almost invariably, is no. It is my greatest frustration as a consultant and my biggest failure as one who offers a vision for tomorrow.

Think about it for a minute. In the past, there was this loosely-affiliated group called "the media." The group had its associations and organizations, each working for the betterment of the whole. That betterment, however, always began with protecting the core value propositions of media, and it worked well for a long while. Like any living subculture, however, relentless inbreeding produces unintended consequences, but when it's all you know, what the heck, right? That's where we're at today with media; we're brain dead and waiting for some one or some thing from within to prove a validation of all that came before, so that we can copy it and be successful.

"So, Terry, who's somebody out there doing this right (so I can study it at my own pace and see if it's something I want to emulate)? Who could blame anybody for wanting that? The problem is that it doesn't exist.

247

Well, that's not entirely true.

One of the most interesting characters I've met recently is Clark Gilbert of Deseret Media in Salt Lake City. Gilbert runs a very effective and profitable business that is owned by the same people who own the KSL media empire, so he's responsible for the digital growth of a legacy media business in addition to new business development. There are a couple of unique things about Gilbert's approach, however, beginning with his background. This is his first media management job. He came from Harvard, where he taught and studied with Clayton Christensen, the disruptive innovation guy ("The Innovator's Dilemma"). People like Christensen and Gilbert wrote the book on how businesses should, but usually don't, respond to core business disruptions, so Gilbert is applying first hand what he's studied and learned about how innovations disrupt businesses. He was part of the Newspaper Next project, where he got a firsthand look at media in disruption.

Welcome to the world of the Internet and legacy media, Clark.

Not bound by any form of legacy media "experience," Gilbert has built an organization of pure Web experts. His company is separate from the brands it represents and has full authority to compete against those same brands in the Salt Lake City advertising universe. This is textbook Clayton Christensen. He simply sees things differently and is very happy to work in a place that allows him to bring theories to life.

We had the chance to talk about other traditional media company organizations, and I asked him about how he would approach managing a large group of media properties. In other words, how do you centralize things to attain efficiencies while maintaining autonomy for individual business units. Is that even possible? His answer, as you might imagine, is counterintuitive:

Clearly you need both local initiative and centralized leverage. The question is what organizational structure is best for this. My working hypothesis is that there is a sequence approach where the "local" unit has to develop the autonomy and identity before you turn back to get the direct corporate leverage centrally.

This is the opposite of most media company thinking, because the properties exist to serve the centralized unit, not the other way around. This opposite kind of thinking is why I am constantly facing the question about naming somebody that others can copy. Perhaps I should point to Clark Gilbert and Deseret Media, but what's right for him may not be right for you. That's the problem. In the world of disruptions, it's more about courage than copying, and that's something I find lacking at the highest levels of most media organizations. Immediate revenue needs trump the needs of R&D, and this is the innovator's dilemma.

I'm not sure what it will take to change things, because by the time desperation arrives, it may already be too late. Driving the car and fixing it at the same time is still the operational mandate, with fixing it becoming more important as we proceed farther down the new media turnpike.

Courage is a central component of leadership, especially for media companies that may actually have to slow the car to make maximum repairs. Who has the courage to do that?

IT'S THE PEOPLE, NOT THE TECHNOLOGY

In the nineteenth century, as pioneers moved their way westward across the U.S., they brought law and order with them. It was, of course, their version of law and order, not that of the current residents. This is textbook colonialism, something about which I write frequently. Whether it was the local sheriff, the Texas Rangers, or the famous U.S. Marshals, gunmen and other outlaws couldn't escape for long. And if the ~~savages~~ Native Americans got in the way of our progress, well, we always had the Army to step in a smooth things out.

Many people look at the world of the Web as similar to the old days of the West, where criminal minds basically have their way. In our attempts to fix the problem, we've created whole industries to protect ourselves, and the sense of danger is so prevalent socially that some find the Web simply too unsafe to explore its many wonders. Malware, viruses, spyware, porn, and other forms of extreme expression are lurking around every corner. This fear is exploited for profit, of course, and that's to be expected.

The Web is, of course, much more than a den of iniquity — vastly more good than evil — but there are forces at work that badly want to bring their version of law and order to an infrastructure that needs something different. Rather than let the market figure it out, there's a movement underway to alter certain core mechanisms of the Web in order to find peace and quiet.

In a provocative piece in the *New York Times* last week, Virginia Heffernan asked if Apple's iDevices could mean the death of the open Web. I don't think so, but she makes a strong argument.

People who find the Web distasteful — ugly, uncivilized — have nonetheless been forced to live there: it's the place to go for jobs, resources, services, social life, the future. But now, with the purchase of an iPhone or an iPad, there's a way out, an orderly suburb that lets you sample the Web's opportunities without having to mix with the riffraff. This suburb is defined by apps from the glittering App Store: neat, cute homes far from the Web city center, out in pristine Applecrest Estates. In the migration of dissenters from the "open" Web to pricey and secluded apps, we're witnessing urban decentralization, suburbanization and the online equivalent of white flight.

The "white flight" metaphor is accurate, and it ought to make us think. By controlling what makes it to the screen of the iDevices via apps, Apple is creating a walled garden within which its sheriff can maintain law and order. The iPad contains a browser, so mischief is still possible on a user-by-user basis, but that decision has nothing to do with the environment in which the device itself works. This is the anti-Web, a response from the world that's being disrupted, and if history can be trusted (and I think it can), such a effort — regardless of how well-intentioned — cannot last for long.

Google, on the other hand, is all about enabling the open Web that the suburbanites wish to escape, and the coming war between the open and the closed will be unlike anything we've witnessed. Since money generally belongs to the suburbs, watch for lobbying efforts to break up Google. It will come in the form of articles and stories suggesting anti-trust violations, and when push comes to shove, it will be a real donnybrook in Washington.

There's another new discussion developing that strikes at the very heart of the Web — that links are a distraction in the communicating of ideas. Nick Carr published an essay this week challenging the assumption that links are necessary.

Links are wonderful conveniences, as we all know (from clicking on them compulsively day in and day out). But they're also distractions. Sometimes, they're big distractions — we click on a link, then another, then another, and pretty soon we've forgotten what we'd started out to do or to read. Other times, they're tiny distractions, little textual gnats buzzing around your head. Even if you don't click on a link, your eyes notice it, and your frontal cortex has to fire up a bunch of neurons to decide whether to click or not. You may not notice the little extra cognitive load placed on your brain, but it's there and it matters. People who read hypertext comprehend and learn less, studies show, than those who read the same material in printed form. The more links in a piece of writing, the bigger the hit on comprehension.

This brought out an almost comical rebuttal from various quarters, including this tweet from Jeff Jarvis:

> Nick Carr wrote that piece about links to get links. I won't link. It would distract you.

Linking isn't good or bad; it's what makes hypertext different than anything before it, and links are the currency of the new world. Debating their value is absurd to most, but perhaps Carr is merely trying to point out that sometimes we can get carried away. Hypertext is the most important communications discovery ever, but just because you can doesn't mean you should. When writers use links without including some summary, I find the practice needlessly time-wasting for the reader. This is the essence of Twitter, and it's fine there, but when it drifts into other forms of writing, I have problems with it.

Like Heffernan's "white flight," this anti-link "undo button" stems from the growing pains of the World Wide Web. Like Gutenberg's movable type, the culture had to adapt, which resulted in a vast shift of power away from the Roman Catholic Church and into the hands of a new elite. It didn't happen overnight, and neither will this cultural shift, but it's important than we maintain a little perspective as the transition goes along.

In an excellent piece that compares the iPad with the early AOL, John Battelle writes that the link represents more than just technology.

The problem, of course, is that Case's AOL, while wildly successful for a while, ultimately failed as a model. Why? Because a better one emerged — one that let consumers of information also be creators of information. And the single most important product of that interaction? The link. It was the link that killed AOL — and gave birth to Google.

It was the link that made the web what it is today, and it's the link — reinterpreted in various new strains — that drives innovation on the web still. The link is the synapse between you, me, and a billion other humans — and the signal (dare I say, a signal one might consider third party data) which allows a million ideas to flourish.

Neither hypertext nor Apple's suburbanization efforts are inherently wrong; they're just opposites. When we look at all of this as media companies, it's attractive to want to drift to the closed, because it feels so familiar. There's nothing wrong with that, but the problem is the choice about media today isn't really ours. It belongs to all of those men, women and children who ARE the links about which Carr, Jarvis, Battelle and others write. The printing press didn't change culture. It was people using the printing press, and so it will be with the Web.

We mess with that at our own risk.

"INVENTORY" IS AN
INDUSTRIAL-AGE TERM

In introducing the concept of Local Ad Networks to media companies — where we place ads on as many sites in the marketplace that will have us — I'm often met with the following response: "Why would I want to increase the number of sites I'm advertising on when I can't even sell the inventory I've got on my own site?" It's a logical question given the world we've ~~created~~ been handed. The answer is simple, but understanding it means thinking outside the conventional realm of reach-frequency in a display advertising model.

Implied in the question are at least seven assumptions, so let's examine them one at a time.

The CPM method of selling and accounting is the best way to handle online advertising. The reality is more that CPM is what we have, and that's just the way it is and has to be. This is a compromise and one that values advertisers over publishers, especially when rates are established by third-party networks. CPM pricing is killing online publishing, but CPM accounting is arguably a good way to keep track of payments and trafficking. It does not necessarily follow, however, that this is the way we should sell advertising on the front end. Simply put, the industry is so accustomed to CPM pricing that the only way for us to increase the value of our content would be to dramatically increase the CPM. That's just not going to work, and that's a problem that we've created for ourselves.

Moreover — and this, frankly, is most important — there's no compensation for the data that's acquired by the server handling the ads, which, to the server, is of greater value that the reach provided by serving the ads in the first place. Data is our future, and we're giving it away by serving only or mostly third-party ads.

CPM is lazy but it's what we know. We sit back and take orders from advertisers and networks that want our inventory rather than fight for the value of what we create.

All ad impressions are created equal. This bogus assumption has been used by the advertising industry to commodify online advertising in such a way that it has destroyed the value of the content around which these ads are served. In order to create a viable accounting mechanism for BIG advertisers, this one-sided proposition serves only advertisers and the networks that serve them. Publishers don't stand a chance, and this became acutely apparent when the economy went south two years ago.

> The tail wags the dog for publishers, and we simply must find a way to break free, or local media properties will ultimately be worth a tiny fraction of what we used to know.
>
> The reality is that all ad impressions are not created equal, and the amazing thing to me is that we already know this is true, or why else would certain ad positions cost more than others. We continue, however, to perpetuate the myth that the ad industry needs to maintain its catbird position.

Eyeballs are eyeballs, and inventory is inventory. Flowing from above assumption, this one is also needed to cement the necessity of easily assembling a mass for the CPM model. We're content with the knowledge that, over a certain period of time, we'll accumulate enough eyeballs that our advertisers will surely be able to hit their targets. This is old mass market thinking, for while we're doing that, third-party ad networks are accumulating data, so that they don't need mass eyeballs to deliver targets anymore.

Cumulative reach is the same as real time reach. This is perhaps the most dangerous assumption we make in cultivating the CPM model, for as the news and information business shifts to real time, so, too, does advertising. The ability of an advertiser to immediately switch out ad copy is already a high value proposition for companies offering these types of ads, but there's no place for it when all you're doing is counting eyeballs over a period of time.

> The shift to real time is one of the clearest online trends of contemporary media, and we must find ways to work with the trend instead of fooling ourselves into believing that the old accumulation of mass over time will protect us. It won't.

Banner blindness isn't a real problem. The notion that people don't "see" the ads on media company websites has been proven by the eye-tracking studies of Jakob Nielsen, and yet we must set it aside to validate the CPM model. After all, if it was true, then the myth would be destroyed, and we can't let that happen.

> Even companies who accept the idea of banner blindness fight it by turning plain banners into whirling, blinking "rich media" ads that fight for attention. All they do is piss people off. And how about those ads that do manage to pop up? It's amazing how easy it is to find the "X" to close the ad without ever actually looking at it.

The value of online advertising is determined by the advertiser, not the publisher. We're getting exactly what we deserve by buying into the myths and assumptions of mass advertising online. We've dug ourselves into this hole, and as the old saying goes, the first thing we have to do in order to get out is to stop digging." In order to "fix" this, however, we need an entirely new way of looking at the real value of online ads, and that won't be found by affixing ourselves to the concept of "inventory."

Local advertisers are happy with the CPM model. As Gordon Borrell says, "Local advertising is sold, not bought," so we automatically run into problems with the model locally, because advertisers who don't or can't "see" their ads don't come away with a real warm feeling. The bigger the portal website we operate, the greater the problem, for ad visibility becomes a serious matter to the local guy whose shelling out money to "see" his own ads. If he can't see them, he assumes nobody is seeing them, regardless of the report we can print from server logs that shows otherwise.

> When your site garners 10 million page views a month, a campaign providing even a half a million impressions doesn't stand a chance of being seen by anything other than the server. Local advertisers want visibility, not to get lost in a vast sea of our greatness.

So inventory isn't the issue that we think it is, and it's certainly the wrong question in dealing with a concept like the Local Ad Network. Inventory is an industrial age term that finds meaning in a world of mass. Data, however, is our future, and that turns the world of inventory on its head.

Of all the issues listed above, none is greater than the shift to real time. This is much more problematic for the print industry than their broadcast competitors, for broadcasters know and understand real time audience reporting. We call it "ratings," the percentage of households capable of viewing who are actually doing so.

So the accumulation of large numbers of sites in a market upon which we can serve ads is both a reach and data play. The reach, however, is both horizontal and vertical, and that stands a much better chance for future relevancy than "inventory" spread out over a single website.

CONTINUOUS NEWS ISN'T
FINISHED PRODUCT NEWS

Much has been written in this newsletter about the AR&D strategic platform known as Continuous News. Our definition of the concept was first articulated in my 2007 essay, News is a Process, Not a Finished Product," and it's a chapter in our book, *Live. Local. BROKEN News.* Continuous News IS the future of online news, because it is designed for the online audience for news, which is Monday through Friday, 8 a.m. to 5 p.m.

We can and should stunt all we like in creating rich content portals, niche verticals, microsites, full local advertising solutions, ad networks and hundreds of other options, but if we're going to be in the online news business, we must be presenting a Continuous News service. We're having some truly wonderful success stories with our clients, but we still run into people who want to fight about the core assumptions of the concept.

While we believe strongly, for example, that Continuous News should be presented in blog format, with the latest entry at the top, this is a difficult concept for many to grasp, largely because it's so different from the "lead story" or "banner headline" of finished product journalism. In the old form, completed stories are presented in ranked order of importance, a ranking determined by the skill, training and intuition of an editor or a producer.

The paradigm of ranked presentation is what the newspaper industry dragged with it to the Web in the mid 90s, which was then copied by the television industry, because, well, that's the way media companies did it. While it's an oversimplification to blame industry woes on how news in presented online, the reality is it hasn't exactly blossomed as a viable replacement for traditional forms of media. Meanwhile, the people who built the Web moved in an entirely different direction, in part because they knew something media companies didn't — that the Web is a real time database, not a transport system for content.

And so, from the very beginning, media companies were going up the down staircase, and the results are not surprising. The analogy of pouring new wine into old wineskins is appropriate, with the predictable result of exploding wineskins.

The database-driven, real-time Web doesn't play well with traditional news items, because the values of the Web conflict with the values of what we call "finished product" news, that which we publish in our newspapers and deliver in our newscasts. Speed, transparency, authenticity and unbundled ubiquity are quite different from that which is bundled, carefully constructed, fully vetted, and complete. It is no surprise that the individual blogs of many media company employees are providing the online oomph for their employers. These are designed for the database-driven, real-time Web, and make no mistake, there is no other kind of Web.

So the conflict between the traditional and the new is innate and deep. Try to convince an old-timer that online news should be presented differently than offline news, and you'll generally get a harumph and horizontal head movement. The resistance can be extreme. We've run into media properties that try to promote a hybrid model, with the "top stories" presented in a block at the top, followed by the continuous news stream.

The perceived assumption with those who resist Continuous News is that people both want and need to have everything summarized for them in one place. We would argue that this is elitist, contrary to evidence, and contrary to the established trends of the Live Web (Seth Godin, Google, Wikipedia-Semantic Web) and social media. The creation of an online finished record, therefore, is a throwback to the days of the Static Web and the logic and reasoning of the late twentieth century. For broadcasters especially, transitioning from the static to the live is difficult, because our instincts and traditions tell us to "gather" an audience. However, television news people understand the word "live" better than other traditional forms of media, so the execution of a vibrant Continuous News strategy can be almost second nature.

Let us also note that "the stream" of information in the Live Web is much bigger than that which any website can produce, which is why we need a strategic approach to Facebook, Twitter and YouTube. Think of it as a giant funnel through which flows a massive flood of information and data that is much bigger than us. Figuring out how to curate the stream is a problem that many are currently working to resolve, but that should not prevent us from shifting our focus to "live," because we want to be rightly positioned for where things are going, not for where they have been. If, for example, Facebook becomes "the Web within the Web" as some predict, we will be prepared to adapt to the environment. Too much is fluid today and too much is at stake for us to remain in a Static Web mode.

In the Continuous News model, everything is a breaking event. There is no "lead" story, for the only thing that matters is the time. Bits of stories are sufficient and they can be tied together through search, tags and a "more coverage" button, if we believe that's necessary. Belief that the audience can't figure out what's going on — what's important — is tied to our finished product news genes, but it's an insult to empowered consumers. Creating news for the Web that appeals to the lowest common denominator is a broadcast mindset. If we challenge people to move ahead and create an environment in which THEY are in control, we will be rewarded by their loyalty. People "get" Facebook's "News Feed." People "get" Twitter. And the numbers for both are northbound, so it isn't really too much of a stretch to make the assumption that they will "get" what we're trying to do in the Continuous News world as well.

And beyond all of that is the need to fully understand that this "real time" stream is where all of the news business is headed downstream. It's much, much bigger than simply a discussion of whether our website output should be a part of it. The Semantic Web itself will be able to harvest all kinds of database files simultaneously to provide facts, context, understanding and knowledge. We must be a part of the stream, and the time to begin is now.

Aside: I just learned that Albritton's new online news venture in Washington, D.C. will be presented in a form of Continuous News. Note this quote from the Broadcasting & Cable article:

> "TBD will never be a finished product," wrote Director of Community Engagement Steve Buttry in its inaugural post April 28. "We'll always be

in motion: constantly updating, improving and evolving. We'll be a place you visit to watch the news unfold in real time."

Here's a caution for Mr. Buttry. The online audience for news is generally at work, so be careful with hot audio on all that video. We don't want to disturb the guy in the cubicle next door.

THE PAGEVIEW ECONOMY —
ENOUGH ALREADY

At the recent SXSW gathering of techies in Austin, Texas, one discussion didn't get a lot of attention from the press. It's a touchy subject — the turd in the punchbowl of online revenue — so most people look the other way and pretend it doesn't exist. I'm talking about what's known as "pageview billing," which along with its companion, the CPM, is the central component of Madison Avenue's way of counting the value of online ads. It's killing media companies, and we need to do something about it.

The advertising industry believes it has an inherent right to interrupt or clutter the lives of everyday people (who ceased long ago to actually be human — to Madison Avenue, we're "consumers"). Web publishers are complicit in this myth, and if you don't think so, take a look at what Lost Remote's Cory Bergman found when looking for breaking news from the paper in Charleston, West Virginia:

Gazette home page during mining tragedy   Disaster story page

No serious purveyor of news and information could possibly believe this is the right way to present things, but this is vastly more commonplace than we could imagine. How did we get here? The pageview.

The SXSW panel featured just two people, John Gruber of Daring Fireball and Jim Coudal of Coudal Partners and The Deck Network. Gruber is a highly regarded Philadelphia blogger and Apple pundit. Coudal's Deck Network is an innovative ad network for select publishers, one of whom is Gruber. The Deck violates all the Madison Avenue rules and yet is very successful.

In the early days of the Web, media companies needed something similar to what they sold in their traditional media models. For print, that's circulation. For television, it's ratings. The essential problem for either is that they are not Web native, but rather than learn about the Web from the people that made it, we decided to pursue our traditional revenue models, and so was born the CPM method of counting pageviews, multiplying that number by the number of ads per page and divided by 1,000 to establish rates. An oversight group was created — the Interactive Advertising Bureau (IAB) — because we needed "standards" in order to maintain an "eyeball is an eyeball" paradigm for advertisers.

In this way, Madison Avenue controls the value of Web properties, not those who run the sites themselves.

Two things happened, neither of them good for publishers or the users of their sites. One, banner ads became a commodity, because the value was with the pageview math and not with the environment in which the ads were presented (despite the hue and cry of publishers). Eyeballs are eyeballs, after all. Two, publishers turned to tactics that increased the number of pageviews, because it was the logical (and easy) way to grow revenue. These things have combined to cripple media company efforts to shift emphasis away from our traditional products and onto the Web, because they work to interfere with the way customers interact with content. This is a bigger deal than you might think.

The Deck overcomes all of this by establishing one unique ad size and providing one ad per page. This establishes scarcity and allows for pricing that is only in part impression-based. The value is set by The Deck, and advertisers can take it or leave it. Given the techie niche that it serves, the network has been very successful, and the advertisers are quite happy to be the only ad on a page of relevant content.

When asked if media companies such as CNN could learn anything from this, Coudal honestly responded, "I don't know."

It was important for The Deck early to get to a certain level of traffic, so that we could be invited to discuss advertising budgets with large advertisers… We had to get to a certain scale in order to have conversations with advertisers, but once we sort of got to that, the cost per thousand thing really doesn't make much difference to us, because we don't pay the affiliates based on pages or clicks and we don't charge the advertiser based on impressions or clicks. Certainly, if our ads aren't being shown, the network doesn't work at all, but once CPM is out of the equation then a lot of this rigamarole that's come along with online advertising becomes sort of silly and unnecessary.

Gruber responded that traffic counts and is important, but "it's not a number that you multiply another number by to get the check that you write."

There are three people involved in the online advertising equation: the reader, the publisher and the advertiser, and, as Coudal pointed out, that which has passed for "innovation" from the industry over the last five years has ignored the first two." One of the big consequences of the CPM system is that publishers must try to game it in order to show growth. In a later blog entry, Gruber was more colorful, calling it a "scam."

Publishers game it with sensational link-bait articles and bullshit tricks like breaking articles into multiple "pages". Advertisers get stuck paying for valueless impressions. Readers get stuck with the sensational bullshit articles, the tricks…and suffer through too many annoying ads surrounding actual content.

The topic has long been a source of discussion among members of the tech press.

TechCrunch writer MG Siegler, writing on his own blog, says it's not publishers' fault. "Pageviews," he notes, "remain the metric by which we're all graded at the end of the day because, right or wrong, that's all advertisers currently care about in the online world."

If sites don't hit pageview numbers, they start losing advertisers. If advertisers are lost, money stops flowing in. If money stops flowing in, people need to be let go. It's that simple. So pageviews remain crucial.

The problem with that model is that it means pageviews have to keep going up. That means that new pageviews must come from somewhere.

And where they come from is a series of tactics that insult the very people they're trying to reach, the audience.

Marco Arment, developer of popular applications Tumblr and Instapaper, writes that pageview billing "incentivizes publishers to distract you while you're reading."

So they take every possible opportunity to try to get you to read their stories, and then, once you try to do exactly that, they try to get you to abandon what you're reading before you've gotten very far so you can go view something else before abandoning it and continuing the cycle.

You're not readers to them. You're "eyeballs."

You're not customers. You're the product.

And that may be the biggest problem of all. Arment offers this illustration of a recent *Time* article on the iPad:

> He notes that publishers are actually saying to readers (without realizing it) that "We don't respect you, and we're trying to aggravate you as much as possible, but not quite enough that you'll stop coming."

What he's talking about is commonly known as the "price of interaction" that users must pay in order to participate in the process of consuming what the site has to offer. Publishers try to find a right balance, but the demand of the pageview is relentless, and so we compromise. In so doing, we're killing any chance at making serious money through our core products, and this has ramifications beyond just the bottom line.

The nut of the issue here is that old bugaboo, copying instead of innovating. Media companies have been guilty of this from the beginning, choosing to bolt everything about the industry onto the Web instead of asking the people who built the thing how to do it. We present content, for example, in the same ways we've always presented it. The geeks created blog software and presentation. We present and sell ads in the same ways we do it offline, and now techies like John Gruber and Jim Coudal are proving there's another way.

This is also why Web pureplay companies are gobbling up local ad spending in record numbers. Companies like Yodel, Local.com, Reach Local, MerchEngines, Yelp and many, many more are putting advertisers together with consumers (and potential consumers) using methods and techniques built on the logic of the Web instead of insisting that things be done some preset, traditional way.

The pageview billing model isn't going anywhere soon, because there's just too much money at stake with the advertisers, agencies, and networks. But that doesn't mean we shouldn't be experimenting — at least at the local level — with new concepts that make sense for everybody, including the audience and the publishers.

THE CONFLICT BETWEEN ENGINEERS AND MARKETING

Before I became a consultant about all things Media 2.0, I ran a Web company specializing in personality assessment. One of our value props was the ability to help companies hire just the right kind of person for the job. We knew that personality — the essential motivations that drive each of us — were critical in getting the various jobs done that make our business world function. Emotional people, for example, while necessary in social or some personnel relations functions, have great difficulty at the top, because their emotions can interfere with making tough decisions.

Analytical minds have different types of issues, because they're always looking for the right process to handle various tasks and problems. This interferes with some forms of creativity, but these people can perform seemingly emotionless jobs. An executioner, for example, could rationalize his job, but an emotional person could not. It's simply impossible.

The right kind of person to run a start-up Web company needs a combination of creative and analytical skills, but all too often they're run by one or the other. In the end, however, it's about risk-taking, vision and cash, and that job is best left to those with a deep personal drive and leadership and motivational skills.

This is important in today's media world, because we've shifted from a management paradigm to one that is much more entrepreneurial. As New York Times Regional News Group exec David Knight told me recently, "It's not about revenue anymore; it's about making money." He's so right.

So who calls the shots with your entrepreneurial digital strategy? Do the people at the top make the decisions — the managers and leaders who came up through the news, sales or marketing ranks — or does that task fall to a person or people who came up through the tech side of things? All too often, in my experience, they come from the tech side, because media executives generally don't have the *knowledge* to drive strategy. While this has certainly been understandable, it has produced less than stellar results for media companies in the grip of disruption, and maybe it's time we took a really hard look at that.

Broadcast companies have been through it before.

I worked for WTMJ-TV in the early 70s and was running the Assignment Desk when the station manager had the idea to create a "Who's Who at WTMJ" booklet, complete with pictures of everybody. TMJ was a combination television, AM and FM powerhouse, and we had a ton of employees. I've kept that old book (dated 1974) and while looking at it a couple of years ago, made a pretty interesting discovery. The largest employee department was Engineering. Over 70 engineers worked there then, dwarfing the news department. General Managers of broadcast stations often came up through the engineering ranks, because, frankly, they were the people who understood the technology necessary to keep the signal on-the-air. Back then, you accomplished nothing — nothing — without the assistance of an engineer.

All of that changed during the 80s, when corporate mandates drove the bottom line to top priority status, and that required somebody other than an engineer to run the place. GM's rose up from the sales, marketing and, occasionally, the news ranks, because they could best move the revenue rock. Technological advancements made it easier to handle the engineering side, and TV stations became massive money-making machines.

I've often written that Ted Turner should go down in media history, not as the man who built CNN and was an early driver of the cable industry, but because he took graphics production out of the hands of engineers and put it in the hands of artists. Until that happened, it was a major project in newscast development to make simple graphics. Turner changed that with his non-union CNN, where artists were equipped with a camera pointed downward, a character generator, and access to images that were either self-created or from a library. Contemporary newscast production owes a lot to that innovation, and it was yet another case of moving technical people away from tasks that formerly they were the only ones able to execute.

Fast forward to today.

We've arrived at that point in the execution of digital strategies, too, and, with deep respect to my geek friends (and my own inner geek), it's time for those who drive cash flow to take over. Why? Because as long as our strategic decisions are made by those in charge of maintaining technology, we'll always default to things least likely to go wrong — the most provable, the most reliable, that which is known — and in today's environment, we need to take chances. The last people in the world to take risks are those whose principal responsibility is to keep things from going wrong.

It's not that engineers aren't capable of risk-taking; it's just that they'd rather not, because their world is bound to that which is known and proven, black and white, and right and wrong. Engineers are highly process-oriented and follow that which is known. Every good entrepreneur has a great engineer on the team, but even where engineers originate some great innovation, the smart ones find a different kind of personality to bring it to market. This pattern has been repeated over and over and over again in Silicon Valley, home of the Web start-up and the largest gathering of techies in the world.

The problem with what I'm suggesting is that the people running media properties — including those that work at the highest levels — lack the knowledge to be able to handle the task of strategy. There are only two solutions to that: acquire the knowledge or hire visionary people who already have it and have run Web businesses themselves. That's problematic, of course, because the people who would hire them are the people who would have to step aside in so doing. Not gonna happen.

That means that the only alternative is a serious commitment to study, something that's especially scary for executives who've worked hard to gain their positions on experience in the old world and would like nothing more than to just manage that until retirement. But study we must, and if it has to be one-on-one, then so be it. The alternative — unless you have a real visionary running the digital side — is to keep letting the engineers call the shots, whether that's operational or strategic.

A COMPREHENSIVE BLOG STRATEGY

When bankrupt Young Broadcasting shut down Nashville Is Talking a couple of weeks ago, WKRN-TV General Manager Gwen Kinsey made a statement about blogs suggesting that we've moved past them in efforts to communicate with the public. Kinsey told Broadcasting & Cable that Nashville Is Talking was a bold statement "way back when."

"I say way back when because if digital technology is teaching us anything it is that specific platforms, unique technologies and the next cool thing all are born, reach maturity and fade or evolve in what feels like a nanosecond of time."

Kinsey says the station—and its viewers—are using Twitter, Facebook and live streaming to connect "in ways that blogs do less and less."

B&C writer David Tanklefsky then added, "Generally speaking, stations' forays into the blogosphere have been inauspicious, with GMs and talent often showing waning interest in maintaining blogs."

Unfortunately, I think this is the consensus of thought, but it's not only dead wrong; it's dangerous in the counterintuitive world of the Web. I would argue that traditional media has never "gotten" the blogosphere, and this is a shame, so let me attempt to explain why.

Ms. Kinsey's statements are spot on — if the purpose of station blogs is to "broadcast" news and information or information about the news to a wide audience. That is much more efficiently done via Twitter and Facebook, although I'd argue that the "notification" aspect of either is a misuse of those two platforms as well. It's all about listening to a community that wants to participate — feels it has a right to participate —

in the news that impacts their world. So what I tell clients is that Twitter, for example, is more about listening than broadcasting, but I digress.

Ms. Kinsey also states that viewers are using Twitter, Facebook and "live streaming" to connect in ways that blogs do less and less. First of all, blogs never were and aren't generally regarded to be a form of social media, so connectivity, while certainly an aspect of any blogging, isn't the main purpose of a comprehensive blog strategy by a traditional media company. Secondly, if connecting with "viewers" is the sole purpose of what we do online, we'll never reach our potential as local media companies, for we'll always be limited to our (competitive) brands. An advantage of having a TV station promote your station.com site is that, well, you have an 800-pound gorilla helping you. The disadvantage is that you can't grow beyond your favorite station status online, because, well, those other TV stations have their viewers, too. Rather than talk about connecting to "viewers," I think we need to be talking about connecting to Web users and, perhaps, using the Web to give people reasons to watch our newscasts. Different approach completely.

But there are three big reasons traditional media companies need to be into the business of blogging. One, **blogs and blogging are a key element in the new news ecosystem** that those of us in the mainstream need to be including in covering the news of the day. The model created by Jeff Jarvis and his students at CUNY identifies the "new news organization" (NNO) that will curate the input from many players locally. Now, that certainly will include Twitter and Facebook, but the people who are serious about participating in "the news" are the bloggers. We tend to forget that "blog" refers primarily to the software that these people use, but from a content perspective, they're doing the news. Nashville Is Talking was a unique aggregation vehicle for what is a very vibrant blogging community in Nashville, but even absent that kind of application, blogging by station personnel puts the company in the midst of this new news ecosystem, and that has value to the company.

Two — and this is perhaps even more important — those employees who work for a media company and blog are **advancing their personal brands and competing in the world of personal media**, where an institutional press entity cannot. I can't possibly overstate how important this is to the people who work for traditional media companies and, by proxy, the media companies themselves. It's so important that I teach they should be doing this on their own time, although I believe the company win is so big that it ought to pay for the hosting, etc.

How does the company win? Here's the third reason media companies need a comprehensive blogging strategy: **these sites are a natural way to grow our local ad networks**, and that, my friends, is the $100-million solution that media companies have been seeking. We want the local blogosphere to participate with us in this venture, and, well, it's just easier if we're involved in the blogosphere ourselves. Companies like GrowthSpur are being funded by Venture Capital to create ad networks for bloggers. Are we going to sit back and let that happen in our markets? If we do, shame on us.

So when I read comments from traditional media executives suggesting that blogs have gone the way of the mammoth, I cringe, because along with such statements I sense a sigh of relief that "the fad" has passed. That is, after all, what all of these things really are anyway, aren't it? Fads? Right? Agree?

THE BEST "DESIGN" FOR THE WEB

It's easy to recognize a media company website: It's the one with all the clutter.

When mass marketing is your world, you only get one shot to "grab" people, and so was born the home page of a media company website. The idea is to put as many links on the page as possible. Whether they are in the form of text links or images, that's the purpose of a media company website. Ads fight for eyeballs. News fights for eyeballs. Promotions fight for eyeballs. Special sections fight for eyeballs. The page is a busy doorway, with each element competing against the next. We want the weather "up top," because that's what people come here for, and so it competes with the video listings, the news headlines, and, well, you get the idea.

The thing that has always struck me about this is that we think that getting people to that page is the solution to all of our problems. This is insanity, and while I'm finding a great many digital vice presidents in agreement, we seem helpless to fix it. That, I think, is because we don't know any other way to do it.

Let's examine four pertinent facts that can help us.

Digital media presentation was created by the newspaper industry. In the early days of the Web, media companies could see its potential, not so much as a disruptor but more so as a way they could extend their brands into this new world. The early Web supported text, and so the written word was supreme, and that played into the strengths of the print media. This is why media sites resemble newspapers in form and function. There is no "fold" in a Web document, but we've convinced ourselves (and our advertisers) that there is one. The display ad model doesn't really "work" in this environment (nobody sees them), but we still sell ads based on size and placement. We tease people on the front page and drive them deeper into the site in order to show more ads (that nobody sees). Nearly every tactical application regarding the presentation and selling of the news online by traditional media companies is birthed in this model, and it's killing us. Even television station websites copy the model, because, well, it's the model, right? We may put a video player front-and-center, but it's treated like any other content block on a portal. Like its predecessor, the newspaper site, a TV site exists to keep people inside the advertising ecosystem that comes with the portal, and that is our Achilles' heel.

The Web is a database. If I could burn only one thought into the hearts and minds of media executives it would be this one. Why? Because once you can bring yourself to this understanding, everything else about the Web makes sense. The Web is not cable TV, nor is it a distribution model for mass media. Oh it has elements of both, but at core, it is a database. Web "sites" pull from the entire database, not just those rows and columns that are run by the media company itself. The AP seems to have had an awakening about this, for the cooperative is now using its Twitter account to push people to its Facebook page, where it distributes full-text articles and builds relationships with its (to date) 9,400 fans. Steve Rubel calls this "brilliant" and notes his earlier references to a "headless" Web, something Paul Gillin calls "the siteless Web." What's happening here is that The AP appears to be discovering that publishing TO THE DATABASE is more natural for the back end of the Web than publishing TO ANY ONE (OR MORE) SITES. This is revolutionary and will lead to a much more efficient delivery system for consumers (and, one hopes, The AP).

> The AP is now changing the game for news by not only going where attention spirals are taking us but by also using their content to curate a conversation on Facebook and — above all — build relationships.
>
> The point is that the database is much bigger and works more efficiently than any walled garden within the database, and

those of us who wish a seat at the table of news relevance in the future are going to have to get into this game. This is the major reason I've always struggled with traditional media companies' refusal to fully participate in the world of RSS. RSS was created to distribute content to the database, and yet traditional media companies only use it to "tease" people and force them to click on a link and "drive" them back to their walled gardens. In so doing, we completely miss the point of the technology, and that has cost us points with the Live Web.

People no longer enter sites through the front door. As the Live Web matures, we're finding that Facebook and Twitter are increasingly feeding people to our stories. However, they're going to individual stories — entering our sites through side doors — and not our home pages. Search also accomplishes this, and at some point, we're going to have to accept that our main doorway is irrelevant. Let's face it: people are hip to what they're going to find on our home pages anyway, so there's no compelling reason for them to explore beyond the story that they came to see in the first place. This is our own fault, for we're the ones who've done the educating by example.

The only "news" style created by the people who actually built the Web is the blog. This is the dirty little secret that traditional media companies wish to avoid, because it's just too simple for our business model. "You mean, Terry, that you actually want us to put our (precious) content on one page?" Yes, exactly. The blog format is ideally suited not only to publish to the database but also to easily follow. The latest item is up top with older items beneath in one long stream. Users scroll to get to the content, not click on links. This dramatically reduces the cost of interaction and makes for a much better user experience. The page itself also focuses attention on what really matters: the output of the news organization.Even if news organizations put a headline and a couple of sentences in blog format, it would still be better than what we offer today, because it would focus user attention where it needs to be and reduce the clutter that dominates media company sites. The right column in the blog format is where bloggers (and blog media companies like TechCrunch or TMZ) do their business. It follows the scroll down the page and doesn't "compete" for eyeballs with the actual output of the company. Anybody that wants to distribute content to users and the database efficiently should be using the blog format. It forces a 100% Web-native product or service, and alone should compel our participation. Surely we've learned by now that repurposing our "real" content gets us nowhere on the World Wide Web. AR&D clients are moving to what we call a "Continuous News" model of website — the TMZ model — which flows in blog format. This is designed to meet the needs of news consumers Monday through Friday, 8 a.m. to 5 p.m. Some sites choose the TechCrunch model of providing only part of the story on the home page and requiring a link to the "complete" story. This is fine, but it is not Continuous News, which uses only parts of stories as items in the stream. I should also note that TechCrunch averages between 35 and 50 completed stories for their site every day.

Traditional media companies need nothing less than an internal revolution to not only extend their brands but also awaken to the possibilities of a database-backed Web. In reality, every element in the database is content, including the advertising, and we'll never learn how to play in that world, if we insist on the walled-garden, news portal approach. It won't be easy, but innovation rarely is.

IT'S ALL ABOUT PEOPLE (NOT "CONSUMERS")

In my early presentations to groups that wanted to talk about disruptions to media, I always began with a slide that said, "It's not about technology; it's about people." For those who've not read or heard me on the subject, let me give you the basics, because I need to answer a question posed to me by colleague Jim Willi over the weekend on his blog.

While everybody points fingers of blame this way or that over what's been taking place with media companies over the past few years, we would all do well to look in the mirror. The Internet has brought Western culture to a new place, and here's what's important to know: the Web is unlocking deeply-held feelings and awakening new possibilities for everyday people. To begin with, people are able to be better informed about a great many things today. And if information is power, then people are more powerful today. On many fronts, they are enabled to do something about their former helplessness. They're involved in their lives and the lives of their friends, families and communities on levels never known before, largely because they're all connected and can respond on a dime to anything. This is new under the sun, and we cannot look the other way.

This is why I say that technology may be providing the means, but it's what's being released in people that's generating the heat. In my view, we are in the midst of the second Gutenberg moment in history, and it will have profound ramifications for all of culture.

So when Mr. Willi wrote this weekend of the failure of Superbowl advertisers to successfully drive viewers to their websites, the question about why is rather simple.

> Apparently Super Bowl advertisers missed the mark in their attempt to extend their ads from the big game by using social media to give life to their brands beyond one multi-million dollar spot within the most-watched event. I leave the diagnosis of why this effort missed the mark to 2.0 gurus like our Terry Heaton — but I find the information fascinating.

Jim wrote of strategies by advertisers to involve social media in their ads, but noted that research after the fact showed that few people actually were moved to do anything. "The advertisers' goal," he noted, "was to drive the viewers to go on line and chat, Tweet and become a Facebook fan."

When marketing people use phrases like "drive the viewers" — and media companies are certainly guilty of this as well — we dismiss any notion that, just perhaps, people don't care to be so driven. In the seminal book of the new revolution, The Cluetrain Manifesto, Doc Searls wrote extensively about this. Here's a key paragraph:

So the customers who once looked you in the eye while hefting your wares in the market were transformed into consumers. In the words of industry analyst Jerry Michalski, a consumer was no more than "a gullet whose only purpose in life is to gulp products and crap cash." Power swung so decisively to the supply side that "market" became a verb: something you do to customers.

If you've never read the book, I strongly recommend you make it your weekend project. It's free as a PDF online.

The point is that people are tired of the relentless carpet bombing of unwanted messages, and so they've turned them off and tuned them out (think TiVo). The marketing world's response is to try and jam more into every conceivable sight, sound, touch, taste or smell. If it can get into your brain, marketing will try to get in there with it, or at least that's the way it used to be.

Newscasts and news departments, for example, that radiate a "watch or you might die" persona are challenged, because people know it's just not true. Hubris is our big enemy, along with the presumption that we can say or do anything — no matter how it challenges the integrity or intelligence of the audience — and they'll respond the way we want them to respond.

This is why Jay Rosen refers to them as "the people formerly known as the audience."

So why didn't people respond to those ads? Well, it certainly could be lots of things, but the place I'd begin is the presumption in the first place that they would. Social media isn't a place where we can butt in and take over. Just because you're a big brand doesn't mean you have a license to treat people as pawns on your self-serving board game. Until mass marketing accepts the new realities of life in an empowered culture, they will continue to find failure with old thinking. People simply need to be treated differently.

Here's Rishad Tobaccowala, CEO of Denuo, and formerly Starcom's chief innovation officer:

> (We've entered) an empowered era in which humans are God, because technology allows them to be godlike. How will you engage God?

Douglas Rushkoff in his book, *Get Back In The Box*:

> The internet is not a technological or even a media phenomenon; it is a social phenomenon. And in this sense, interactivity has changed everything.

Chris Anderson in his book, *The Long Tail*:

> As the tools of production and distribution are democratized, institutions lose power and individuals gain it. As the Web becomes the greatest word-of-mouth amplifier in history, consumers learn to trust peers more and companies less.

So I'm not surprised when marketing fails today, and the lessons for all of us are pretty clear. Old assumptions about people, especially those that involve fun verbs like drive, move, shift, and my favorite "reposition" must be carefully reconsidered in our dealings with our audiences. New words like participate, involve, transparency, and friend are strong but only if we deliver what we promise.

I can still remember sitting in an office at Nielsen in Dunedin, Florida and reading comments in diary after diary from viewers in the Northwest **begging** for the TV stations to stop insulting them with teases. I asked myself, "Do station managers ever *read* this stuff?" Because if they did, they might have a different view of how we interact with viewers.

(Now that's not to say we shouldn't do "teases," only that we might want to try less insulting approaches than "15 dead in an accident on highway 101. The story at 11." And it turns out to be pigs. You get my drift.)

In the old world, people couldn't escape that nonsense. Today, not only can they escape, they are — and in big numbers.

"Spam" is a nasty word for unwanted messages via email — or any other delivery system. Think about that before you create some clever way to "drive" people from here to there.

CONTINUOUS NEWS IS A SOCIAL LOOP

The next step for a newsroom participating in the "news as a process" business is to include the audience in the process of gathering and reporting events as they're occurring. This may seem obvious, but Continuous News is a continuous loop that includes consumers on a scale with which traditional media companies are unfamiliar.

Traditional media is a one-to-many paradigm, and this influences our use of social media. We "get" that Twitter, for example, is a great notification system, so a part of its appeal to us is its one-to-many side. We want to get a message "out," and Twitter is very good at that. It's the feedback loop that we fumble with, and this is even true in the Continuous News model. To begin today's lesson, let's back up a bit.

News is evolving away from what I've called "finished products" for several years. To be sure, we'll always have newscasts on TV, some version of a "daily record" in print (after all, we need that first writing of history), and websites that offer completed stories, whether they are blogs, like Duncan Riley's wonderful Inquisitr or online newspapers, such as the Huffington Post. What the news is evolving "to" is a continuous stream of elements that need no finished packaging, as is practiced by the gossip site TMZ.com. You can laugh all you want about the content of TMZ, but they are masters of the concept of continuous news.

Social media is also driving the news business to the continuous stream. This is a new form of news, which, I suppose, is why it's so hard for media companies to explore. We keep defaulting to finished stories and everything that goes with that, and we're missing the opportunities of professional life in the stream.

One thing we must all learn about the stream is that it's not exclusive, because our contributions are just that — our contributions. They're part of a vast linear timeline that is here and now. We don't wait for anything; our deadline is always "now." So if we are but contributing to a much bigger stream than our own, what are our responsibilities to others participating in the stream? This is a critical question, as it relates to our future relevancy as professional journalists in the ongoing stream of consciousness that is the Web. We may even have to interact one day with, OMG, our competitors!

One problem we have with this feedback loop is that we don't control it, and this is counterintuitive. We may not control it, but we can influence it. For example, let's say a television station airs a segment in one of its finished product newscasts that shines a light on the best local tweets of the day on that particular story or issue. We certainly can use such — and we should — but how many of us go the extra mile and notify those people that we're using their creations? What happens when we do that? Lots of things:

- We acknowledge that the stream is bigger than just us.
- We give credit to those who participate, thereby encouraging others to do so.
- They get a chance to notify their friends about "being on TV."
- Our Twitter street creds grow exponentially.
- Our "finished" presentation is better served, and we're better off for it.

The same holds true for comments on our sites. Merely acknowledging their presence is big, but connecting back with them is even bigger. Interaction begets interaction. If we have none, we must look in the mirror. The stream is alive with people — our people — each of whom has a place in the infrastructure that is Continuous News, and we're smart if we lead that all that participation by example.

When big events take place, do we create hashtags that everybody can use? Do we engage those on Twitter through the use of hashtags or through replies or direct messages? The people formerly known as the audience are waiting to be invited in, but not just to become our pawns (let's face it — that's what they mostly are have been to us).

In the stream, we're all equal. Let's not forget it.

Continuous News is a work in progress. We're all learning as we go along. The AR&D clients who practice the concept are, we believe, far ahead of their competitors who don't. "News as a process" is a lot different than finished product news, and that includes the way it's monetized. The sooner we learn how to drop commercial messages into the stream, the better off our bottom lines will be served. Our clients are figuring all this out as they go along.

Others in the business are waiting for somebody to figure it out first. What they don't realize is that by the time "the book" is complete on Continuous News, it'll be too late for them.

IT'S ALL ABOUT YOUR ADS

The digital disruption has given clarity to what is the artificial belief that a media company's advertising infrastructure is tied to its ability to create content. This is important on many levels, so I thought it would be useful to take a step back and examine its essence.

In the broadcast world, it's how many commercials you can run inside the closed system that is a broadcast signal. Since the signal can't expand, the only thing to do to make more money is to buy other channels, raise rates or add more commercials. I recall a study I did a few years ago of the program *Law & Order*. When the show first aired in 1991, the average program length was 48 minutes. By 2008, that had declined to 43 minutes. What happened to the other five minutes? It had evolved into commercial time.

We can call this many things, but the motive for NBC was to increase its advertising infrastructure. The ad infrastructure inside a newspaper is limited to the pages of the paper. To increase the infrastructure, you must add pages, whether they are in the form of more "news" or special sections.

The important thing to understand from an historical perspective is that advertising infrastructure was tied to the properties owned by the media company. The value of that infrastructure was the size of the audience it delivered, whether in total or specific demographics within the whole.

It's a different world online, however, because the reach of one's advertising infrastructure doesn't have to be tied to property ownership. In fact, it's actually more beneficial (and profitable) that it not be. This is why I'm so adamant that the most important product we can create as media companies in 2010 is a local online ad network, a business that leverages our relationships with local businesses and our roots in the local advertising community.

A story in the New York Times this week spotlights the issue. The piece, about how a newspaper in Manchester uses a third-party content provider to boost traffic, quotes Doug Hardy, the paper's Internet director, as recalling the general thinking when website traffic declined:

> "We needed new strategies," Mr. Hardy said. "We needed new ways to draw traffic to our site and to improve our product and make it more compelling."

What Mr. Hardy is really saying is that their advertising infrastructure was shrinking with declining traffic. This comes from the belief that a media company's ad infrastructure is tied to only the content it creates or hosts. Strategies were needed to create more page views and keep people around, the only two ways to increase an advertising infrastructure within a closed system.

If I'm in a university town, it might be a good idea to create a niche vertical site dedicated to that university's sports teams. But it might actually be better to serve ads on the other niche sites that already exist in the market. Think about it. The purpose of creating such a vertical, in all likelihood, would be to grow our advertising infrastructure with ad impressions dedicated to loyal university sports sponsors. I mean, why else go to the expense of building and maintaining such a site? Such a venture would certainly fulfill that purpose, especially with a TV station or newspaper to drive traffic to it.

But if such an audience already exists on one or more other such sites, why not avoid all the expense and simply split ad revenue with them? This carries no risk, because the job of generating the content lies elsewhere. You might be able to make a case that you could do both, and I'd probably agree. But Google has learned that, as the Web grows, it's better to put ads on everything rather than try and control the growth, and this vision can apply to local markets as well.

The point is that there is no way we can create an advertising infrastructure that will compete with the entirety of the Local Web. This is what Yahoo! discovered and why it works with a consortium of newspaper companies to increase its reach. Half a loaf is better than none, but Google's way is preferred. Why? Because in the end, online advertising is all about data, and you can get much richer data from a wide variety of websites — especially if many of them are retail — than you can from a combination of media sites.

AOL's "anti-portal" strategy relates only to content; its advertising infrastructure is the same across all of the vertical sites it runs. They recognized the truth about online advertising: that you can separate your brand from your advertising and do quite well.

So the lesson for today's 101 is this: *Revenue is not (necessarily) about your content; it's about your advertising.*

IT'S NO LONGER
ABOUT SELLING INVENTORY

I had the opportunity to speak to a group of top-level newspaper executives on Monday in Naples, Florida at the annual conference of the Southern Newspaper Publisher's Association (SNPA). Most of my work has been with broadcasters, so it was nice to have a different audience. The problems are all the same, however, and so are the solutions.

I spent two hours talking to them about things that you've read about here, especially the value of understanding the Local Web and how the creation of local ad networks is a potential goldmine for somebody. At the end of the presentation, one gentleman asked, "How can we be expected to sell an ad network when we can't even sell the inventory that we already have?" It's a great question, and I did the best I could to answer it, but it's one that requires a little thought for a really good response. Why? Because of the assumptions that exist within the question itself. So let's begin there.

The phrase "selling inventory" envisions store shelves stocked with items that consumers walk past and place into baskets for later purchase. In some cases, inventory is kept in the back room, with only samples on the showroom floor. Inventory represents the items that you're selling, but even more so, inventory represents the items people are buying, and that's why it's a problematic concept in a local online advertising sales environment.

When a company or an agency comes to us to "buy" some inventory, they usually know exactly what they're looking for, including the ad placement, size, and the reach and frequency objectives. This is the role of third-party ad networks, who are also very good at setting the value for that inventory as well. It's machine-like buying and selling, but it's fraught with issues as it relates to local media and local advertising. As Gordon Borrell puts it, "Local advertising is sold, not bought."

Advertising "inventory" also brings with it an assumption of scarcity. Otherwise, why would anybody want it? In the case of online media sales, if the content being used to "host" the inventory was scarce and in demand, we might be able to make a case that our inventory had high value. We could, therefore, offer it to the highest bidder, which is the model of broadcasting and newspaper sales. The problem is that eyeballs are eyeballs and inventory is inventory, and there's a ton of it in all sorts of contexts online.

So the question being asked is actually framed from an old world, old media perspective. We're not creating an ad network to bring new "inventory" to the table; we're doing it to enable commerce in the community, and that's a very different animal than taking orders for inventory from people who need it or are hungry to get it. Selling the Web this way is also difficult, for there's little evidence that it actually works for clients.

Gordon Borrell and I strongly agree that revenue generation at the local level isn't about content; it's about advertising and the enabling of commerce. Borrell pushes a consultative sales strategy as the road to profitability and has the data to prove that those who practice it consistently outperform those who are into simply selling inventory. In fact, the fastest growing sellers of online advertising — companies like Yodel and AT&T (the yellow pages people) — are all about helping local businesses grow through the versatility of online advertising that works. Likewise, Google's platform and tools are designed to give local businesses ways to grow their companies through online search and advertising. For these companies, it's truly about enabling commerce and not about selling inventory.

The longer we insist that our content is sufficient to generate revenue growth in the Media 2.0 world, the farther down the slope we'll slide in an environment that's proving every day to be just the opposite. Ads adjacent to or that interrupt scarce content is a model with which we're both familiar and comfortable. It's a model, however, that's increasingly difficult to justify in the world of possibility known as the Web.

THE DISRUPTION IS PERSONAL

I created the image below over five years ago to illustrate the disruption that media companies were facing. I still use it today, because it represents — perhaps even more clearly today — the fundamental problem that we have in trying to adopt new media tools to what is essential an old media model.

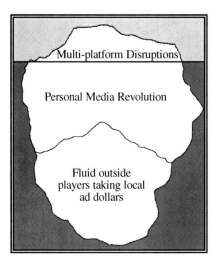

Personal media is an umbrella term that includes social media, for all social media applications are personal, but not all personal applications are social. Personal media also includes personal publishing, as in the creation and maintenance of blogs, personal broadcasting, as found on YouTube, and the use of any form of personal media in the enabling of commerce. It is, after all, the simplifying of and reduction of cost in the ability to "make media" that's at the heart of what's tearing apart mass media. eBay is another form of personal media in that it gives anybody a storefront.

One of the biggest disruptive factors of personal media is how its tools are used by the business community to by-pass the filtering mechanisms of mass media. Using simple — and in many cases, free — personal media software, businesses can create elaborate and sophisticated methods of reaching potential customers. Where they have to pay, the money comes from, you guessed it, ad money that used to go to mass media companies.

Personal media was created to disrupt mass media; it's as simple as that. Giving a voice to the formerly voiceless has just begun to alter our culture, the fruit of which we won't really understand for years. When asked to speak at Universities, I talk about the "Second Gutenberg Moment," for that's what I believe we're experiencing today. Every institution in the West will be impacted by this, with media taking the initial blows.

In the following illustration, which was first given to me by Gordon Borrell a few years ago, I've relabeled the circles to show what's taking place. Instead of Media 2.0 disrupting Media 1.0, the view is now personal media disrupting mass media. It's an important illustration for two reasons. One, the "green" circle WILL overtake the "blue" circle, so opportunity lies WITHIN the green circle, WITHIN the disruption. Two, the gray slice where the two circles overlap is illustrative of how media companies are merely taking the tools of personal media and using them in furtherance of their Media 1.0 mission, rather than embracing the disruption itself.

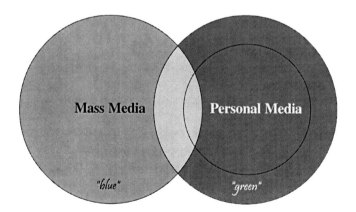

Nokia's prediction that by 2012, one fourth of all entertainment will be created and consumed within peer groups is easier to imagine in light of the personal-disrupting-mass concept. Personal media is where the growth is at, both in real time usage but also in where the tech community — and its funders — are headed for the future.

And then there's Google, the ultimate enabler of personal media. Rather than become a big content company (content is expensive to create), Google has chosen to offer applications that further enable the growth of personal media. Every purchase or innovation coming from its campus in Mountain View, California is designed to strategically grow the disruption, because one of those innovations happens to be a way for people to place ads on what they create, in effect monetizing the disruption. Google, of course, gets a cut.

For media companies, personal media poses serious issues, because to actually enter the disruption means giving up on some long-held advantages that come with owning a broadcast tower or a printing press. Nobody's eager to do that, so what we have is a textbook example of driving the car and fixing it at the same time. That's not easy. In fact, nothing about adapting to personal media is easy, which is why a lot of what Steve and I see is contained only in the gray area where the circles overlap.

Here are ten examples of trying to bolt the disruption onto a model in decline rather than embracing it:

- Building a big list of followers on Twitter but following no one.
- Restricting videos to brand-extension websites instead of turning them loose on YouTube.
- Using RSS only as a way to "move" people back to a brand-extension website.
- Denying the significance of personal branding in furtherance of the corporate brand.
- Overly restricting what employees can do or say via personal media.
- Blogging only within the ad infrastructure of the portal.
- Building neighborhood sites within the framework of the portal.
- Expecting that people who are deeply involved in personal media will work for us for free.
- Using Facebook only as a one-way platform for announcements.
- Not allowing users to participate in our work by restricting online comments.

Contrary to the view that the disruptive innovations brought about by technology are merely new distribution channels for our work, personal media offers not only challenges but also opportunities for local media companies. Do you operate, for example, a community channel that represents your market, either on YouTube or Facebook? If not, why not?

We've got to get outside ourselves, if we're really going to make an impact within the disruption.

LOCAL MEDIA IS
ABOUT LOCAL AUDIENCES

There has always been an understanding with local media companies that local eyeballs were their source of revenue. Account executives for the *Nashville Tennessean*, for example, wouldn't generally travel to Seattle to manage clients. Their clients are obviously in Nashville. Likewise, WBRZ-TV in Baton Rouge wouldn't generally be selling advertising to businesses in Austin, Texas. Local media is about local business, and local businesses are really only interested in local consumers.

The Web, of course, interferes with this notion, because Web distribution is global and not limited to the geography assigned to a license or fancy printing press. A local advertiser on a media company website can't be sure his ad is being seen by local eyeballs, unless he asks for that data from the company serving the ad, and media companies are not real eager to share that information. That's because a larger percentage than you might think of the page views and their accompanying ad impressions that are delivered on local news and information sites come from outside the local market. While many media company managers are completely unaware of this dirty little secret, many know full well its potential ramifications.

I attended a meeting a few years ago at the offices of a third-party website provider during which the GM of a top-20 market expressed this very concern. Local news on his website was made available to Yahoo! News, which fed out-of-town eyeballs to his site. One month, he said, during a big national story from his market, 70 percent of the traffic to his site came from out-of-the-market. Seven out of every ten page views that month were irrelevant to his advertisers.

This is a big problem, if we're ever to become a viable advertising platform for local businesses.

The same thing happens when a local story "goes viral." Most media companies make it easy for people to refer their stories to Digg or Fark, big user-referral and rating sites capable of sending millions of people to a story that makes it to their home page and stays there for awhile. High fives usually follow "getting farked," because the event can boost traffic statistics incredibly. The problem, of course, is that those people aren't local, and local media companies aren't prepared to monetize that traffic without hosing their local advertisers. This will not continue for long, because as the sophistication of the local advertiser grows, so will their unwillingness to participate in anything that doesn't directly benefit them.

And even worse is the illusion that such events create in the minds of the people running the websites. We are fooling ourselves to count such traffic, and we would be well advised to look at ONLY local traffic instead of overall numbers that are inflated by out-of-town guests.

There's another factor that must be considered. All those remote visitors come at a real dollar cost, and this is especially true when they come to watch a video that has gone viral. Bandwidth overage charges for a single story can run into the tens of thousands of dollars in some cases, and while the ad for Joe's Automart gets a lot of traffic, nobody has asked Joe if he really wants to advertise to viewers from Taiwan.

I've occasionally argued with media company executives about this. A local video story goes viral, and I suggest they might want to put it on their YouTube channel and embed that version of the video on their own site. This feels like heresy to them, but it's honest and it's smart. Put a quality version of the story on YouTube with your branding all over it, and let YouTube handle the bandwidth charges. How does this hurt the local media company? It doesn't, and it actually saves the bandwidth costs while letting its account executives deal with making money via local users. It will boost the value of the YouTube channel and give the station the same street creds with users everywhere — perhaps even more — than if they'd forced people to view the story on their own website, complete with the ad from Joe's Automart.

It would be nice if we had a few national accounts in our back pocket to use when such things happened, but the reality is that we don't. Besides, we really need to be spending more energy and resources in enabling commerce *locally* than trying to stunt our way to page view growth.

At AR&D, we profoundly believe that online revenue growth is a local opportunity for media companies, and this is why Steve and I are always talking about local control for local media. Third-party website providers — and we put company-operated digital divisions in that category — make the bulk of their revenue by selling their network of sites to national advertisers. In this world, Digg and Fark are best friends, for the location of the eyeballs being counted is mostly irrelevant. This puts the network at enmity with its nodes, for the node cares deeply about the location of those eyeballs, and sooner or later local media companies will be required to give an accounting for the audience to which they are serving local ads. This day of reckoning will not be pleasant, and we believe smart companies should be anticipating its arrival and behaving accordingly.

Why not even be the first in your market to tout the fact that you are selling only local eyeballs?

Google, Yahoo!, and a host of other companies are aggressively pursuing local online advertising dollars, and we're mostly just sitting by and letting this happen. We cannot, or, as we have been saying for many years, we will find ourselves creating expensive content without the ability to pay for it.

THE QUESTION OF CREDIBILITY

In discussing the reinvention of media with media types, the question of credibility inevitably surfaces. News industry people are willing to do just about anything to survive, but a firm line is drawn when it comes to doing anything that might jeopardize the credibility of the organization. I've written plenty about this previously (The Assumption of Trust), but the subject is coming up almost everywhere these days and demands revisiting.

This week, for example, the people at Pew Research came out with a new study of public attitudes about the media that seems to dovetail other recent studies. The image below shows that perceptions of both accuracy and fairness continue to slide. From the report:

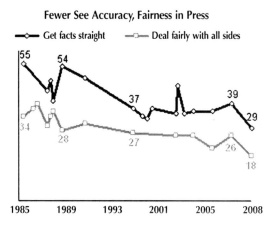

Fewer See Accuracy, Fairness in Press

The public's assessment of the accuracy of news stories is now at its lowest level in more than two decades of Pew Research surveys, and Americans' views of media bias and independence now match previous lows.

The study also examined partisan attitudes about news outlets and found a widening gap between the right and the left and "their" media favorites.

Partisan differences in views of Fox News have increased substantially since 2007. Today, a large majority of Republicans view Fox News positively (72%), compared with just 43% of Democrats. In 2007, 73% of Republicans and 61% of Democrats viewed Fox News favorably. Three-quarters (75%) of Democrats assess CNN favorably, while just 44% of Republicans do so, which is little changed from two years ago. MSNBC also rates substantially higher among Democrats (60%) than among Republicans (34%).

Gallup has been tracking this issue since 1973, and when last polled in 2007, responses were at an all-time low. In fact, more people now distrust the media than trust us to be fair and accurate.

This has brought out all kinds of responses, including the interesting notion that the press has a "public relations problem." This comes from Gene Foreman, former editor of the Philadelphia Inquirer and author of the textbook *The Ethical Journalist.*

Although publicly confessing your own mistakes is almost unheard of in other businesses, it's nothing unusual for a profession in which "corrections" are prominently posted every day.

As morally necessary as these disclosures are, it is ironic that they only reinforce the public's perception that those transgressions are commonplace. Studies have shown that what journalists see as exceptions, the public sees as the rule.

As for other causes of the news media's public-relations problem, that is a matter of conjecture. Roy Peter Clark, a scholar at the Poynter Institute for Media Studies, offered his educated guesses in a 2008 essay. He wrote that the attacks were coming from many directions, with a persuasive cumulative effect on "a public that has been conditioned to hate us."

Foreman admonishes journalists to stay the course and that "self-respect is reward enough."

What's always interesting to me in these discussions is how immediately the industry dismisses the public as being wrong. The argument that there might actually be bias, inaccuracy or unfairness in the press is simply never considered, and so we come up with a series of other reasons for "the problem." It's Hollywood painting us as slime balls and lumping us in with the paparazzi. It's talk show hosts inflaming the emotions of the right (or the left). We never stop to consider that, despite our best and most honest efforts to be otherwise, we're actually human and capable of real and inherent bias.

And now, as we're all facing other very serious problems as media companies, this issue seems like piling on. But is it really? Could it perhaps be at the heart of what's killing the professional press? Given the evidence, can we really expect that hanging on with the reward of self-respect is nothing less than suicide? People are turning away from us in droves, and yet we're conditioned to somehow blame them, while turning a blind eye to what they're telling us.

In his brilliant 1990 essay, "The Lost Art of Political Argument," historian Chris Lasch elegantly deconstructs the myth of objectivity, while making the bold statement that "What democracy requires is public debate, not information." The blogosphere has brought argument (not to be confused with opinion) back into the public discussion, and Lasch, who died in 1994, would've loved it.

As we're reinventing ourselves for a better tomorrow, maybe it's time we looked at the core principles that drive us as news organizations. Can we be "fair" while taking a stand? Of course. Can we be accurate? Ditto.

Whatever we do, we need to be building credibility, rather than assuming that we already have it.

AN OPEN LETTER TO NEWS EMPLOYEES

I'm filing this in the wake of an "open letter to Rupert Murdoch" from Mark Sudock, a senior editor at Fox 11 in Los Angeles about severe job cuts expected to hit tomorrow. In the letter, Sudock waxes nostalgic about things like competence, quality and "the gold standard" for news. "The envy (of their work)," he writes, "is palpable." Due to the pending cuts (117 jobs), however, he adds, "Chances are very real that our reputation and our legacy is at risk." The letter is heartfelt, passionate and very sad, and Elisabeth Kubler-Ross would argue that it comes from the "bargaining" stage of grieving.

The cuts are so severe that virtually no one remains on-site to technically maintain the facility. The cuts are so deep that our ability to cover the news as we did this past week (with pursuits, brush fires and the Michael Jackson funeral happening simultaneously) is in absolute jeopardy.

While Mark's grieving is certainly understandable, the longer he (and many others) cling to the belief that what we're going through is "cyclical" and that "things will be okay, if we just hang on," the longer we delay the acceptance that necessarily precedes change. Before I can change, I must believe that I have to change, and that's true whether it's losing weight or fighting addiction. In that spirit, I offer the following open letter to news employees:

> Dear newsroom employee, whoever and wherever you are,
>
> News people are by nature curious. At times, we can also be quite skeptical, cynical, thin-skinned and resistant to authority, and while that may make us hard to manage sometimes, those can be

healthy traits for journalists who are asked to probe various aspects of life in search of truth. And probe we do. We may have our biases, but most of us are able to set those aside in the performance of our jobs.

One place where we don't do that, however, is in examining our own potential demise. We seem unable to bring an open mind or a genuine curiosity to the discussion, and our distrust of those who "manage" us gets in the way of a realistic examination of the events contributing to the need for change. Somehow, we're convinced that this is some sort of a trick designed to squeeze us for the sake of profit.

So let's look at just ten facts.

1. The market share of people watching television news is off 35 percent in just ten years. Like everything else, there are exceptions, but the truth is people aren't watching what we're producing at levels we used to enjoy.

2. Profit margins for broadcast companies have shrunk from 50 percent to 40 percent to 30 percent to 20 percent, and while the slide is slowing, it's still headed south. Now it's true that our companies still make money, but running a business is always about growth, not just standing still, much less sliding backwards.

3. The automotive ad category used to produce 40-45 percent of our revenue. That's gone to 15 percent, and while car dealers will always advertise on television, they've discovered whole new ways to talk to potential car buyers, so that money is never coming back.

4. The morning news is now the second most important newscast of the day, and yet we haven't shifted resources accordingly.

5. The six o'clock news is no longer the newscast of record, yet we behave as though it is.

6. National advertising used to be 45 percent of a station's revenue. It's now in the 20-22 percent range.

7. The personal media revolution has touched advertisers, who are now increasingly becoming their own media companies and finding ways to better reach people without us.

8. Network compensation — where the networks paid us to carry their programming — used to be a seven figure source of revenue for most stations. Now it's zero.

9. News has become a commodity, and while we're convinced that nobody can do it better than we can, the reality is that scarcity as a business model can no longer produce the kinds of profit that we used to realize.

302

10. The demand for positions within the news industry continues strong, despite a reduced number of positions available. Newcomers coming up through the farm system have skill sets and attitudes about work that are foreign to many of those already employed, and this is a problem for mid-career journalists.

There are many other factors involved, and it's time we had the courage to face this and just turn the page. This is nobody's "fault;" it just is what it is. We can't blame our companies. We can't blame our managers. We can't blame "the consultants." We can't blame the Internet. And we can't blame the audience. We're all in this together, and we're all just trying to do the best we can with a lousy situation.

Perhaps the business has changed so much that you truthfully can't stand it any longer. If that's the case, take it as a sign that maybe you should find other ways to pay the bills.

But whatever you do, do something, because standing still won't cut it, and cursing at the moon puts you in the way of those who have decided to move forward. Fear is tissue paper disguised as a brick wall, folks. Walk through it, and let's get on with reinventing ourselves.

—Terry

PERSONAL BRANDING
WITHIN MASS MEDIA

The exploding world of personal media is the greatest threat to mass media companies. If you've followed this newsletter for very long, you already know that, but the picture of what to do about it is getting clearer as the months tick by. The reality we all face is that anybody can be a media company today, including the people formerly known as our advertisers.

But the bulk of personal media is personal, meaning it's individuals doing their thing, either alone or with others. Mass media is not personal, and therein lies the rub.

Nokia has predicted that by 2012, one-fourth of all entertainment will be created and consumed within peer groups, and already we see evidence of this via that repository of all things video, YouTube. We're also seeing some growth in the area of collaborative efforts, as discussed in a recent CNN report.

Twitter users are banding together to write an opera for London's Royal Opera House. Bands like My Morning Jacket and Sour, out of Japan, are turning to fans to help film their music videos. Programmers are pulling quotes from online social networks to make automated poems.

More than 50,000 animators are divvying up work on an upcoming animated film called "Live Music," and amateur videographers are re-filming "Star Wars" in 15-second bites.

Within personal media is the personal brand, something graduating college students are now being encouraged to develop. I wrote about this subject a year ago in an essay called Your Personal Brand.

The farther we get down the road of a networked culture, the more we're going to see our identity being shaped by what we do and how we interact with others in the network. In the industrial age, one's identity was more often associated with status than anything else. He lives in the big house up the street. She drives that beautiful Porsche. He's the youngest millionaire in town. Her family is old money. He doesn't have a pot to piss in.

Status also means "connections," and only those with the right ones can advance. In a networked environment, true meritocracy has a chance, and it puts the ability of a person to influence his or her reputation with the individual, for better or for worse. The Web levels playing fields, or at least it can.

The Huffington Post is a perfect example of a media company built upon the personal brands of others. It is the personal brands of the writers that "make" the publication, not the other way around. At best the relationship between writer and publication with the HuffPo is symbiotic, but which is the host and which the symbiote? In the world of mass media, the brand of the company is what matters, for it "lifts" the work of its employees. Those who write "for" The Huffington Post may benefit from their association with the other writers, but it is not the Post itself that provides that benefit.

Personal media and personal branding are here to stay, and while our companies struggle to compete with the explosion of all of this, our employees find themselves unable to even stake a well-earned claim in this new landscape. After all, they don't work for themselves; they work for us and our brands, so the digital land grab is taking place largely without them. Their work isn't "personal," and while most could run circles around the amateurs of this new world, they don't, and we miss out. Oh a few anchors, especially meteorologists, have stand alone websites, but most of our work is attached to our employers' brands.

Perhaps this is not a good thing. Perhaps the brand of a legacy media company only "works" offline. Perhaps we should be helping our employees establish and grow their brands instead of forcing everything into ours. Some will argue that this is heresy, that the growth of personal brands in the marketplace harms the brand of the mass media company, so why participate in what amounts to a form of self-destruction? Why should we promote JohnSmith.com when we could be driving people to WWWW.com?

The brand of a media company exists apart from the connectivity of the Web. This is the reality of all legacy media. People in our communities "connect" with us via our distribution systems, but that's a different kind of connectivity than the Web provides. Online, it's personal. It's social. It's interactive. You can have a conversation with an individual, but you can't speak with a television station. What makes us think people can socialize with one?

We are who we employ, and the hyperconnected world doesn't "see" a mass media brand as any different than an individual brand. Both are nodes on the network. More nodes is always better. Always. We tend to think that people who connect with "us" are connecting to more than one, but that's not the way the network sees it. Therefore, the aggregated value of personal brands may actually exceed that of our mass media brand, for those who connect to one aren't necessarily interested in connecting to the other. That's not to say that any single writer is equal to the brand of, say, the *New York Times,* only that the *Times'* dot on the infrastructure of the network isn't any greater than any other dot.

Moreover, developing the brands of employees grows the Local Web and gives us advertising inventory that we wouldn't have otherwise. Ten personal websites with 1,000 page views each a week is small potatoes until you begin to aggregate them, and there is no evidence whatsoever to support the idea that if you just put those pages on a media company site, they would do the same traffic. Sorry, it doesn't work that way.

In addition, people who are writing to help themselves are motivated to keep the content fresh and current. We struggle with trying to motivate our employes to write Web stuff "for" us. Maybe, it's time to let them write for themselves and harness that energy in other ways. In the end, after all, we gain from the growth of those who work for us.

And let's not forget the great line from Steve Jobs when asked why he created the iTouch to compete with the iPhone. "If anybody is going to cannibalize me," he said, "it's going to be me."

Do we have the courage to cannibalize ourselves by promoting the individual brands of our employees?

BUT IS IT REALLY CHAOS?

Mentioning the word "chaos" to the organized mind of a professional manager inevitably generates beads of sweat, for where order produces smooth efficiency, disorder produces waste and unnecessary headaches. But is chaos really disorder, and if it isn't, how can we set aside our fear and exploit chaos to move our businesses forward?

We addressed this issue at some length in the opening chapter of our book, *Live. Local. BROKEN News.* We wrote of the need for leaders and leadership in today's media environment, one that is governed almost entirely by managers.

Managers and leaders are different. An entire industry of consultants have studied the matter for decades, so anything here will seem oversimplified. For purposes of this discussion, however, let's assume that managers flourish in the world of process and use it to accomplish goals, while leaders begin with the goal and work backwards, often wreaking havoc with processes and systems designed to go the other way. Both can accomplish great things, but where managers work very well in times of known parameters, leaders seem to function better with the unknown. Chaos is the enemy of managers, a barrier to progress, but to leaders, it represents, at worst, a blip in the path to the goal. The assumption of the leader is that chaos is expected and welcomed and that it will no longer seem chaotic when the goal is reached. Leaders seem to work "around" chaos while managers are thwarted by its very presence.

The spreadsheet is the tool of process in the same way that ingenuity is the tool of vision. I once ran a company that specialized in personality research. We were hired by a large engineering firm to help them find a certain "type" of engineer based on their experience with a curmudgeonly loner on their staff who could solve any problem thrown his way. The guy dressed like a bum, drove an old clunker and preferred a tiny, cluttered office in the back, far away from the cubicles that housed most of the staff. When the systems of other engineers failed to produce a certain desired effect in the development of a product or device, the company always turned to this fellow. He'd work for days without food or sleep and eventually resolve the engineering problem, and when he did, the reaction of the other engineers was usually shaking heads and the muttered word: "Impossible."

To this fellow, resolving engineering problems had nothing to do with processes, because the processes WERE the problem. The desired accomplishment of the device was all that mattered, and back in his little office, he was God in determining how he met that goal. We were told that he often by-passed many "mandatory" steps in the solving of problems, but to him, these "steps" only interfered with the desired result. What the other engineers viewed as chaos in a world the "known," this guy viewed as a sign that perhaps something was wrong with the steps themselves.

Chaos has an image problem. It has no brand except that which comes from individual experience, and while the scientific community — those faithful practitioners of rational processing — is romping and playing in the world of "chaos theory" — and with significant accomplishments — chaos is still thought of in the same category as words like criminal, disobedient and counterproductive. In so doing, we miss that there are *degrees* of chaos, some of which may be critical on the path to progress.

There is no question that — to the managerial minds of media company executives today — that the Web, social media and the vast disruption of personal media all work together to form a bubbling caldron of pure chaos. We have no choice, however, but to jump in with both feet and deal with the consequences as they come along, because if we wait until all of this sits still (so we can measure it and create comfortable processes), we won't have a seat at the media table anymore. It's that simple.

And that's why we say that our industry today desperately needs leaders — or at least leadership from its managers. Our companies are filled with talented, capable, professional people who, if we turned them loose, could run circles around those who are leading the disruptions that are killing us. It is our insistence that we force our rules, our systems, our paradigms on them that blocks the path to our own progress.

For people with a great deal of discomfort with the word, I can only say that a, it is not your enemy and b, there are varying degrees of chaos, many of which can flourish within limits. Sometimes, the best thing a manager can do is to get out of the way. The trick, I suppose, is to know when.

FORGET YOUR "SITE."
IT'S ALL ABOUT YOUR FOOTPRINT!

The term "footprint" has many definitions, including the obvious one — the image left by a foot or shoe. Who can forget the scene from King Kong where the adventurers first find one of the beast's footprints? Another definition is a trace suggesting that something was once present or felt or otherwise important, like "the footprints of an earlier civilization." The area that a satellite signal covers is called its footprint, and then there's the area taken up by some object: "the computer had a desktop footprint of 10 by 16 inches."

A popular twenty-first-century term is a "carbon footprint," the total set of greenhouse gas emissions caused directly and indirectly by an individual, organization, event or product.

In Media 2.0, a Web company's overall presence, whether global or local, is called its footprint, and it's an important term for media companies to understand. It's important, because traditional media is all about the brand. It's well defined and tightly controlled. Its marketing is all about promotion of the brand, drawing people to it. I like to think of media brands as stages with an audience. In the stage metaphor, the only thing that matters is what occurs on the stage, because the performances there are scarce. Scarcity attracts an audience, which can be sold to advertisers, and so it goes.

But as I've explained before, in the hyperconnected, networked world of Media 2.0, people aren't looking at the stages, because they're looking at each other. This means its essential to disconnect from the stage, to "unbundle" so that people can pass individual items along from person-to-person.

A website, especially a media company website, functions like a stage. No matter how much effort goes into it, a local media company's website is just too small to be revenue effective in the world of the Web. There's no demand for stages on the Web. There's no NEED for stages on the Web, because doing business in Media 2.0 has little to do with websites and everything to do with Web footprints. A website is a valuable part of a company's Web footprint, but there's so much more.

RSS feeds take content from the site and distribute it elsewhere. They are a part of our footprint. Our Facebook fan page and our YouTube channel are two other parts. Keyword-generated microsites are, too. Our Twitter account is another. Assuming we have employees blogging (we should), those blogs are also a part of the company's Web footprint. Here's one that you might not have considered, but every time someone from our company leaves a comment on somebody else's website, that is a part of our Web footprint. Why? Because comments link back to a source. Every tag of every piece of information "out there" pertaining to our company is a part of our Web footprint. Do we have a Wikipedia page? Linked-in account? Individual employee Twitter accounts are a part of our footprint, just as are their Facebook accounts, whether those are used for personal or professional reasons. If we serve our own Web ads, those, too, are a part of our footprint, and the more, the merrier, especially if we can serve those ads on other people's websites. Do we operate any unbranded niche verticals? How about a local search site? Do we partner with anybody? Do we provide content widgets for other sites in the market? How about text message alerts? Email campaigns? The list is endless, and the farther out from the stage we get, the more we begin to realize that every element of the footprint is important. It all works in sophisticated harmony to leave its mark on the community, and we want out footprint to be dominant in the market.

So when we speak of the Web at our place of work, let's move the discussion away from our portal website and onto the more important matter of our Web footprint. Big foot is good! In fact, we want our footprint to be so big that they don't make a shoe that size.

THE WEB IS NOT A NEWSPAPER
(OR A TV STATION)

In my presentations with television stations, I always find receptive ears when discussing the fact that traditional media websites are all built on a newspaper paradigm. Why TV stations have spent 15 years trying to be newspapers online is beyond me, but that's exactly what's been taking place. How did it get that way? Simple.

Firstly, the bandwidth of the early Web was conducive only to text. Secondly, newspapers were the first to see the handwriting on the wall as regards the viability of the Web as a communications medium. That they squandered it by using the Web to add value to newspaper ad sales is a sad commentary, but the point is the traditional media Web functions like a newspaper. TV stations were too busy making money in the late twentieth century to pay attention, which allowed third-party ad networks to move in and provide newspaperesque websites to stations that gave the impression the stations were actually working the Web. We were not, but that's another story.

Everything about a mainstream media website comes from the print industry. Information is displayed on "pages," but they are not really pages. We say there is a "fold;" there is not. Even the idea of driving people deeper into a site is born of a newspaper's practice of printing a few graphs on page one and forcing readers to move to page eight for the rest. Sales come through display ads, the nomenclature of which comes directly from the newspaper play book. Television stations come from the world of interruptive advertising. We don't sell ads around our content; we interrupt it to deliver ads. Banners, buttons, skyscrapers, and

311

leaderboards are all valued by placement on "pages," and this hasn't been good for either newspapers or television stations. Why? Because the Web isn't either.

To determine what it "is," we have to delve deeply into the world of the nerds and geeks who created it.

Their mechanism for communicating "news" was first called a blog, and it functioned very differently than fixture websites governed by newspapers or TV stations. Blogs don't pretend to be finished products; they're always a work-in-progress, for the Web enables the process of journalism more than it does any finished product. This is why innovations in media coming from the geek culture are advancing the process. Twitter and all forms of social media function to enable the process, not to grow a finished product. Attempts by media companies to reverse this — to turn the Web into a fixture-based, finished product news and information service — are vanity and chasing of the wind.

This has not prevented mainstream media companies from attempting to seize the blogosphere and control it, and already there's evidence of a subtle shift from a blogosphere that was once renegade to that which is increasingly the purview of the mainstream. Rather than run with the technology, however, traditional forms of media that are now "blogging" continue to try and ram the concept into its existing, tired newspaper model. Frankly, this is why many old school bloggers have moved to Twitter and other forms of social media. The process is advancing, but traditional media wants it to sit still or, better yet, move back into an old model.

The key to the process Web is unbundled content, and the key to future revenue will be unbundled advertising, for advertising IS content in the Media 2.0 world. To those who aggregate and process it will go the spoils. We're fighting over content when the battle is really over advertising. We can't see that, however, because to us advertising must be adjacent to or interrupt content. Not so with the Web.

Media companies must wake up to the reality that not only does the proliferation of newspaper-modeled websites not get us anywhere; it actually devalues our legacy platforms by moving content from a paradigm where it can be monetized to one where it's free or worth a mere pittence of its original value. If we're going to do news for the Web, then let's do news for the Web. If we're going to make money on the Web, then let's enable commerce via the Web.

There is a need for newspapers to maintain archives and "be" a newspaper on the Web, but it is secondary to the need to aggressively advance the medium. Television stations must first stop trying to be newspapers online, but we, too, must realize that the need to participate in the advancing medium is far more important than merely extending our brands.

THE DE-PORTALIZATION OF THE WEB

I get questions from clients all the time about whether it's better to create a bunch of niche vertical websites or put them all into a single domain. Our answer is always the former, for we're deep into an era where the all-encompassing portal is increasingly irrelevant. Search by-passes portals, and a series of niche verticals offers many "home pages" for monetization. AOL — the original portal — is now growing business through what we've noted is essentially an "anti-portal" strategy. The company is expanding its ownership of niche verticals.

Fred Wilson is a New York venture capitalist that is quoted often in this newsletter. He's one of the smartest and most open people in the VC business, and his blog is widely regarded as a "must read" by those who wish to live on the cutting edge of this developing space. With his permission, we're republishing a recent post on this very topic, one in which he gives spot-on advice to Yahoo!.

THE DE-PORTALIZATION OF THE INTERNET (AKA WHAT I WOULD DO IF I WERE RUNNING YAHOO!)

Back in the first Internet era, it was all about amassing as large an audience as you could on your website. That's when Yahoo! was built and still to this day, Yahoo! is a "portal" where you can get almost anything you might want; email, chat, stock charts, news, instant messenger, shopping, jobs, etc, etc. Some of these services were bought instead of built, and after being bought they were integrated into Yahoo! adopting its look and feel and its URL structure. Today, according to comScore, Yahoo!

has the largest Internet audience in the US, with 130 million people in the US visiting Yahoo! at least once a month.

But the first Internet era was at time when consumers weren't that comfortable with vastness of the web and they wanted a safe clean place where they could experience the web easily and comfortably. If AOL was the web on training wheels (it wasn't really the web at all), then Yahoo! was the web you graduated to when you were ready to shed your training wheels.

Google and others changed all of that. Today most consumers are comfortable with the web and all of its complexity. They simple type a search query into Google, Yahoo!, or some other search engine and off they go. In October, according to comScore, there were 6.8 billion searches done in the US alone.

I don't have the data to prove it, but my guess is if you looked at the percent of all pageviews that are generated each month, a much smaller portion exist on the top 10 properties today than in 2000, at the height of the first Internet era.

Today, we shop directly with the Internet merchants we like or we use a shopping search engine to find what we want. We can look for jobs on Indeed, meet people on MySpace or Facebook, find roommates on Craigslist, and use Meebo for instant messaging. It's rarely true that the best of breed service exists on a "portal." The portals continue to buy best-of-breed services like Flickr, but now they let the service continue to exist on the web with its own look and feel and URL structure.

The other thing that Google did to foster this de-portalization was introduce a monetization system that existed off its own network. Dave Winer says that "web 2.0 is really nothing more than an aftermarket for Google." While I don't agree with that assessment at all, it does point out how critical an effective monetization system Adsense has been and how important that money has been to building a de-portalized web. What Adsense does is provide a revenue stream early on in the life of a new web service, long before the founders can focus on building their own monetization system. And that has led to a proliferation of high quality web services that do not ever need to end up on a portal.

So if you buy that the web has been de-portalized, what do you do if you run the largest portal in the world? I think its pretty simple actually. Yahoo! needs to offer its users and customers (advertisers) the ability to get the same experience they get on Yahoo! all over the web. They need to stop thinking about keeping their audience on Yahoo.com and start thinking about serving their audience wherever they are on the web. They need to stop thinking about selling ads on Yahoo.com and start thinking about selling ads all over the web.

I know that they are doing all of this, but I do not believe they have made a strategic decision to "de-portalize" their business model. For one, it will cost them in the short run. There are partnerships, deals, and relationships that produce millions of dollars in revenues that would go up in smoke if they really de-portalized with a vengeance. AOL faced the same issue, but much worse, with their ISP revenue and finally realized they had to give up on an unsustainable revenue stream in order to be a player on the web long term. I believe that Yahoo! needs to make that same kind of strategic decision. And I think their stock will react positively if they articulate it correctly.

So what are some concrete things they need to do? Well first, they need to improve their search service. On a de-portalized web, it all starts with search. I never hear of companies that have 80 percent of their traffic coming from Yahoo! I hear of companies all the time that have 80 percent of their traffic coming from Google. Yahoo! may have 28% of all Internet searches, but for some reason that I am not sure I completely understand, Yahoo! does not generate 28% of Internet traffic.

When most people talk about the fact that Yahoo! needs to improve its search system, they focus on the monetization piece (ie Panama). That's clearly critical as Google monetizes search something like 10 times better than Yahoo! But I think Yahoo!'s search itself is inferior to Google's. I have tried to use Yahoo!'s search as much or more than Google's over the past year as I want to support Yahoo! as much as possible. But I do not get the results I want from Yahoo!, particularly on advanced searches or complex search queries. Yahoo! needs to make it's search product as good as Google's (ideally better) and they are not at that level today.

Yahoo! also needs to start building properties that exist outside the Yahoo.com orbit, like the new Mixd service they launched last week (but Mixd still has a yahoo.com URL).

And Yahoo! needs to get its YPN (Yahoo Publisher Network) service in gear. They need to offer advertisers the ability to reach people when they are not on Yahoo! They've done some things recently, like the eBay partnership, that suggest they are headed in that direction. But I would urge them to move faster in this direction than they are moving now. It might mean buying some ad networks instead of just investing in them.

I believe AOL's purchase of Ad.com was the single best thing that AOL has done since launching AIM ten years ago. Yahoo! should look at that move closely. I think there's a lot to learn about what has happened to Ad.com inside of AOL.

These are some examples of the moves that Yahoo! needs to make in order to leverage their considerable assets onto a de-portalized web. They are not the only things they need to do, but this is not a McKinsey strategic plan. It's a blog post. And it's gotten too long already.

DATA IS THE DIFFERENTIATOR
FOR ADVERTISERS

The role of the ad agency in the Media 2.0 world is evolving, and like media companies themselves, ad agencies face an uncertain future. The problem for agencies is that they exist as middlemen between advertisers and media, and the uncomfortable reality is that the Web tends to route around those who used to make their fortunes by being in the middle.

There is considerable debate about all of this, and of course, agencies aren't giving up without a fight. At the very core of that fight is the world of data, the Holy Grail of the Web, and whoever or whatever is able to manage data for the benefit of clients in a cost-effective way will likely have a seat at tomorrow's media table. Even this, however, is uncertain, for one of the big unanswered questions of the day is who owns the data about visitors to a website, the publisher or the advertiser who's running ads on that site? This is one of the issues in the publisher revolt started last year by ESPN in announcing they would no longer accept ads from 3rd-party ad networks. The networks think the data belongs to them. Publishers think otherwise.

A recent *New York Times* article (Put Ad on Web. Count Clicks. Revise.) featured the work of an ad agency built on the use of online data.

From the "Mad Men" era until now, advertising has been about a catchy tagline, an arresting image, the Big Idea. But Mr. Herman (Darren Herman, president of Varick Media Management) and his competitors are bringing some Wall Street-like analysis to Madison Avenue, exploiting the huge amounts of data produced by the Internet to adjust strategy almost instantly.

If your site is part of an "ad exchange," your remnant ad spaces will be grouped together with others of similar demographic and psychographic nature and sold through one of these data-centric agencies. The idea is that the eyeballs that visit your site are more valuable when grouped with other similar eyeballs, and the exchange allows publishers to earn more per ad impression than they would otherwise.

Jarvis Coffin of Burst Media wrote in response to the *Times* article that this data-centric approach should eventually lead to offline as well. He took the *Times* to task for missing the real story, which is the use of data in behavioral ad networks.

Indeed, searching for the new heart of Madison Avenue has been the past-time of many people inside and out of the industry for years. Maybe love has finally found a way. Once again, information is power and much of it derives from the sort of relationships that ad agencies have continued to enjoy — albeit in serf fashion — with their clients. Sitting atop copious amounts of campaign data, which they have watched get turned into fortunes by vendors with shifting attachments to the strategic welfare of a client, ad agencies have decided they are — and ought to remain — media planning and buying vendors of first and last resort.

Good for them. Now they just have to figure out how to get paid for it, but the excitement and opportunities increase when they consider how data can begin to play a livelier role given the expansion of digital media technology to all places offline, especially TV.

One of the cornerstones of Media 2.0 is data, and local media companies are facing the dawn of the database age with no idea of its requirements, scope or the tools necessary to compete. This needs to change and change quickly, 'lest all local media companies find themselves at the wrong end of the online value chain. The making of expensive content is not the best revenue position for tomorrow. That seat belongs to those who manage the data of the local market.

Gordon Borrell has seen this evolve in his own work. One of the characteristics of what he calls "Green Zone" performers — those media properties that do above average online revenue market share — is an incredible thirst for data. He told me in an email that most media companies are still stuck in the past.

I think analog media reached the zenith of their youthful beauty a few decades ago, and what we've seen since the mid-1980s is an obscene amount of cosmetic surgery and make-up. Newspapers moved from talking about "subscribers" to a much bigger metric called "readers," figuring that if a newspaper hit the doorstep of a household had 2.5 adults in it, there must be 2.5 readers in it. TV started talking about TV households, figuring that if a household had a TV in it, people must be watching it. And radio invented cume — which is a fancy way of saying that if the radio is left on long enough, a lot of people might actually listen at some point.

The Internet isn't as lucky. It has things like pageviews, clickthroughs, unique visitors, time spent online, "bounce" rates, and connection speeds. While some of those statistics can be misread or manipulated, there's a helluva lot more to go on than a mere telephone survey or diary sent to less than one percent of the population.

Borrell added that data has become incredibly important and that he's witnessing "a great divide" between those who know how to collect and read that data and those who don't.

Helping advertisers understand just how many people saw their message, how many clicked on it, what times of days produced better responses, and what people did after they clicked — are all wildly powerful pieces of information. The collection, analysis and manipulation of data will continue to be more important in the media landscape, thanks to the application of computing power to advertising. I think information is still power, but the collection of vast amounts of data magnifies the potential.

Add to the equation the reality that some well-informed local advertisers are themselves becoming extremely well versed in data, and you can see the problem for media companies who just sit on their hands in the Media 2.0 world.

We feel strongly that the window is open for smart media companies to move in and seize this space at the local level, becoming, if you will, ad agencies themselves. That window won't stay open forever, and the sooner we adapt to a data-driven marketplace, the sooner we'll be able to grow significant revenues online.

THE WEB IS (ALSO) A MARKETING TOOL

We've always believed that the Web was just another delivery vehicle for our content, one that would allow us to monetize that content the old-fashioned way, through advertising bundled to it. But ads next to content don't "work" unless many, many eyeballs are exposed to the ads and it can be reasonably inferred that those eyeballs have actually seen the ads. It's this belief that has led mainstream media companies down various rabbit holes in attempts to unlock the wonderland of profit in a universe that is both foreign and dangerous. The best it can be said for the result is that we're trading, as Jeff Zucker put it, analog dollars for digital pennies.

This belief is also at the bottom of sincere but foolish efforts by the AP and its members to impact the link economy of the Web by altering search results and limiting the use of their material by aggregators (a.k.a. "text pirates") such as Google, who are really just trying to send them traffic. The latest is a Cheshire Cat, a "secure widget" of content — with the bundled ads — that so-called "content pirates" (bloggers) can use on their own sites for referencing stories. Raw text cannot be copied from the widget; bloggers wishing to write about an article must include the widget with the whole article and the ads. The widget smiles, but its body disappears, because nobody in their right mind will actually post such a widget.

Links are the currency of the Web, the very nature of its structure. Those links have a real dollar value, when viewed from a marketing perspective. I wrote of this in the 2007 essay, "Links, the Currency of the Machine."

The professional news industry is, of course, quite content to sit back and let others link to it. It's a traffic strategy. This despite the fact that many in the business criticize the linkers as parasites who build reputations and audience by linking to their work. This is an absurd and dangerous perspective...

The mainstream press views outbound linking as irrelevant — or worse, suicidal. The idea is to assemble crowds in one place rather than disperse them to the winds. Besides, the mere thought of actually linking to another person or organization is anathema to the concept of original reporting or scarcity of content, and the whole traditional press suffers as a result.

It suffers, because the news is bigger than that which any limited, single organization can get its arms around. It suffers, because its unwillingness to participate in the conversation that is news leaves it isolated, naive and mere pawns of the status quo. It suffers, because without participation, the press will never discover the wonder or the tools of the Personal Media Revolution. And it suffers, because in the end, the Machine will calculate its value downward in the overall scheme of importance.

The *New York Times* is the most linked-to media publication on the planet, and if you pay attention, you'll notice that the company creates dynamic pages of its content that it then links to, which adds to the volume of inbound links. Every newsmaker, for example, has his or her own New York Times "page," so their name becomes an automatic link in any story containing it. Wikipedia doesn't show up in the top of the search rankings by accident; it is an internal linking machine. Every entry contains links to hundreds of other entries, which work together cumulatively to create a massive database that the search engines recognize as authoritative.

Is this gaming the system or playing by its rules?

The latest iteration of all this is the growing value of short message system applications in determining the authority of participants. Michael Arrington wrote of this in an important entry in TechCrunch, Topsy Search Launches: ReTweets Are The New Currency Of The Web. Arrington examines a new search engine (Topsy) and makes the observation that the real-time chatter of Twitter reveals much.

The 30 million or so Twitter users are an army of little content-finding machines. Topsy says those users are sending tens of thousands of unique links per day to interesting things around the Internet.

Some of those users have more influence than others. And some links are sent by lots of Twitter users, others just sent once. Those links, combined with the information in the Twitter message itself, is what Topsy uses as the basis of its search engine.

And the results are…amazing.

For media companies of every stripe, this is proving that participating in the conversation that is news will bring people to us, although the best we can do is simply seed the mix. We can't manipulate this; we just have to participate. Unlike conventional web linking, however, there's nothing here (so far) that values one retweet as greater than another. That's just a matter of time, however, because technology loves data, and there's plenty here to play with.

So if we have a valid linking strategy and we're tweeting and retweeting with the best of them, where's the money in all that? Think of it as marketing, the positioning of ourselves as valued and trustworthy partners in the conversation that is news. Instead of driving traffic to our web applications, we should be driving traffic to our legacy applications, which is how we make a living. Think of it as a way to listen to that conversation. We've spent decades listening to police radios. Isn't it time we expanding that listening? We need to do this to be relevant in the community, and if we want to establish the news agenda for that community, we'd better be prepared to hear what our readers and viewers are saying.

For media companies, it doesn't appear (yet) that there's a real solid and sustainable revenue play via the content we create on the Web. And maybe that's a good thing. One, we'll be motivated to creatively explore using the Web to enable commerce within our communities and in so doing reap rewards ourselves. Two, we'll regain the trust we've lost by participating WITH the community in the news gathering and creating process. Three, we'll use the Web as the powerful marketing tool it is to drive traffic to our legacy platforms.

THE WEB DRIVES
TRAFFIC TO OUR BRANDS

One of the key strategic mistakes local media companies have made regarding the Web (especially TV stations) is the assumption that driving traffic to a brand-extension portal is smart business. It's not, and we can see this today, whereas we perhaps couldn't a few years ago. In the early days of the Web — before we knew what this thing really was — the Web seemed just another distribution channel for our goods and services, and smart third-party ad network companies were there to make sure we had everything we needed.

But these ad networks made money through aggregated ad impressions nationwide, so the driving of traffic to properties containing their ads was smart strategy — for them. Tactics to do just that came with the software, and so was born a consistent practice of using the legacy property to move people to branded corners of the Web.

In so doing, however, we've harmed the value of legacy media, for a media company can only "drive" those eyeballs that it already reaches. When NBC Universal president Jeff Zucker proclaimed his fear of turning "analog dollars into digital pennies," he was really holding up a mirror to himself and all other media moguls, for we have all been participating in a process that does exactly that. If web users in our communities have the idea that they can get everything online that they can offline, then audience convenience becomes the only determining competitive factor, and whose fault is that? Pay walls and micropayments won't solve what bad strategy has created.

At this point, it's a case of water under the bridge, but the essential lesson is one we should heed moving forward. We simply won't survive, if we shift everything we have to the Web. To be sure, some companies have made a lot of money in building and maintaining brand extension websites, but the long-term efficacy of such sites is not a sure thing. Most are tied to banner advertising, which has a questionable future. Most exist to make it efficient for ad networks, such as Centro, to move national and regional ad money to local markets. This symbiotic relationship (and easy money for media) depends on a certain status quo in the world of advertising, a world that is facing disruptive innovations similar to what have been eating away at the foundation of traditional media for the last 20 years. Betting the long-term health of your media company on a strategy that emphasizes only brand extension portals is a dangerous move.

If we are to be truly successful downstream, we must begin to enable a fundamental shift in our strategic thinking:

> The Web drives traffic to our brand.
> Our brand drives traffic to the Web.

We don't use the Web to grow legacy media, because we don't believe in the power of the Web to do so. Moreover, we don't have legacy products that work "with" the Web to accomplish this end. TMZ.com is a web business that built a television show and brilliantly uses the Web to drive traffic to that show. The Continuous News model that effectively meets the news and information needs of the community during the Web's "prime time" — Mon.–Fri., 8 a.m.–5 p.m. — is the perfect vehicle to drive people to early evening newscasts. One of the key purposes of any web business we create ought to be to promote the legacy business we already maintain.

The new value of local television airtime is to promote the web businesses that the station runs as part of its business portfolio. This is the right use of legacy media, for the reach of the traditional property is being used to drive eyeballs to businesses that don't compete with the products and services of the traditional property itself. This is the key competitive advantage local media has over the internet pureplay companies. This presupposes, of course, that we're creating such online businesses and not merely parroting our traditional news and information services on the Web.

While industry insiders focus on the content side of what we do and craft clever strategies and tactics to that end, we simply must start looking at advertising as the driver of anything we do tactically. Advertisers are an increasingly empowered lot (just like consumers), and they won't suffer the rates of ad-supported content forever. Whether it's online or off, the game today is about enabling commerce. We enable commerce when we use the reach and frequency of our legacy products to help businesses expose their products and services to a mass audience. Online, however, we enable commerce by connecting those who want to buy with those who want to sell through a variety of means, including local search, email, video, contextual targeting and behavioral targeting.

The Web is so much bigger than we think it is.

SELLING SCARCITY AND PASSIVITY IN
AN OPEN AND INVOLVED MEDIA WORLD

The oldest newspaper in Tarrant County Texas (home to Fort Worth) is shutting down this week. The *Grapevine Sun* has been in existence since 1895, and it cannot sustain that existence given the current state of the economy and newspapers. Even though it serves my community, I never read the *Grapevine Sun*. I guess I'm just not that interested in neighborhood news.

Community newspapers are having as much difficulty as the big dailies, and the hand wringing over what's happening to newspapers has gotten so loud that it's become a net liability to an industry in decline. To read some, you'd think democracy itself was at stake, while others suggest that print will never die. Michael Josefowicz's recent piece in PBS's MediaShift falls into the latter category.

Josefowicz begins his argument by stating that "common sense tells us that print is not going away." Hmm.

> ...most of the public discourse tends to be dominated by information junkies and there is little doubt that if you're an information junkie, the web is the way to go. But the reality is that info-junkies are only a small tribe. They consume the news at a prodigious rate and the web is the fastest way to satisfy their appetite. Thus, they're also the most vocal tribe — so it's easy to get the impression that theirs is the most widely held conclusion.

It's pretty hard to argue with that point, but what follows ought to be of concern to everyone following any mainstream media difficulties.

When I was 20, I wore a T-shirt that said "Don't trust anyone over 30." It seemed to be completely clear at the time. It made so much sense. Anyone who didn't see what I saw was destined for the dustbin of history. I was wrong, but it happens every 40 years or so. 1920s, 1880s, 1840s, 1790s. A new cohort enters the global arena. They think the way they see the world is the Truth. It's the error of clarity in a very complex world. The same thing is happening today with young info junkies so eager to discount print.

I don't believe this is true.

In 2005, IBM issue a heavily-researched body of work called "The end of TV as we know it: A future industry perspective," in which author Dr. Saul J. Berman examined the issue of young turks and concluded that instead of the rebels moving toward the masses, the masses will be moving toward the rebels.

The image below is a grid displaying limited-to-open access to media and passive-to-involved participation by consumers. Not only will the open/involved quadrant be growing, but the researchers projected that the masses in the lower left quadrant will be drifting to open and involved. There is considerable evidence (can you say Twitter and Facebook) to suggest that the masses are warming to open and involved media.

The Generational Chasm: Future State for 2012

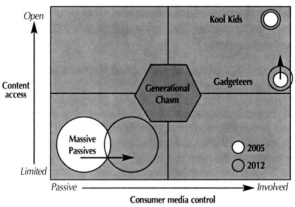

Source: IBM Institute for Business Value

This is why it's so dangerous to cling to the hope that we're ever going back to the days of limited access (scarcity) and passive participation, which is the market for newspapers. Television lives in that world, too, which is why Steve and I are constantly pressing for a better understanding of Dr. Berman's open and involved corner.

As for the *Grapevine Sun* and others of its ilk, community news is springing up from the grass roots, and at least some of it is driven by journalists who used to work for traditional media companies. In Dallas, we have Pegasus News, which does an excellent job of covering my neighborhood. Pegasus is a complex machine, but the simplicity of the neighborhood sites in, for example, Seattle provides a glimpse into the future of local journalism. Check out the West Seattle Blog, Cory Bergman's MyBallard.com and Exit 133. In New Jersey, take a look at Patch.com, featuring three communities. There's also a wonderful site called Neighborlogs, a turn-key software solution for anybody wanting to create a neighborhood site.

Newspapers are dying quickly in their scarce and passive corner of the world. The news business, however, is doing well in the world of open access and involved consumers.

REINVENTION INCLUDES JOURNALISM

The name "Marvin Kalb" was synonymous with network news when I was a young man. He spent 30 years with CBS and NBC and now hosts The Kalb Report, a monthly discussion of media ethics and responsibility at the National Press Club in Washington, D.C., sponsored by Harvard's Shorenstein Center and George Washington University. Last months' session was entitled "Down to The Wire: Journalism in Crisis," with guests Jon Klein of CNN, Alberto Ibargüen of the Knight Foundation, Vivian Schiller of NPR, and Tom Curley of the Associated Press.

The transcript is a fascinating view of the old versus the new, with Kalb bemoaning the state of the press and democracy, and the guests defending change. These kinds of sessions are useful in pointing out the assumptions made in certain arguments that are holding us back, and that's what I'd like to do here, for old school journalism is not above disruption. The canons were not etched in stone by the finger of God. Contemporary journalism is a modernist invention, and we must be willing to accept that, if we're to be relevant downstream.

Challenging assumptions ought to be the first duty of everyone in a postmodern world, for it is often very revealing. Here's Kalb:

> Joe Nye, has written about the paradox of plenty. And let me quote him for a second. "A plenitude of information leads to a poverty of attention. Attention, rather than information, becomes the scarce resource. And those who can distinguish valuable information from background clutter gain power."

...how do you help the public work its way through the clutter and get to what is substantive, get to what is news, get to what is important to them to make up their minds about this country?

Ms. Schiller responded that Kalb's question demonstrated a "lack of trust in the intelligence and the discerning power of the audience. I actually think that most of the listening, viewing, using audience is pretty good at discerning clutter from real stuff and they will self select." Well said. The assumption of Kalb's question is that people are incapable of such and need to be guided, which comes right from the lips of Walter Lippmann, the social engineer and dean of professional journalism. Technology is increasingly able to filter the fire hose that Kalb fears, and that will only continue to improve.

The press is sincere in its belief that democracy needs it to sort through this clutter, but that is merely an assumption.

A similar assumption is behind this statement:

Ed Murrow and Walter Cronkite: There was no question about the trust that they engendered in the American people.

The assumption here is that it was Murrow and Cronkite, not the market with its limited choices, that engendered the trust. All of the network anchors were trusted back then, but what's ignored in making such a statement is that people really had no other choices to trust. The network anchor chairs were all there was. Of course, newspapers were trusted back then, too, but then came Watergate and the birth of gotcha journalism. Trust went south, and we nostalgically remember a less complicated time.

When AP's Tom Curley noted that "somebody" would step in to fill the gap in governmental coverage, if newspapers go under, Kalb responded, "but will this someone be a trained journalist who was there to cover news, understands the difference between opinion and the acquisition of hard information?"

The assumption here is that only one "trained" in journalism is capable of covering news, and that's simply a myth. Kalb then asked if the panel thought "the old values of journalism" would be around in ten years. Klein responded that "the audience is going to demand that those values are preserved because they demand accuracy above all else."

Klein's right, but he's referring to the same audience that has rejected those "old values" as horse poo, because the evidence doesn't support contemporary journalism's claims of righteousness. The "audience" isn't nearly as stupid as we think, and we need to honestly accept their rejection for the sincere criticism that it is. Those old values may not be as valuable as we once thought.

The panel took questions from an audience of journalism students and practitioners. One referenced the "first rough draft of history" often ascribed to newspapers. This student/journalist was worried about the future.

> ...what will future historians do and the wider public, without this rich contemporaneous depth of coverage of what it was like to live through these times, so we can go back and create a picture of what this piece of history was like to live through if we don't have those newspapers to draw on?

This argument ignores the broader picture of a history that's being more accurately written and recorded today, thanks to the marvelous technology of the Web. Rough draft? Who edits that rough draft today? Everybody, that's who.

Journalism and history have always been problematic for the serious researcher, because history has always been written by the powerful. As Napolean (I think) used to say, "The victor gets to write the history in war." We're experiencing the difficulty of that today in the Middle East, because anybody can publish their version of events, which forces a broader spectrum of opinion and limits the ability of anyone to manipulate the truth.

And what is truth, after all, if not the greased pig that professional journalists chase?

BUILDING A WORDPRESS BLOG

When we look at the enormity of the disruption that's attacking the mainstream media business model, people are often confused by the nature of the disruption. It seems so staggering, because we view it as technology, and who has the time to learn all that? Television people are generally those who sided with the bad guys in "Revenge of the Nerds," and who knew we'd need them so badly today?

Every time some engineering whiz opens his or her mouth, we shrivel up into a ball and want to cry. The world of technical acronyms is a foreign language, and who has the time or energy to learn all that?

I faced this fear and won when I bought an internet company many years ago, one that required the boss know everything, including how to write code. At age 52, I became a hands-on student of things I never imagined I'd be learning, but the secret to my success was in learning by doing, not by studying.

This same method can be applied to everything that a reporter in Louisville or Tallahassee or Dallas might need to know to transform herself into a multi-skilled, multimedia journalist. And here's the thing: it doesn't require taking courses at the community college. In fact, I'd argue that's the wrong way to learn.

The first recommendation I'd make to any budding multimedia journalist is to start a blog. Don't go the easy route (Google's "Blogger"); go to a hosting company, like Bluehost, buy a domain name, and lease monthly space on a shared server. It costs $6.95 a month. Like other newer breeds of hosting companies, Bluehost will set you up automatically with WordPress or other forms of software. I like WordPress; it's powerful and easy to use.

You will now be in business as a blogger, but more importantly, you'll have a very powerful and flexible content management system at your fingertips. WordPress is "open source" software, which means it has an enormous community of geeks working to improve it every day. You can find thousands of "plug-ins" that will do amazing things, simply by adding them to your installation of WordPress.

When entries are published in WordPress, all kinds of cool things happen. A searchable archive is created automatically. The software will "ping" search engines, a way of telling them that you have posted new content. Your RSS feed will come alive with fresh content. It operates the way your station's website should operate, but probably doesn't.

You'll want to put images in place, and it'll do that for you. You'll want to customize the look of your website, and there are tons of places to go for help with that.

You'll learn two important concepts: templates and CSS (cascading style sheets). These two elements control the way your content is presented online — the look and feel of your website. Templates control where things are placed on the page. CSS controls how they are displayed, including colors, fonts, spacing, line sizes and such.

In a simple two-column WordPress model, the page you deliver is divided up into four parts.

- The header controls the top of the page.
- The footer controls the bottom of the page.
- The sidebar controls the right hand column (or left) of the page by default. This is created by simply adding the widgets that you like. It's far easier than you might think.
- The index controls the actual blog content. It sits to the left of the sidebar and between the header and footer.

You can find all kinds of design models for WordPress, including multiple columns or whatever you wish to present as a design. These models come fully equipped with templates and CSS.

Eventually, though, you'll want to customize these elements, and that's a whole lot easier than you might think. Just remember one rule. Always keep a copy of the original file you're customizing on hand, because you may need to put it back the way it was. It happens to everyone.

You can learn customization many ways. Just let your mouse do the walking in a search on "customizing wordpress" and see what you can find.

The best way is to find somebody who knows HTML and have them show you hands-on. If you don't know anybody so skilled, you'll learn a whole lot quicker by paying a pro than by going to school. Always learn by doing, and work using your own WordPress blog. Check your local Meetup.com. You'd be surprised how many Wordpress advocates exist in your market. Of course, you can always learn on-line, but the fastest way is in person with an expert.

In just a matter of days (really), you'll be familiar with more things that you ever anticipated, plus you'll have your own customized publishing system.

The reason I recommend this path is for the eye-opening revelations that come with it. As you work with the same tools that the personal media revolution is using, you'll have a new appreciation for the sheer magnitude of the disruption and a new respect for those who work therein. You'll see how easy it is to create a standalone business, and you'll also find it increasingly difficult to work within the restraints of centralized, command and control web software. All of this is good for you and good for the company that's paying you.

"IT'S JUST A BLOG" IS A
DANGEROUS POINT OF VIEW

The argument over whether blogs constitute journalism or not has been waged online since before the turn of the century, and just when I think it's been put to bed, it rears its ugly head again. For me, the latest example took place in my classroom at the University of North Texas, where I'm teaching a course this year on Media Ethics in a Networked World. In every fictional, ethical dilemma that I pose to my students for discussion, no journalist works for a traditional media company. For these young people, I think that's their future reality, so fictional cases are presented in which the protagonist is an "independent journalist," and in many cases, a blogger. Ethical dilemmas are very different when a traditional news "force" isn't there to advise or back you up.

So we got into the "bloggers aren't journalists" debate last week, and I felt like I'd been rocketed backwards to the old discussions. It occurred to me, however, that these were journalism students facing a declining marketplace, and if they were clinging to the idea that journalism is reserved for the "trained" professionals, then this argument about amateurs versus professionals is really quite alive.

So let's review.

The idea of professional journalism — as it exists today — is less than a century old and came from debates in the 1920s between Walter Lippmann and John Dewey. Lippmann was a social engineer and believed the press must play the role of elite middleman between the cultural elites and the general public. His fundamental reasoning for this necessity was a profound belief in the ignorance of the public and their inability to do anything other than vote. Dewey, on the other hand, had much more faith in the wisdom of the·people, not only to understand the issues but to bring creative ideas to the surface in resolving problems.

So professional journalism has prospered with Lippmann's perspective, but all of that is changing. It's changing because technology has now enabled Lippmann's "ignorant public" to arm themselves with knowledge and shape their own arguments. Dewey's vision of journalism is the future, and it much more resembles the blogosphere than the contemporary professional press.

Last Spring, I attended a conference about the state of broadcast journalism that opened with a video from NBC anchor Brian Williams addressing the attendees. I was shocked when he referenced blogs as a threat to democracy and quoted from a blog about nose hairs to "prove" his point. Such condescension is rampant among the Lippmannites of professional journalism, those who would prefer it if the public would just get (back) in its place and let the educated, trained elites handle things.

For anybody reading this who still clings to this belief, that horse left the barn years ago, and if you continue to claim some special privilege because you have a degree, you will be run over by that which is rising up from the bottom. Witness, for example, what's happening in Seattle with the rapidly evolving "neighborhood blog" phenomenon. Check out the West Seattle Blog, Exit 133 and Cory Bergman's MyBallard.com network (five neighborhood news sites, all next door to each other). As Cory noted recently, these sites have "large audiences, dozens of advertisers and zero startup investment."

This is not to say there aren't problems with independent journalists who make assumptions rather than check facts. Fred Wilson recently wrote of this — on his blog — because some tech bloggers had taken a PowerPoint slide of his out-of-context, and he chided them for not talking to him first before writing. This may be an issue, but the reality is that this also happens in the professional world.

We're hung up on the word "blog," a pejorative term (depending on your point-of-view) that refers primarily to software that allows a chronological display of entries. In early years, it was primarily used as a publication — or "log" — of one's private or professional life. While the genre has evolved, the chronological display has not, and it's all tied to extremely powerful and easy-to-use software that makes a perfect connection with not only other such pieces of software but also the Web itself. That's because it was built by the people who built the Web, and I'm mystified as to why people in media can't see this. It's like walking into a baseball field expecting to play basketball.

So folks, let's get past this argument about journalism and blogs. Anybody who chronicles any aspect of life is a journalist. We can talk about ethics and history and laws, but the act of making media is not reserved for an educated elite. And if the defining factor of professionalism is getting paid, then thousands and thousands of blogs are very much professional. Lippmann's "manufacture of consent" is a broken dream. Perhaps once necessary for the industrial age, it is now as obsolete as landline telephones. Can we please just turn the page?

SIMULPATH™ EXPLAINED

In our work with clients, we've taken the thoughts and teachings of people like disruptive innovation expert Clayton Christensen to heart. Reinvention isn't a static process, nor is it a blow-the-whole-thing-up-and-start-over idea. Local media companies need to "drive the car and fix it at the same time," and Simulpath™ — our strategic approach — provides an executable model for doing just that. Everybody knows that a dual path model is what's needed, but there's not agreement on the tactics that are necessary for the execution of a true dual path strategy.

If you're interested in this for your company, please drop us a line, because Simulpath™ is all-encompassing and vastly more complex than I could or would reveal in this newsletter. I want to give you a brief summary today, however, because the economy is forcing decisions I've been reading about that could make it more difficult to implement it downstream. Companies forced to downsize need to keep this in mind, because there are certain areas that not only should be untouched but even expanded.

A lot of people look at the idea of "dual path" and assume that one path is the company's traditional output, while the second path is new media. There are lots of problems with this, but the biggest one is the assumption that the business of media is only ad-supported content. We argue that traditional local media products are really fruits of a much bigger business mission — the enabling of commerce in the community. As such, advertising is our business, not merely the creation of scarce content that can be used to "carry" advertising. The earliest forms of local media were subscription-based, but those evolved to the advertiser-supported model, because it worked so well at enabling commerce in the community.

So the two paths necessary for downstream success aren't different versions of the same thing; they're based on different ways of enabling commerce in the community through advertising. This is the dividing line — the one that separates the two paths — that makes the most sense for local media, because ad-supported content — that which governs path one of Simulpath™ — is diminishing in its viability in a networked world. To be sure, there's still a lot of money to be made in this arena, but that revenue stream will never return to its former glory. Its value proposition has always been based on delivering scarce eyeballs to ad messages, and people are increasingly able to tune them out. As Doc Searls says, "There is no market for unwanted messages."

Looking at the dual paths as separate business channels, therefore, is what separates our thinking from that of most conventional media types. Mass marketing, ad-supported content — in whatever form and however delivered — is the business model of path one. Direct marketing is the ad model of path two. So while most companies are working to blend their staffs to successfully execute both their legacy content and that which is on the Web, our position is that this is really all just path one. Path two is entirely different, and it is what will provide sustenance of the work of path one in the future.

The most important governing principle to understand with Simulpath™ is that it's not an all-or-nothing thing, and this is where most problems exist in dual-path execution. Christensen, for example, writes that a separate business unit with authority to "kill the mother" is what's necessary to overcome true disruptions. We think that means a separate entity for the Web. But information isn't a product, and neither is a delivery system. Did radio "kill" newspapers? Did television "kill" radio? Will the Web "kill" everything that came before it? Moreover, it takes precious resources to enable a separate content business unit for the Web.

In our view, everything that relates to the creation of content all belongs in path one. It involves the company's brand and the use of technology to extend that brand. Since your brand is associated with your traditional media output, efforts to extend your brand largely involve the products and services you normally create. If your product is a newscast, for example, then this path would include efforts to extend that product into all things new media. This includes multi-platform distribution of ad-supported content. Even the Continuous News model that we promote is a brand-extension play. Multi-purposing content to create niche verticals is also path one, because the business model is aggregated mass and ad supported content.

So path one, therefore, consists of many tactics, which, when assembled together, resembles the double-helix of DNA. Each "tube" may be separate, but they are interconnected and held together by the staff and resources assigned to create and support ad-supported content.

Path two, though, is an entirely separate path, driven by the laws of direct marketing. To play in this space locally, one needs only the ability to serve ads and build a database of web users in the market. This is the future cash cow of local media, and it operates under different rules than that of ad-supported content.

- Its infrastructure is the Local Web, not any individual property therein.
- It seeks out individual members of the community, so it doesn't require any form of mass.
- It is action-friendly, which advertisers love. Brand-friendly, not so much.
- It's cost effective and highly profitable.

Online advertising is evolving at a frenetic pace and at such a level of sophistication that local advertisers can "target" whoever they wish, based on behavior and known interests, and they increasingly don't need media to make their online reach/frequency goals. This is what we hear directly from the horse's mouth.

And it's why we so strongly endorse Gordon Borrell's admonition for a separate sales unit dedicated to the Web. A separate sales staff can handle both forms of online advertising and deal with both dual path business models. That's why any path two application should flow from the revenue-generating unit, not the content unit. We need to train and free our sales people to become effective agents in the enabling of commerce in our communities via the Web. That is our new mission.

I've written previously that the most valuable current asset of any local media company is its sales department, and I hope this has given you a little clarity about why I feel that way. A highly skilled sales force with the right technology will make the difference between those who survive and those who do not in the years to come.

Business development is all about path two right now, folks, because this is where we're getting killed by outside pureplay companies. We need to stop them, because our future depends on it.

FULL FEED RSS IS A JEWEL THAT
MEDIA COMPANIES REFUSE TO EXPLOIT

The *UK Guardian* shocked many people two weeks ago when it became the first major newspaper in the world to offer full text RSS feeds, something Steve and I have been wondering about for years. This is a significant milestone, and it is absolutely inevitable that every media company will go this route sooner or later.

The depth and potential of the subscription (RSS) Web — in which people can bring content to themselves rather than "visiting" websites — has been held back by companies who heretofore have only used RSS to "tease" people. The hope is that they will click through to the company's portal website, where the eyeballs can be counted for advertising. This has been traditional media's downfall in the use of RSS, because the technology has advanced to the point where it's possible to serve and count ads in feeds.

Tech media and bloggers have been providing full feed RSS for years, having gone through the pro and con arguments long ago. Media companies didn't participate in this, because RSS for media has always been restricted to a marketing tool. I subscribe to 40 RSS feeds, and very few are partial text. I keep those in my reader only because I have to, but I very rarely click through to read the full text. I've long thought it was an insult to provide only partial text, but I've grown to believe it's much more than that. Those companies who provide only partial text feeds are shooting themselves in the foot, because on the Web, authority and relevance go to those who play the game the Media 2.0 way.

Broadcasting and Cable, for example, provides many feeds, but they are useless in terms of communicating information, which is what RSS was created to do. RSS isn't a manipulative marketing tool. It's an end unto itself, and until we start using it as such, we're going to miss the opportunities it offers.

The *UK Guardian* has opened the door, although only partially. They're not including images, and they've decided that they'll only offer full text on stories they feel they can legally distribute. The paper has also announced that they'll begin running ads in the full text stories, which will be the big differentiator. Sooner or later, they'll discover that they can also offer as "as items" in the feeds, and then a real business model will be established.

The place-based distribution available through RSS is the future, folks. The mobile Web forces the issue, because browsing on a portable device offers virtually no business model, and the only question is who will get there first at the local level. This is another reason why we so strongly advocate a blog-based, continuous news model for local media. Its output is an RSS "river of news," that plays well in the place-based distribution model.

Let me repeat: RSS is not a tool for driving traffic to your portal; it's a valuable way of communicating your products and services to an increasingly networked culture. Ignore it at your own peril.

"HUSTLE" IS THE MOST
IMPORTANT WORD — EVER

As I have for many years, I try to examine the world of technology from the side of the disruption, not the side of that which is being disrupted. The longer I do that, the more I'm convinced that media people need to come over here — at least occasionally — because the view of what's happening is entirely different than what traditional media people see.

One thing that has never changed for me is the reality that the tech community — and, by proxy, tech media — is way out ahead of traditional media, both in terms of vision and practical application for the flow of information. Media is so driven by revenue (and that means revenue attached to content) that it will always lag real technological innovation. But what's troubling is that once media latches onto something from the disruption that can be monetized, all else is set aside in favor of what may or may not be the gravy train that media companies seek. If it doesn't make money, it's ignored, so the best we get is elements of the disruption bolted on to the increasingly archaic business model of ad-supported content.

Many people wrongly interpret these events as where the two worlds (the disruption and that which is being disrupted) "touch." The reality, however, is that the worlds never touch, for one is overtaking the other. Think of those giant alien ships from the film "Independence Day" as their shadows loomed over the world's biggest cities. The only time they "touched," was when the aliens destroyed the cities. A shadow is not touching, not in science fiction and not in disruptive technologies.

Broadcasters and print executives live in a static world. The templates for success need only to be filled with fresh content, but everything else sits still. Elaborate and sophisticated industries have sprung up around this, not the least of which is advertising, but the essence of what drives business is the foundation of a static world.

But the disruption does not sit still and routes around this static world. There was a time when the Web consisted of static sites with static pages, but that's long been replaced by the live, dynamic Web. Browsing has been replaced by searching and subscribing, but media companies cling to static representations of their core businesses. To the tech community, the Web is cyberspace, a fabulous and innovative place where people meet, information flows and commerce is conducted. To the media community, the Web is a series of pipes for the transportation of content, or perhaps more realistically, a series of pipes leading to their distribution points.

So you see the conflict and why there's really no "touching" taking place whatsoever.

"Where's the money?" is the relentless cry from media company board rooms, but it's the wrong question. The only answer is the same one that everybody involved in the disruption knows well — it's all about hustle. Gary Vaynerchuk (a.k.a. "GaryVee") says it well in this video clip from the Web 2.0 conference. Do yourself a favor and watch it, but if you can't, here's the relevant part:

> Stop crying and keep hustling. *Hustle* is the most important word — EVER. And that's what you need to do. You need to work so hard. Guys, we're building businesses here. This isn't about parties. We're building businesses!

Traditional media people don't know how to hustle, and this is where we're getting beat. The disruption doesn't ask for the business model; it goes out a makes one happen, even if it takes a whole lot longer than anybody thought. GaryVee's two key words for business success in the new world are "patience" and "passion." Of these, we cannot possibly have too much.

I had a discussion this week with the head of a major media web unit who made the comment that he knows what he could and perhaps should be doing, but that he's making too much money doing things the traditional media online way to just up and stop. He knows, as most of us do, that the world of online traditional media — as is — will never replace the dollars being lost by our legacy platforms, even though the revenue we are making may be significant. It's damned-if-you-do and damned-if-you-don't.

But we've got to stop crying and keep hustling, especially in these times of uncertainty and opportunity, for to do otherwise is to cede defeat to the alien spacecraft looming overhead.

WHY TRADITIONAL MEDIA
NEEDS SOCIAL MEDIA

The following was lifted directly from a Cone LLC press release, and it is highly, highly relevant for local media companies:

> Almost 60 percent of Americans interact with companies on a social media Web site, and one in four interact more than once per week. These are among the findings of the 2008 Cone Business in Social Media Study.

According to the survey, 93 percent of Americans believe a company should have a presence in social media, while an overwhelming 85 percent believe a company should not only be present but also interact with its consumers via social media. In fact, 56 percent of American consumers feel both a stronger connection with and better served by companies when they can interact with them in a social media environment.

> "The news here is that Americans are eager to deepen their brand relationships through social media," explains Mike Hollywood, director of new media for Cone, "it isn't an intrusion into their lives, but rather a welcome channel for discussion."

This is an old song for Steve and me, but you'd be amazed at how few television stations or newspapers pay attention to this space. They'd rather create their own social networking "section" (and perhaps they should) than take the time to "work" MySpace and Facebook, and that's a shame. We keep trying to force our model on younger generations, rather than experiment where they all gather.

This study ought to be required reading for media companies, because it's rich with information that marketers can use. People said they wanted interaction with companies, but what kind?

- Companies should use social networks to solve my problems (43%)
- Companies should solicit feedback on their products and services (41%)
- Companies should develop new ways for consumers to interact with their brand (37%)
- Companies should market to consumers (25%)

We can no longer only make ourselves available via our portal websites; we must go where the people formerly known as the audience live and breathe. And increasingly, that's in the world of social media. Individual news people and the institutions they serve should all have MySpace and Facebook pages and YouTube channels. But, but, but… "Where's the money, Terry?"

As Kevin Kelly notes, "Where Attention Flows, Money Follows."

IT'S TIME FOR A NEW ONLINE MODEL

The earliest iterations of online media were all text-based, because that's all the bandwidth could handle. This suited the newspaper industry, and it's the principal reason that the presentation of information online follows a model that is essentially a newspaper. Content is presented on "pages." The idea of a "home" page — front page — that serves as a doorway to everything inside IS a newspaper. Online advertising is the same. Display ads, artificial page folds, value based on page placement and so forth are all newspaper concepts.

Most importantly, the portal model of organizing information is very much built on this foundation. In many ways back in the 90s, AOL was a glorified online newspaper. Inherent in this model is an advertising ecosystem that is limited by the "walls" of the portal, its URL.

Even television stations have been dragged into this model, and understanding this is critical, if you wish to understand the disruption of Media 2.0.

A few years ago, Gordon Borrell's company and the Harvard Business School created the illustration on the next page. I've altered it a bit to make a point, but what we have is essentially a enlarging circle that I've labeled "Media 2.0" moving into the circle representing Media 1.0. I think it's farther along today, but the message that both Gordon and I were trying to deliver five years ago was that opportunity was within the expanding "green" circle, not the "blue." But here's the point: generally, what we see today from media companies is the gray overlapping area — Media 1.0 disguised as Media 2.0.

Another very important point to understand is that the green area is not being created or funded by the traditional media of the blue circle. Consequently, it doesn't give a hoot about what the blue does, and the view from the green is very different than the view from the blue. And the view from the green is finding its way into publication with increasing frequency, and it is apparently not even read by those coming from the blue. That's a shame, for how can you truly enter the disruption unless you're willing to accept its point-of-view.

Here's what I mean.

The Inquisitr is a popular tech and pop culture online media company featuring some of the best and most tenured writers in new media. A few weeks ago, Duncan Riley began looking at television and wrote a chilling entry called "Television Will Fall." I don't agree with everything Duncan wrote, but I'd be a fool to dismiss it as ignorance. Riley's article was followed this week by one by JR Raphael called "Could Television's Fall Be Closer Than We Thought?" Understand that when the tech media writes about traditional media, it does so from its place within that green circle above. Raphael's article is about new media efforts by Gannett, and it contains a really important observation.

Another trend you'll notice is Gannett stations heavily promoting a new concept branded as the "Information Center," which is basically just the idea of their local Web site combined with the broadcast news. It's really the same stuff with a new name and new promotional push. Ironically enough, most of the stations are operating with far fewer people, so while

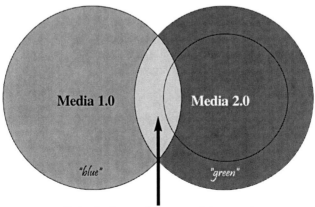

Doing business only here won't be enough.

the Web sites have a slightly updated look, their resources are not as robust as one might be led to believe. In actuality, most modern mainstream journalists just do double duty, splitting their time between broadcast and online work. Still, the notion highlights the industry's attempt to at least outwardly rebrand itself away from its long-standing primary interest.

So what Raphael "sees" (and frankly, what others in the green see) is questionable strategy in the "Information Center" concept that Gannett is following. It's just another version of the old newspaper portal idea that's been around since the beginning, another effort that lies within the gray zone.

This does not go unnoticed by the venture capital community that is funding the disruption. Rockefeller family investor Rich Moran told Beet.tv a few weeks ago that the best media companies could do was "bolt new ideas onto the old," and, as a result, online video was in danger of passing by traditional media completely. This is the kind of thing that happens when you insist on maintaining your view entirely from the blue circle.

I'm passionate about this, because after I left television in 1998, I spent three years inside the green circle running an internet start-up. It was an amazing crossover experience, and it keeps me encouraging others to examine the view from over "there." It's why I think the way I do and why my RSS reader is likely filled with feeds that you don't read.

Local media needs reinvention, not just new ways of doing old things. Why everybody in media sticks to the online newspaper model is the biggest mystery of all to me. Just because it's safe, everybody else is doing it, and it "seems" to be working (much of the online revenue growth in recent years has more to do with newness than sound strategy, IMO) doesn't mean it's good strategy for the future. At AR&D, we recognize that media companies must operate in both circles, which is why our strategic thrust is Simulpath™, but you'd be amazed (perhaps not) at how hard it is to move minds into the "green."

THE "BUSINESS" OF
MEDIA IS ADVERTISING

While media companies struggle to find the magic distribution element or the content mix that will "work" in attracting audiences, the advertising industry continues to move forward without them, and this is my greatest concern for the well-being of anybody in the media business. The "business" of media is advertising, and we ought to be paying more attention to that than trying to rescue our ad-supported platforms.

So let's put together a few news items this week to make a point.

According to Online Media Daily, "Carat has revised its global and U.S. ad spending outlooks for 2008 downward, but has slightly increased its projections for online ad spending in 2008 and 2009."

Carat said it now expects the global advertising marketplace to expand only 4.9%, and U.S. ad spending to rise by 2.1% in 2008. In its preliminary forecast released in March, Carat had projected worldwide ad spending would grow 6.0% and the U.S. would rise 3.8% this year.

"It's clear that the worldwide economic issues affecting businesses are having an impact on where and how advertisers spend their money," Jerry Buhlmann, CEO of Aegis Media, stated in the report.

> ...By medium, Carat reduced the outlook for every major medium with the exception of the Internet, which it now predicts will rise by 23.7% in 2008 vs. its early projection of 23.3%. For 2009, Carat now predicts online ad spending will expand 18.6%, vs. its earlier forecast of 17.8%.

So the Web is where it's at, but there's nothing really new there. However, take a look at what's happening in the online newspaper world this summer. Media Daily News reports what it's calling a "drastic slowdown" in online revenue GROWTH during the first month of the 3rd quarter. While display ads are strong, the newspaper industry's loss of print and online classifieds revenues are simply hammering media companies.

But there's another issue that online newspapers face that I've written about previously, and that is the inventory wall that some companies are hitting, because the online ad paradigm for media companies is based on page views and ad impressions. In order to sustain growth in such a paradigm, you must have more, more, more, in terms of inventory, and that duty falls to the editorial staff in cranking out the pages. This is also the source of the need to annoy users with page clicks and other stunts that generate statistics at the risk of alienating audience. It's a tough world.

Meanwhile, that friend to all online businesses, Google, has taken another step forward in rewriting the rules for online ad distribution. In a TechCrunch article, Google Will Now Manage Your Website's Ads, Mark Hendrickson writes that Google's "Ad Manager" service is now out of Beta and available to everyone.

Since its unveiling, Google Ad Manager has been seen as a direct threat to OpenX, an on-premise software solution (known previously as OpenAds and phpAdsNew) for managing the advertising campaigns on websites. Both solutions serve and track the performance of ad units sold either directly or introduced by third party networks like Federated Media or Google AdSense...But only Google can "use AdSense to fill unsold inventory or compete on price against other ad networks," optimizing returns for publishers by serving up the most profitable ads from campaigns vying for the same space on a page.

This image from Google demonstrates what Ad Manager does for website publishers.

Google is providing a easy-to-use platform that allows publishers to control ad inventory on their websites, and this is going influence every level of the Web, including local.

Running into an inventory wall? How about the inventory that exists on every website in your market?

And so I say again that the advertising industry is moving forward without institutional media companies, because as far as the Web is concerned (Google, too), everybody with a website is a media company. The opportunity for local companies to explore this at the local level is staggering, but most media companies are still stuck in the rut of "monetizing" their content. Content is not our business; advertising is our business, and the sooner we embrace that, the better off we'll all be.

THE WEB IS COUNTERINTUITIVE TO TRADITIONAL MEDIA THINKING

When dealing at the strategic level with all things Web, it's wise to step outside the conventions and norms that govern traditional media thinking in order to get a real understanding. The moment we apply convention to this new world is the moment when we miss the possibilities that it offers. The online world is almost entirely counter intuitive to traditional media thinking, and nowhere is this reflected more than in the business practices of Google. In a fascinating interview last week with CNBC's Jim Cramer of Mad Money (you either love him or hate him — I love him), Google CEO Eric Schmidt made statements about the company's fundamental beliefs that probably will leave media company executives shaking their heads.

He said the company gives up billions in revenue by keeping ads off the home page. Why? Because it would upset users. "We prioritize the end user over the advertiser," he told Cramer. This simple statement — if truly adopted by media companies — would revolutionize all of online media. We'd have a race to see who could better serve the wants and needs of the people formerly known as the audience, and that would be a refreshing change from words like capture, drive, and my favorite, monetize.

Google doesn't provide any guidance whatsoever to stock analysts, and Schmidt's answer, again, is profoundly simple when he says it would "get in the way" of running the business, adding, "If we started giving quarterly guidance, all of a sudden the whole company would start focusing on the quarter rather than trying to change the world."

On the company's heretofore unsuccessful attempts to make money from YouTube, Schmidt said it didn't matter, at least not right now. He said they make plenty of money already, because YouTube places users in the stream of Google's other businesses, and that cannot be overlooked. "I'd be worried if people weren't using to YouTube," he told Cramer. "Since it's an enormous success globally, we know we will eventually benefit from it."

Cramer began the interview with a personal story of how his 5th grade daughter was prohibited from Googling the topic of a class project, which evolved into a discussion of whether Google is "dumbing down" people. Schmidt disagreed and compared academia's complaints about access to knowledge with the complaints about portable calculators in the 70s. I agree with that, which is why you'll often hear me reference that we're in the midst of a second Gutenberg moment in Western Civilization.

Do yourself a favor and go watch the interview. Note Schmidt's constant but subtle references to Google as an advertising system.

THE KEY TO MEDIA'S FUTURE
IS A TEACHABLE MACHINE

In his remarkable 2005 *Wired* essay, "We Are The Web," Kevin Kelly weaves a prescient tale of where we're all headed with this amazing technology known as the World Wide Web. I think this is one of the seminal pieces of original thinking that defines the future, and I always recommend that people read and study it carefully. Kelly's piece forms the basis of another brilliant piece of work, cultural anthropologist Michael Wesch's 2006 film, "The Web Is Us/ing Us."

The farther downstream we get from these thought-provoking gems, the more brilliant they seem. I find that when I immerse myself in the ideas they express, the more centered and focused I become.

Since one was built on the other, let's go back to Kelly's original piece for a few minutes to make an important observation about Media's future. Kelly's metaphor for the Web is a Machine (he capitalizes the word for emphasis), a Machine that is powerful, always on and learning constantly. To science fiction writers, it conjures dreadful images, but to Kelly, the Machine is us.

What will most surprise us is how dependent we will be on what the Machine knows — about us and about what we want to know. We already find it easier to Google something a second or third time rather than remember it ourselves. The more we teach this megacomputer, the more it will assume responsibility for our knowing. It will become our memory. Then it will become our identity. In 2015 many people, when divorced from the Machine, won't feel like themselves — as if they'd had a lobotomy.

…There is only one time in the history of each planet when its inhabitants first wire up its innumerable parts to make one large Machine. Later that Machine may run faster, but there is only one time when it is born.

You and I are alive at this moment.

The vision of both Kelly and Wesch go beyond the scope of media, but there's a lot to learn (big picture stuff) from what they've created.

In the new world, the only property that matters for media companies is their form of the Machine, and it is here where our investment in dollars and knowledge matters most. The only successful media company of tomorrow will be one with a teachable Machine, because how well that Machine connects with the people formerly known as the audience (TPFKATA) is the key to not only our place in the culture but also how we'll make money. Media companies without a teachable Machine will drift into the unenviable position of simple content creators and eventually blend into low-margin oblivion.

To "teach" a Machine, it must have input while it is outputting, and this is where everybody in media misses the point of the Web. The input is the only thing that matters. It has value, big value, and it is what we will sell downstream. When we carry ads from third-party providers, for example, we're freely GIVING away this input to somebody else. The cookie data from website visitors belongs to the publisher, not some outside agency. In declaring earlier this year that it would no longer run ads from third-party ad networks, ESPN announced to the world that it was no longer going to give user information away. I fully expect companies will follow suit.

The teachable Machine is central to the strategy of developing local ad networks and to place-based distribution. Traditional media people look at place-based distribution (putting my content on your site) as a way to aggregate mass, but that's short-sighted. The real and lasting value is in the user data that is fed to our teachable Machine. That Machine is what will drive revenue through a vast understanding of the habits and demographics of the Local Web.

The creation and maintenance of a teachable Machine will determine who survives in the years ahead, and there's no time like the present to get started. Every strategic and tactical move we make should have this as its ultimate goal. In that way, we'll know that we're always moving in the right overall direction.

So stop chasing page views and start collecting data. It's the only end game that matters.

SIX PRINCIPLES TO LIVE BY

I've often found that bullet points succeed where vast prose does not, and this is especially true when communicating with busy executives. Here are the six strategic principles that I pose to every AR&D Media 2.0 client as fundamentals to downstream success:

The Web is our platform. Simply stated, we cannot generate enough "pages" to offset revenue losses to legacy platforms. Our online platforms are just too small, so we must be willing to pursue strategies that take us beyond our branded content.

Value creation is the top priority. Does our strategy simply move something we already create from point A to point B, or are we actually bringing NEW value to the table with our online innovations? What new value are we bringing to our customers, both consumers and advertisers?

Revenue flexibility is at the property level. Many media companies operate with a centralized online entity as a way to avoid duplication and group eyeballs for national ads. Online revenue's big growth area for the next five years, however, is at the LOCAL level, and in order to capture that money, individual properties must have more flexibility that many have today.

Our audience is at work. This one ought not need explaining, because it ought to be obvious. The problem is that while we may understand it, our behavior doesn't reflect it. Only the continuous news model perfectly fits this consumer demand.

Focus on the goal, not the process. If media business planners are going to miss the mark, it is generally here where it happens. Managers are process people and require a clearly understood path from here to there. Leaders, on the other hand, are comfortable with the goal and figuring out how to get there along the way. Our industry needs leaders today.

Make informed tactical decisions. We need to be fully up-to-speed on all things new media, and that means digging into tech media like never before. We've got to expand our knowledge base to include that which is coming from Silicon Valley, or we'll be easily led astray by clever gimmicks and smart salespeople.

So there you go: a few principles upon which to chew this last week in July.

HOW TO MONETIZE
USER-GENERATED CONTENT

Every media company everywhere (how's that for sweeping generalizations?) is struggling with the question of making money off the free work of others. It's such a nice thought, isn't it? The problem is that the people creating the content — especially local bloggers — are hip to what we're trying to do, so we often end up with egg on our faces.

The problem is that the concept of displaying ads around content is the only thing we know. We see content, and, BANG! We want to slap an ad on it.

Scott Adams wrote this week that in the future, news organizations will share revenue with bloggers, and I think this is a great idea:

In the future, I can imagine bloggers opting in for a system where they allow newspapers to grab their content any time the newspapers want, move it into the newspaper's own content model on any given day, surround it with their own ads, and pay the blogger a percentage of ad revenue. In other words, every blogger (and cartoonist) would be self-syndicated, but newspapers wouldn't print the same bloggers every day. They'd grab only the best writings of the day based on social voting and the newspaper's own editorial opinions.

But bloggers are but a tiny, tiny segment of the personal media revolution, and this isn't where we really should be looking to make money off content created by others. There are two examples in the news this week.

363

1. Mark Burnett, creator of the modern reality show, is working on a program for next summer called "Jingles." According to *Variety*, "teams of players will be given weekly jingle-writing assignments — coming up with, say, the next Oscar Mayer wiener song or a new pitch for Coke — and will then have to perform them in front of a studio audience. Viewer votes will determine a weekly winner (whose ditty will end up in a real ad) and loser (who will go home)."

   Think about this for a minute and imagine what types of contests advertisers in your community would support. Remember that everybody's a media company these days, and they all have technology that enables them to do many things. I'm not saying do the Jingle thing, but let your imagination run with the idea.

2. This summer, Friendly's Ice Cream ran an interactive campaign called iScream, during which customers were encouraged to "show their love for Friendly's ice cream or life itself" by posting original photos and videos to the iScream microsite. Todd Nissen of the Michigan ad firm Valassis said at least 75% of the submissions that came in were high-quality and effectively integrated the Friendly's brand.

   "The first batch of submissions had us worried, but they got better over time. By the end of the program they got phenomenal on brand and exactly what we were looking for," said Nissen. "It's a wonderful thing as a brand to see a lot of people literally screaming your virtues."

Now again, I'm not suggesting you run out to the local ice cream parlor, but think about the possibilities here for advertisers in your community.

One of the fundamental facts of Media 2.0 is that everyday people are making the types of things that only those of us "professionals" were able to do just a few years ago. We don't need to co-opt what they're doing in order to profit from it; we simply need to create platforms for them to show off what they can do.

This is the proper mainstream media use of User-Generated Content.

CREATING NEW VALUE IS THE MISSION

My friend Gordon Borrell is projecting growth for newspapers and television companies over the next five years and says that's news. He's right. Borrell is projecting that newspapers will show annual revenue gains of 1.6% over the next five years, TV will show gains of 3.6% and radio will stay pretty much flat.

> The fact that newspapers and broadcast media aren't dead is "news," which means that all this stuff about new media killing old media must be hogwash.

Hogwash, perhaps, but it depends on your definition of the word "dead." It's true that legacy media is experiencing a pretty good year with an enormous political season just beginning. 2010 should end well for companies that have seen very, very hard times in recent years.

But Borrell's projections — and others I've seen — all assume that we're in recovery, and the jury is very much still out on that. Money is very tight, and if you don't think so, try to get a mortgage. Loans fuel our economy, and right now, they're only going to those with the very best credit. Like other pendulum swings, we've gone from a place of lending money to anybody to lending money to virtually no one.

Unemployment continues to be the dark secret that nobody wants to talk about. There's no "recovery" for people without jobs. Umair Haque says we're living in a " zombieconomy" and that an even bigger collapse is very much in the cards. The bank bailout accomplished nothing, according to Haque, except reward the people who created the crash in the first place.

Picking up Haque's meme, Matthew Continetti wrote of The Zombie Economy this week for The Weekly Standard, saying that the life jacket the government handed to the private sector has changed.

> What the Obama administration doesn't want to acknowledge is that the life jacket has become a straitjacket. Remove it, and more people will lose jobs and livelihoods and health insurance. Maintain it, and the mounting public debt, combined with the sense that the economy is split between government insiders and everybody else, will provoke a political backlash. It would be easier to remove the jacket if the private sector were leading an economic boom. But that isn't the case. And so the economy is in twilight.

Deloitte & Touche's John Hagel sees no recovery, writing that businesses run significant risks by only focusing on the near-term.

> We continue to be seduced by near-term news, while losing any perspective on longer-term trends. These longer terms trends tell a very different story and suggest that we may be lulled into complacency by the short-term news of recovery.
> ...In our new book, *The Power of Pull*, we summarize the metrics that we developed for the (Deloitte & Touche) Shift Index — the first attempt to quantify the longer-term trends that have been re-shaping the business landscape over the past four decades. Of the 25 metrics in the Shift Index, one metric in particular stands out: return on assets for all public companies in the US. **Since 1965, return on assets has collapsed by 75% — it has been a sustained and substantial erosion in performance. There is no evidence of any flattening of this trend, much less turning it around.**
> What does this mean? It provides strong evidence that any "recovery" is merely a short-term relaxation of pressure and that there will be no "back to normal." We often hear executives talk about the Red Queen effect where they feel they are running faster and faster to stay in the same place. The actual situation is far worse: we are running faster and faster and falling farther and farther behind. **There is absolutely no reason to believe that the long-term performance erosion will not continue.**

Those are sobering words from people watching the short term posturing in Washington and beyond. Meanwhile, media companies riding the "recovery" and hoping their business model will sustain them are rolling the dice once again.

What I'm sensing is a "back to normal" managing of the bottom line: grow revenue and reward those who do. Let's get as much revenue as we can while we can. In so doing, however, we're continuing to milk a business model — mass marketing — that has seen better days, and we're doing so without consideration of creating new value for our companies.

This is the essential problem I see, and it's why I'm not as inclined to believe that ascribing death to legacy media companies is entirely hogwash.

Until the top levels of media companies begin associating management compensation with new value creation instead of just meeting revenue goals, we will continue to place ourselves in positions of extreme vulnerability for the future. We need new value, because the value of our current business model is rapidly maturing, and it will never again produce the kinds of growth it once did.

I realize this message isn't popular, but in ancient times, leaders used times of plenty to prepare for times of want. In the media business today, consideration must be given for new business models, because the attaching of advertising to scarce content fails when content is no longer scarce.

We're building local ad networks and encouraging clients to explore the world of advertising as content. There's money to be made in enabling the personal media revolution locally, too. All of these — and more — are available, but nobody will touch them until management compensation is tied to new value creation instead of just milking the existing cows.

Squeezing every last drop of revenue isn't necessarily a bad thing, but it's a net liability, if that's all you do. And the problem is exacerbated by an advertising community that seems content to continue playing the old game. How long is anybody's guess, and there's nothing wrong with taking money that's willingly offered. It's doing so without an eye on creating new value that's the problem.

So what can or should we be doing and rewarding? Here are five ideas to get you started today:

Data is a big part of the future, so start building databases. Begin with identifying and defining the Local Web. If we must attached an immediate purpose to it, then build a simply application that searches the database. The point isn't to create an immediate revenue generator; it's to build new value, and trust me, there's value in databases of knowledge.

Build networks of people, beginning with a loyal amateur journalist following. Equip them with knowledge. Invite their participation in what you do. Build blogs for them, if that seems smart, and aggregate their content. Show them how to shoot and edit good video. Always be recruiting new members into your group, for they will become your eyes and ears in many ways downstream.

Build networks of websites for advertising. We recommend a horizontal ad network that serves the whole market, but vertical ad networks are there for the taking, too. Is your market home to big regional medical facilities? Create a vertical ad network to serve that community.

Teach advertisers what you know and how to do what you do. The reality is that anybody can function as a media company today, and who better to teach the amateurs than the professionals? If advertising is content in the new world, then there's a market for teaching advertisers how to make content. Who should have a YouTube account rich with videos related to its business? Everybody.

Create an online video archive business that offers uncut video to those wishing to make their own shows, films or whatever. There is a market for this, because the shift to personal media is only going to get stronger, and you can create new value for your company by repurposing some of your old, raw footage. Assign somebody as keeper of this and pay them a cut. It'll pay off downstream.

And, managers, start rewarding this kind of innovation with bonuses, and you'll be surprised at how quickly you'll see your business portfolio expanding. It's not just smart; it's the right response to the disruption of our core business.

MARKETING BY ATTRACTION

NEW THINKING FOR A NEW MEDIA WORLD

One of the lessons that the Web is teaching marketers is that attraction can be successfully used to market products and services in unconventional ways. The best example is the growing understanding and use of viral marketing, but this is just the beginning. Viral marketing is a new industry built on what appears to be a chaotic foundation — that people will carry your message for you if given a compelling vehicle. You don't "buy" rating points, page views or any other scientific measurement with a viral campaign. You simply put it out there and let it happen.

People are seduced by viral campaigns, not hit over the head, and this is the key component of any tactic based on attraction.

In learning the various aspects and tactics of attraction, we must first accept that they will be — in many ways — the opposite of what we know as marketers in the world of promotion. But the two are not mutually exclusive, and successful marketing in the current economy demands knowledge of and action in both promotion AND attraction.

Attention is the goal of either, but promotion calls attention to itself, while attraction shines its light on the one whose attention is desired. Seduction is the means to attraction's end. Think "I want you to want me more than I want you."

Marketing is really just the art and science of what individuals practice in everyday life:

How do you "attract" attention?

Tantrums. This is the earliest learned behavior in human nature, although the attention it receives is usually just short term. Pitching a fit (today called a "rant"), however, is a common form of expression in our culture.

Show Off. This one takes many forms, from the Superbowl to "Jackass" and "flaunt it, if you've got it" to the spelling bee.

Threaten. This can be both overt, as in bullying, to helpful, as in a warning about some real or imagined danger.

Gossip. This behavior flows from the "I know something (about someone) that you don't know" mindset and will always find an ear to bend.

How do you seduce?

The currency of ego. Helping others feel good about themselves is the most powerful tool of seduction. Who doesn't want to be with someone who makes them feel important?

Listen. The method of the currency of ego is listening, something media companies don't practice very well.

Massage the soft spots. When we listen, we uncover specific wants and needs that we can explore to enhance a sense of well-being and importance in the one(s) we pursue.

Chemistry. This includes all of the tangibles and intangibles present before an introduction is made. No matter how much we try to attract attention, it will all fall on deaf ears without agreeable chemistry.

There is certainly the potential for conflict between the two, and this is something that requires a great deal of our own attention. If, for example, our seduction successfully attracts the object of our desire to our home, we would not want them to have to immediately confront an angry attack dog, our pitching a fit, or the trapeze act we've developed in the back yard.

There isn't much science on the subject, so marketing by attraction has largely been the realm of the touchy-feely crowd. Life coaches and others who teach unconventional methods of developing business relationships have preached attraction with varying degrees of success for years. While some of these elements are obvious (e.g., make yourself look nice), this paper speaks to a much deeper level of business strategies and tactics.

We must also add here that we're not talking about so-called "push" versus "pull" marketing, which are two sides of the same coin. It isn't about directly creating or building up any form of demand for products or services. Attraction marketing is subtle and indirect, and it's more about creating an environment conducive to attention than directly seeking that attention.

Hence, we're not talking about direct sales as much as we are about creating lifelong customers.

BACKGROUND

To fully understand attraction as a fundamental marketing concept for media via the Web, we must first take a step back and examine a basic trend of contemporary postmodern culture — the power of tribes in the creation of influence.

Modern tribes share little in common with their historical counterparts, for postmodern tribes are determined solely by the individual. Membership is based entirely on how each serves the interests of the individual. They may be family members, co-workers, friends, teachers, mentors, celebrities or complete strangers. The only thing each shares in common is the trust of the individual around which the tribe is built.

This creates a sphere of influence that guides the individual through all aspects of life. It should be noted that tribe membership isn't automatically permanent, for the beliefs and passions of the individual ebb and flow with the currents of life itself.

The Web enables the connectivity required for this to function efficiently, and entrepreneurs know it. Sites such as Yelp.com, for example, offer a mechanism for people to rate businesses, products and services, so as to provide a recommendation or referral system for postmodern tribes. All the marketing dollars in the world can't overcome a lousy product or service, and those who advertise on sites like Yelp do so with that knowledge in mind. Attraction marketing begins with a quality product or service.

Social networks are deeply aware of the power of tribes and are doing everything they can to artificially mimic their actions. This is what got Facebook into trouble with users with its "Beacon" advertising program. Facebook made software available to businesses who could then "report back" to Facebook the activities of its members. If someone bought a book, for example, at Amazon.com, that purchase would appear on Facebook, which caused uproar among privacy advocates and Facebook members alike.

What Facebook was attempting to do was create an artificial "recommendation" environment based entirely on the actions of members. If one of my tribe members bought something, the thinking goes; I would be more inclined to do likewise, because I trust that person. Efforts like these will continue, because very smart people with considerable resources understand the value of infiltrating tribes and their behavior.

As media companies, these two factors — the organizing of people by collage and tribes — are crucial to future business success, but serving the information needs in such an environment is very different than one based on the gathering of mass or groups of mass. More importantly, it's critical to the future health of the businesses that've used our mass to conduct commerce — advertisers.

We must never forget that the disruption isn't about distribution, disintermediation or technology. It's about people.

THE PRINCIPLES OF ONLINE ATTRACTION

If we are to be truly effective in attraction marketing, everything from website design to how we behave with the people we're trying to serve needs to be in line with the following five basic principles. There are many other principles to successful attraction (or seduction), but these five represent the fundamentals necessary to the development of successful strategies and tactics.

1. The lower the price of interaction, the more attractive the web experience.

When users interact with any website, they are required to pay a real price in terms of time and energy. According to the developers of TMZ.com, AOL research reveals that the lower this "price," the more actively users will engage with a site. While this makes great sense and seems obvious, the behavior of companies that produce websites is often quite the opposite.

Blogger Li Evans of Search Marketing Gurus has listed six reasons why she votes down websites that she comes upon via the serendipitous site StumbledUpon.com. Each involves a violation of this first rule of marketing by attraction:

1. Your Page Has More Ads than Content
2. I Have to Scroll Past Ads to Finally Get To Your Content
3. Your Ads Suggest/Show Porn Sites
4. Your Page Takes Too Long to Load
5. Your Page Is an Obvious Rip-off of Someone Else's
6. Your Page Is A Dumbass Marketing Attempt

What Ms. Evans is really saying is that the price of her interaction is beyond that which SHE is willing to pay, and this is a key to basic site design in the new world. By our own actions, we actually push people away — the very people we're trying to reach for our clients.

We do this when we "optimize" our websites for page views, making users click through numbers of pages in order to read our stories. We do this when we create pages that look like the side of a NASCAR race car and, in so doing, make finding anything far more difficult that it needs to be. We do this when we load our sites with content they can (and do) get elsewhere. We do this when we pretend to be a portal to everything and then deliver only that which helps us make money.

We can create marvelous viral campaigns and be the best at attracting people to our offerings, but if the price of interaction is too high when they arrive, it will be worse than if we'd never attracted them in the first place.

2. The audience is smarter than we are.

Number 6 in Li's list above recognizes a marketing attempt for what it is, and in this sense alone, the audience proves they are smarter than those of us who believe the hype we create. After decades of the relentless pounding of unwanted "messages," people are declaring that they recognize it for what it is, and they're using technology to flee the bombardment. The people formerly known as the audience are vastly more hip to marketing than we can bring ourselves to admit. The question is why do we continue to do it?

But smarts aren't limited only to our tricks. There may have been a time in the gatekeeper news world when the gatekeepers had more access to knowledge than the audience, but that is a myth in today's world. The morning paper or the 6 o'clock news is often "olds" to the readers and viewers, and more and more, the audience is contributing to the news itself. "More people on the street" seems hopelessly self-serving in a world where everyone is a reporter of news.

Bloggers — those leading edge activists in the revolution of personal media — are increasingly setting the agenda in some fields, and this will only accelerate as the culture takes on the ability to inform itself. In the arena of sports, for example, the arbiter of what matters is increasingly shifting from the mainstream media to the blogosphere, according to a study by Sports Media Challenge, a marketing firm that tracks sports blogs. More and more, the fans are "setting the agenda now."

And the sense of superiority that gatekeepers generally assume for themselves is viewed increasingly as a creepy form of arrogance to consumers, and that is hardly an attractive attribute.

Humility is a powerful magnet, so we'll always be more attractive, if we behave as though the audience is smart, informed, empowered, connected and willing to participate in the process that is local media. And this leads us to principle number three:

3. The value of other voices combined is greater than that of our own.

In a world where "content" is being created in many places, the real new value is not in tweaking or bettering our own content but in the aggregation of all those voices. This is a natural role for media companies, because it fits within the functions and duties of a news editor. Rather than rely on just the AP, his or her own staff, and the output of other professional organizations, today's editor can pull from literally thousands of sources. The skill required today includes the ability to sort and group for niche consumption, because one who is attracted to fashion is not necessarily attracted to sports.

The real winners in the new world will be those who use their resources to smartly aggregate — whether strictly through technology or by the insertion of some human element into the process — the many voices, professional or otherwise, who make up the participatory process known as "news" today.

The output of aggregation is a filtering of that which is being aggregated. When we built Nashville is Talking, for example, its core "product" was an RSS feed that summarized what 400 bloggers were talking about on any given day. This form of aggregation has value to users who don't have the time to read through all 400 blogs.

By valuing all of these other voices, we make ourselves highly attractive to news consumers.

However, there is one fundamental roadblock that inhibits the value of any media company aggregation project, and that is the exclusion of content into the filter for purely competitive reasons. This is why internet pureplay companies have an advantage, especially at the local level, for any aggregator claiming to filter news in a market that doesn't include all voices — professional or otherwise — is merely a self-serving marketing attempt that will be ultimately rejected.

4. You can't talk your way out of something you behaved your way into.

This truth was first articulated by Steven Covey in his *Seven Habits of Highly Effective People,* but it is on point in determining the attractiveness of any media company effort in the online world. Again, people understand hype for what it is, and they care only about our behavior, not our intentions or what we say.

Attraction is about being smart, not spending money to say that we're smart. Besides, what other people say about us is more valuable than what we say about ourselves anyway.

People such as new media economics guru Umair Haque and *The Long Tail* author Chris Anderson effectively argue that the creation of blockbusters — the ultimate goal of mass marketing — is becoming increasingly difficult and that a snowball rolling downhill is the new metaphor. Attention to the product itself is what begins the snowball rolling, not what is said about the product.

What this means is that money spent on marketing in attempting to create blockbusters is better spent in the new economy on creativity and product itself, and this is an essential truth about attraction.

5. Transparency makes amends for great offenses.

To many of us in traditional media, our processes, systems and practices are protected forms of knowledge, but the truth is that everybody knows what we do and how we do it. Special interests manipulate us regularly, while we insist they can't and don't.
Despite our pleas of objectivity, most people view us as biased and slanted.

Transparency — the opening of us and our systems for review and comment — can be a humbling and eye-opening experience. Allowing people into our secret world is a form of honesty that resonates with people who view us with cynicism and disdain. It is a practical form of attraction with ancillary benefits, for it forces us to examine our assumptions and argue our positions, whether publicly or privately.

Transparency also opens the door to conversational language and dialog with the people formerly known as the audience. John Robinson, Editor of the *Greensboro News & Record*, has been blogging since August of 2004 and it has opened a dialog with readers that didn't exist before. He's open, honest (sometimes painfully so), and approachable, attributes not normally ascribed to such a powerful person in the community. "When people question something, he writes about it in his blog," said Greensboro journalist Ed Cone in *American Journalism Review*. "He's in the game. He's not just waiting for his column to come out next week to answer a challenge made yesterday."

Not only does he respond to commenters, he also frequently comments on other local information blogs. He's involved and transparent.

When the curtain was pulled aside from the Wizard of Oz, revealing him to be just a man, he was still able to grant the wishes of Dorothy and her fellow travelers. Transparency doesn't change the duties, responsibilities and possibilities of media companies either. It just makes us more human.

TEN TACTICS TO GET STARTED

Think more about page rank than page views. Page rank (often referred to as "Google Juice") is a Google measurement of page "importance" that takes into consideration many factors specifically tied to the nature of the Web. Chief among these is inbound links, which is also Technorati's measure of value. The higher our rank, the more we are playing the Web by its rules, and not those of gathering and monetizing mass. Any practice that will boost page rank will, by its nature, be attraction marketing.

Undergird, support and enable the rise of personal media. As local media companies, we are the professionals in our markets and can make inroads with people who don't currently consumer our products simply by taking a proactive role in the making of media by everyday people.

We can host meet-ups for anybody interested in learning the basics. We can bring in experts and let them share their knowledge. We don't have to limit the initiative to bloggers. There is a community of content creators just waiting to be grown.

Strip away impediments to an attractive user experience. We need to recognize that our sites have value beyond page views and sell advertising placements sparingly. Site design should be based first on user-experience, with advertising inserted in such a way as to not interfere with that experience. We want lifetime customers, people who will enjoy an experience that doesn't give them ANY reason to not return.

Link to others, even competitors. There are several tactics that will help us acquire inbound links, the prime currency of the Web, but nothing inspires reciprocity like a professional media company linking to content other than its own. To be sure, we should link to our own content — even creating special internal pages that allow for this — but if we want to grow our influence exponentially, it'll need to come from outside.

Unbundle our output, so that users can spread it around for us. Again, a key component of attraction is to assist others in the creation of their own media, and providing, for example, a video player that can be embedded in other sites is an important step in that direction. One of roles in the news-is-a-conversation paradigm is to *start* conversations, and the best way we can maintain a leadership role in this is to make our videos and stories exportable to other sites.

Help people to know what we know and do what we do. Any business model that is created on this foundation will be successful downstream, for the personal media revolution is only going to get stronger. What better way to make ourselves attractive to potential customers than to help them grow. We can teach Saturday morning classes on video, video production, writing, reporting and editing.

Involve ourselves in the conversation on other people's sites. This may be the responsibility of an editor-level management person, but it's a smart tactic for two reasons. One, it says to the community that our voice extends beyond our own publications, and, two, every comment on another site includes an inbound link to our site, which will boost our Google Juice.

Regularly ask people for their help in our operational processes. This tactic and the next directly incorporate the currency of ego in our dealings with the people we're trying to serve. The more we value the input of the people in our communities, the more they feel a sense of ownership in what we do. But beyond smart business, the tactic also produces fruit in the way of more stories, better stories, relevant stories, satisfied viewers or readers, new energy, creativity, and a more involved role in the community.

Listen, listen, and listen some more. The gatekeeper world of professional media has produced a separation between us and our audiences, because the flow of information has generally been one-way. We've built our codes of conduct based on maintaining a certain distance from our viewers and readers, and this has cost us in the struggle to maintain relevance in a changing world. The process of re-engaging our communities begins with listening, and this is 24/7 commitment.

Share revenue. In a time of extreme pressure on our bottom lines, this is a tough concept to grasp, let alone implement. But tactically, it's a smart part of business development, for shared revenue is better than none. Assuming we're following the Media 2.0 development of Simulpath™, we're trying to grow a local ad network, where we'll split the revenue with sites in the community that are hosting our ads. But we should also be sharing revenue with anyone who is helping our efforts, be they hyperlocal, niche or any brand-extension effort.

Each of these tactics is designed to improve our attractiveness to our audience and align our resources and our thinking with the nature of the Web.

This is the new role of marketing for any media company, and marketing departments and specialists are the proper overseers of the strategies and tactics employed by the company. This means new skills and skill sets, including Search Engine Optimization (SEO), and Social Media Optimization (SMO). Schooling and training in these areas will produce dividends for everything the company does online.

Viral marketing is another new function — certainly a part of overall attraction efforts — and it, too, isn't nearly as random as it might seem. Even now, manipulation techniques are being practiced every day on YouTube, for example, by people who are writing the book on using the nature of the Web to position their videos with the YouTube audience.

Some of these techniques may be questionable ethically, but we would do well to understand them anyway.

Dan Ackerman Greenberg is co-founder of viral video marketing company The Comotion Group in California. Typical of young entrepreneurs, Greenberg is not afraid to push the envelope to accomplish tasks and has published his controversial methods online. Nothing is by accident in driving client videos to YouTube success. Here's an excerpt:

So how do we get the first 50,000 views we need to get our videos onto the Most Viewed list?

Blogs: We reach out to individuals who run relevant blogs and actually pay them to post our embedded videos. Sounds a little bit like cheating/ PayPerPost, but it's effective and it's not against any rules.

Forums: We start new threads and embed our videos. Sometimes, this means kickstarting the conversations by setting up multiple accounts on each forum and posting back and forth between a few different users. Yes, it's tedious and time-consuming, but if we get enough people working on it, it can have a tremendous effect.

MySpace: Plenty of users allow you to embed YouTube videos right in the comments section of their MySpace pages. We take advantage of this.

Facebook: Share, share, share. We've…built a sizeable presence on Facebook, so sharing a video with our entire friends list can have a real impact. Other ideas include creating an event that announces the video launch and inviting friends, writing a note and tagging friends, or posting the video on Facebook Video with a link back to the original YouTube video.

Email lists: Send the video to an email list. Depending on the size of the list (and the recipients' willingness to receive links to YouTube videos), this can be a very effective strategy.

Friends: Make sure everyone we know watches the video and try to get them to email it out to their friends, or at least share it on Facebook.

The point is that marketing by attraction is both a state of mind and a growing new science, and our internet pureplay competitors are vastly more familiar and comfortable with the concepts than we are. That needs to change, if we are to be successful media businesses in the twenty-first century.

The paths of influence and the nature of authority are changing in our culture. What seems like a time of great uncertainty is actually a time of great opportunity, but only if we get in front of the disruptions and cultural changes that are before us today.

Influencing a single tribe member, for example, may be worth far more than attempts to influence the entire tribe. It certainly is a whole lot more cost-effective. But this is a new path, one that requires knowledge and the expertise that can only come through trial and error, and the book on it is being written with every passing day.

THE WEB'S BUDDING
STREAMS AND FLOWS

AR&D clients are enjoying great success with the concept of Continuous News, with LEX18.com leading the way. We're also delighted to see other media companies doing the same, and note especially the new design of KSL-TV's website, the biggest TV station website in the world. This is still in its infancy, and we're learning as much as we're teaching. What follows is a continuation of the thought stream that began a couple of weeks ago.

As the news business evolves to real time, we must begin thinking of the news product differently. This will alter everything about the news business itself, because since the dawn of the printing press, the news business has been constructed around the production cycle of newspapers and later television stations.

Deadlines are meant to serve the production cycle, which means the definition of "the story" is too. The story includes that which we can put into it by the production cycle's deadline. We "go with what we've got" multiple times for TV news and daily with newspapers. The delivery cycle — be it via the printed word or broadcast video — sets in motion everything about the news business itself. We call it "the news cycle," and the ecosystem that is news is built around it. Newspapers went from afternoons to mornings, which changed the cycle completely, just as TV stations are now shifting from evening to mornings. When deadlines change, the business changes.

This "news cycle" is fed by the other side of journalism's coin, the public relations industry. Events are timed for live coverage or to "fit" everybody's deadlines, because the cycle is what really matters. If an event occurs close to the deadline, it wears the coveted title of "breaking news," the marketing managers' dream.

All of this is changing today, thanks to the real-time Web, the disinter-mediation of news delivery and the hyperconnectivity that puts all of us just a few bits away from each other. It is the most amazing time in communications' history, and yet those who cling to the product cycle have difficulty appreciating it. The product cycle is manageable. Real time is not. In my discussions with executives and in observations at various conferences, I find this to be the core disruption that puzzles media companies most.

This was first evidenced by how media companies originally attacked the Web marketplace. We built "pages" and determined that the product cycle of news could be simply moved to an online version of what we did offline. This was a critical, but understandable miscalculation and one that many venture-capital-supported "new media" entities exploited to suck money away from the news ecosystem. We look at Web "pages" and connect everything with that. The flows and streams of the Web, however, aren't driven by the page concept, so it makes no sense to us.

The point at which "the news" is consumed today may be a "page," but it's also every bit as likely to be something else, some application that updates in real time. It's very likely to be via a smartphone or PDA. It may be alongside something else, augmenting the other content or not. Everything about addressing the news consumer in this context is quite different than addressing them via "the page," and everything about making money via the stream is likewise different.

- The page is vetted and finished. The flow or stream is constant, un-finished and may or may not be vetted fully.
- The page is shaped by "the story," whereas the flow or stream con-tributes to the story, allowing users to put the pieces together for them-selves.
- The page is created for adjacent advertising. Advertising is a part of the stream, not adjacent to it.
- The page assumes consumers will browse and look around. The flow is here one moment and gone the next.
- The page exists to help people make sense. The stream assumes people can make sense as it flows along.
- The page is all about pushing content. The flow is about what people want to pull to themselves.

Twitter is a great example of a stream and flow. Constantly moving, people can decide what messages or people they wish to have in their stream and use software such as Tweetdeck to help them accomplish it. Twitter feeds the bigger stream that is the real-time Web, and the technologies designed to serve the bigger stream are still being created. Traditional media companies would do well to think about this as they begin to conceptualize news of tomorrow.

Perhaps the biggest practical difficulty that legacy media companies have with "the stream" is the need to own it. We can understand the live nature and perhaps even agree that it is a very efficient method of getting news to the consumer, but we cannot bring ourselves to see that "our" stream is but a part of "the" stream. We stop at what we see, which has always been the curse of traditional media and the Web. We confuse the page with the flow, which produces an artificial sense of accomplishment for those who've made the leap to, for example, Continuous News. It's artificial, because we're merely creating a new kind of "page."

I often encounter those who are desperate to place a "top story" block atop the Continuous News section of their news websites. The argument is a good one, if "the page" was all that mattered: we'd need to be able to show people coming to our site what we think is important. I don't argue that there are still people who view the Web this way, but in emphasizing the page over all else, we overlook the pertinent concept that it's not what's on our page that matters but that which is distributed raw into the stream. We simply cannot do this and expect to be relevant in a universe that is shifting to real time.

Deciding "what's important," moreover, is increasingly the purview of the news consumer, thanks to technology. Our editorial decisions are a part of what has led to 57% of adults in the U.S. distrusting the press, an all-time high. The idea of journalists being the unquestioned guides of the news is a relic of the past, yet those who view the web as a "page" insist that our "top stories" are a measurement of our relevance in the world today.

The technology that "sends" our content to "the stream" is RSS. If you want a clear illustration of how important any news organization views the stream, take a close look at its RSS feeds. Chances are you'll find a headline, a couple of sentences, and a link back to a story page. News businesses that do this are telling the Web that they want nothing to do with its wild and wooly real-time and that they're quite happy, thank you very much, to keep things just as they are. This is handing the future over to the upstarts by default, because we just won't view the Web as anything other than the page.

The concept of "flows and streams" applies equally to videos. Who will produce the real-time videos? We all will, and the two-fold challenge for those in the video news business will be similar to those of print today. One, how do we winnow the wheat that fits our needs from the chaff that's only relevant to the people who created it? Two, how do we contribute to the stream ourselves?

On the answers to these questions hang our future in the news business. With real-time delivering what's new, we won't get to call our later analysis thereof "news," because anything beyond real-time will be "olds." I think this is actually a blessing, for it will help us determine the essence of the finished products we currently call "news."

Meanwhile, we need to get busy immersing ourselves in the business of the streams and flows that are the strength of the Web.

SOCIAL MEDIA BY MEDIA, WHOSE BRAND SHOULD WE USE?

Sometimes in executing this thing we call Media 2.0, the managing of processes isn't enough, and it requires something else. Our training and instincts as mass marketers can fool us into thinking that black is really white, because all assumptions are driven by the past or by that which is known. The problem, of course, is that decisions we make today can have a lasting impact in our ability to adjust downstream, so we need to think very carefully about each and every seemingly obvious tactic.

Witness the case of who "owns" the pathways through which newsroom (and other) employees engage "fans" or "followers" via social media. It's a case of whether the company brand should supercede the individual's brand or vice versa. Should "my" Facebook page, for example, or my Twitter feed be branded as mine or the company's? To the traditional mind, the media company owns those, even to the extent of — as a condition of employment — requiring username/password combinations to assure back-end access. The thinking is entirely logical. Media companies retain contractual rights to control the image of those who represent them, in part, because they spend considerable money to promote those people to the community. It does so, because it's in the company's best interests. We control who they speak with and what they say, because it all reflects back on our marketing efforts. One voice. One effort. That's the way it works.

Social media, however, is a different animal. It has elements of "media," because it's possible to reach big numbers of people with a message, but it's different because everybody's connected, not only back to us but to each other. This makes it possible to actually recruit fans or followers of other local media companies, something that can't be done with any form of branded mass media. That recruiting, however, can't be done conventionally.

AR&D research proves that the vast majority (up to 90%) of our online "audience" is comprised of our own fans. We spend tons of money, as a result, serving the online news and information needs of people we already serve offline! Those audiences are shrinking; in fact, they have been shrinking for a long time, and this should tell us something about our brands. While still impactful in the community, their influence is waning, especially among young people, most of whom don't even know who we are. The net and potential reach of the many exceeds that of the one, for friends have friends have friends, etc.

Therefore, attaching ourselves to our employees via social media as a condition of employment is actually a net liability, because we want them free of our baggage in order to compete in the world of personal media, which is what social media really is. Baggage, Terry? Yes, baggage. According to Gallup, trust in the press is at an all-time low. 57% of Americans have little or no trust in the press. Baggage? Ask anybody under 21 to name the call letters of any TV station. They can't do it. Baggage? If we're a TV station — even if we're number one — people attached to our brand are always identified as TV people, and if they're not from the users' favorite station, there's no way they'll wish to connect with our people. "TV people," by the way, aren't as highly regarded as they used to be. Baggage? A newspaper is an archaic relic from the last century. Like vampires, they must be invited into your home, or they can't come in. When was the last time you welcomed a newspaper?

Social media connectivity can remove all baggage, but only if our people aren't required to play a certain role. so the more we allow and enable our employees to be real people, the better their chance of competing in its invitation-only world.

Remember, too, that our brand refers to our stage — the pulpit from which our people do their work. That stage can be whatever we want it to be, for it only speaks in one direction. If we wish to be "on your side," we can, but in the conversational social media world, that's problematic, because artificiality in any form is a curse in a hyperconnected universe, and we clearly aren't actually on anybody's "side" except our own.

It will seem like utter heresy to purists, but we must give control of their personal brands to our employees. Ownership produces pride and value. Besides, if we want people to "perform" for us 24/7, we have to pay them to do so. You want people working on your behalf on their own dime? Give them ownership of their brands.

Somebody will say, "But, Terry, wouldn't we just be creating monsters who could turn against us or hold us hostage?" Good question. Howard Kurtz this week announced he's leaving *The Washington Post*, where he's worked for three decades, to take a position with Tina Brown's on-line-only Daily Beast. He's taking the brand he built for himself and using it to help grow Tina's, which is exactly what we're discussing here. Did *The Washington Post* "make" Howard Kurtz, or was that something he accomplished on his own? It's obviously both, and the paper certainly got its money's worth, but the point is we've arrived at the day of the personal brand. It's a reality of today's journalism world, and much of this is springing up from the bottom in the form of bloggers, neighborhood sites, YouTube channels, Twitter accounts and Facebook pages. Professional journalists can't participate in this, because we've tied their hands by connecting them to our brands.

One of the most prolific network users of Twitter was CNN's Rick Sanchez, who got the axe last week for unfortunate comments made during a radio interview. Most people think he got what he deserved, but he also lost access to all those Twitter fans, because the Twitter address was owned by CNN: "ricksanchezcnn." That's a shame, really. CNN gained nothing from that, so why piss all those people off?

My advice to my students at UNT and to the people who work in the industry is to not wait one minute to start building your brand. Start a blog. Tweet. Facebook. You decide who you are and go out and work it. If your employer insists that you participate in social media for them, be the best you can be on their behalf, but don't forsake your own career either. Some day this will all be clearer, and nobody will question the value of the personal brands of our employees.

To media companies, my advice is to take a step back for a minute and consider that forcing everything we do through the funnel of mass media may not always be the best strategy. Hyperconnectivity is something really new, and we don't fully understand its fundamental essence and ramifications, much less its nuances. Personal media is, above all else, personal, and we need to respect that.

And mostly, when we don't have all the processes in place, maybe it's time to pull out our leadership courage and push forward knowing that we'll be rewarded in the end.

WHY DO BLOGGERS BLOG?

Over at PBS Mediashift's "Idea Lab," writer Brad Flora published a post last week designed, I suppose, to help bloggers be more successful. "5 Mistakes That Make Local Blogs Fail" is designed to help "local" bloggers by suggesting that such things are actually businesses. The problem is that it assigns traditional media ideas of success to the concept of blogging, and this is problematic. To be sure, some blogs and bloggers are in it to make a living, but to overlook — or, worse, deny — the primary reason bloggers blog is to lump all media together, and that misses the point entirely.

Flora's advice is good, assuming creating a little business is what you're after, but as we learned back in the days of the A-list, B-list, C-list controversy, many, many bloggers don't wish to be lumped in with anybody. Blogging can be, but it's not usually a "business," in the conventional sense. So let's revisit some of that discussion before looking at Flora's advice.

The most interesting and useful understanding of the difference between bloggers and traditional forms of media is this: bloggers write because they have something to say; traditional media writes because it has to — they get paid to write. People with something to say write differently than those who are paid to write, so from concept to prose itself, there's a big difference between disruptive bloggers and the media being disrupted.

Old media looks at this with the blinders of tradition and says, "Well, they COULD make money. After all, they're building an audience." The problem here is that when you bring advertisers to the table, they tend to have a governing effect on the content. Walter Lippmann's "objectivity," after all, was designed to create a sterile environment in which to sell advertising. Bloggers don't want such restrictions, and kudos to those "blog businesses" who've been able to maintain their voice despite advertising being present.

Bloggers write because they have something to say. The purpose of my blog, for example, is to challenge my assumptions. I publish my thinking, because it's the best way to refine that thinking. If I get an audience, fine, but I'm not starting out planning to build an audience. It's just not my goal. Could I grow an audience? Absolutely, but that's not the mission, and to say that I'm unique in this form of media is to disregard the reality of some really major players in the blogosphere.

If you blog to make a business, the only difference between you and any traditional publisher is one of size. If your measurements for success are audience size and revenue, then, of course, you're going to approach things differently. If you do that, however, you're much more closely aligned — in every respect ‐ with traditional media than blogging. Blogging challenges the status quo; it doesn't augment or supplement it.

Flora writes in his "5 Reasons" that local blogs fail, because they don't treat the blog like a business. It's right out of an MBA program. You're doing it alone. You don't know your market. Your content is weak. You haven't thought through your business model. And you have no distribution strategy.

In the end, the main mistake is looking at it wrong. You are not starting a blog, you are launching a small business. You are no different from the guy opening a bar up the road. You are both starting small, local businesses. You need to know something about blogging and social media, yes, but what you really need to bone up on is what it takes to run a small business. Instead of going to the local blogger meetups in your city, you should go to the local small business owner and entrepreneur meetups. Instead of following the latest social media news, you need to read up on the latest advertising, marketing, and search strategies showing results for actual media entrepreneurs in the field. This is the main mistake local bloggers make that dooms their efforts.

For us in media, the idea that we can create many little businesses with an internal blogging strategy is a good one, but we can't and shouldn't look at them from a traditional perspective. There are two overriding factors in a traditional media blogging strategy. One, will the blogs help advance the personal brands of our employees who blog? This is a much bigger issue that you may think, because personal brands take on enormous significance in a hyperconnected universe. Two, will the blogs produce data from users that we can use in advancing our database-driven advertising solutions. KOAA in Colorado Springs, for example, runs the "Colorado Dog Blog," and the people who visit that site provide rich data for advertisers who want to reach pet owners. Anchor blogs may help advance personal brands, but niche blogs create user data that helps advance the advertising cause.

Blogs are "blogs," because they're written using software that is incredibly easy to use and publishes the items in a descending order, based on date and time. The software is versatile enough that you can use it to create a site that "looks" like any news organization's site, so it's easy to understand why a neighborhood blog, for example, would be considered to be just like the business of traditional media.

It is a mistake, however, to assume that these types of sites are what are really driving the disruption caused by blogging, for bloggers aren't in the business of competing with traditional media. They simply write because they have something to say.

IN FOR A PENNY, IN FOR A POUND

The longer I teach media companies about the world of Media 2.0, the more I'm convinced that there's no middle ground, no way to straddle a fence between the two worlds, no way to "test" the waters. Partially working the Media 2.0 space is a little like partially pickling a cucumber or partially housebreaking a puppy. No matter how much we stare at it and try to connect the dots back to our core competencies, it just doesn't work very well in that capacity. New media is just that; it's new, and to treat it otherwise is not only disrespectful, it's a trap.

As we chug along with an old model that, by anybody's measurement, isn't doing what it used to do on any level, we can't bear the idea that there's a better mousetrap out there. Better for whom, you ask? Better for the people who really matter — those who used to be our audience. It's better in so many ways that it's hard to put them all in an essay.

New media levels the playing field, so that anybody can be a media company, including advertisers. The Web doesn't play well with artificiality, and so it routes around various middlemen (and women) and takes their jobs. It's interactive. People can talk back to authority of almost any kind. They can resist the carpet bombing of ads that so dominated the end of the twentieth century. But most importantly, it's connected; we're all connected. That's what's really "new," and unless we adjust our business models to embrace it, we're running counter to the culture overall.

This week, Andrew Keen posted five videos on TechCrunch that are worth watching. The interview subject is Justine Bateman, the "Family

Ties" actress from the 80s. Justine, it seems, has become an Internet evangelist and is in the thick of producing things for the Web. Andrew Keen, on the other hand, while showing up everywhere that new media is discussed, is a relentless voice of dissent, as evidenced by some of his questions to Justine.

She spoke of how the old "business grid" for entertainment has been disrupted, and went on to explain how things are different:

> As everyone who works in new media knows, you can't apply the old model in this area. It just doesn't function that way. The old model works only if you have control of distribution. In new media, it doesn't work that way. In fact, you need people to be passing your stuff around in order to have the maximum amount of distribution. There are so many layers, and it's a totally new business model that you have to invent or adopt from somebody who's done something recently that you think will work for you.
>
> You also have to be a multitasker. You can't just come in as a content participant and only do acting or only do writing. In new media, you can't make a living like that, so you need to be able to design a website or you need to be able to know how to edit or you need to have an knack for following Twitter and know how to manage that. So you need to be able to bring something else to the party.

In pressing her on the new business model, Keen asked her to name an example of something new that "made lots of money" and "had a huge audience." This is exactly the type of old thinking that I find with many media companies. People seem incapable of looking at media in any form and not coming to the conclusion that it's all about putting a big audience together and making "lots of money."

The same is true about YouTube. Television people think they understand video, but what they really understand is the old model of video distribution. Everything is about creating something that gathers a big audience, so even when the press reports on YouTube, the stories all tilt towards the "look at how many people watched this" account, proving that they really don't understand how YouTube is creating communities via video exchanges and changing the world.

"What Gutenberg did for writing," Wired editor Chris Anderson told the TED Conference earlier this year, "online video can now do for face-to-face communication." He was talking to a great extent about YouTube.

What I think is underreported is the significance of the rise of online video. This is the technology that's going to allow the rest of the world of talents to be shared digitally, thereby launching a whole new cycle of crowd generated innovation. The first few years of the Web were pretty much video free, and the reason is simple. Video files are huge; the Web couldn't handle them, but in the last few years, bandwidth has exploded a hundredfold, and suddenly here we are. **Humanity watches 80 million hours of YouTube a day.** Cisco actually projects that within four years, 90 percent of the data online will be video. If it's all puppies, porn and piracy, we're doomed, but I don't think it will be. Video is high bandwidth for a reason. It packs a lot of data, and our brains are uniquely wired to decode it.

Eighty million hours of YouTube, and the people who follow culture for a living have completely missed it. What's going on?

Jay Rosen's "people formerly known as the audience" are making media and sharing it with others in interest groups. People are learning and the arts are blossoming throughout the world, thanks to the ability of people to share video with each other. This is why Nokia predicted that by 2012, one-quarter of all entertainment would be produced and consumed within peer groups.

But that's not mass media, so we don't get it. Instead, we try to bolt things that we think "work" onto our tried and true business model, so we're creating that partially pickled cucumber.

When I explore Media 2.0, all I see, frankly, is opportunity, but it means the willingness to detach from the old and look at the new for the "new" that it is. In for a penny, in for a pound. There's no holding back, and those who are able to do so will write the book on the future while occupying the catbird's seat today.

ENDNOTES

EVOLVING USER PARADIGM

1   Weinberger, David. *Everything Is Miscellaneous.* New York: Holt, 2008.

2   Lasica, J. D. *Darknet: Hollywood's War Against the Digital Generation.* Hoboken: Wiley, 2005.

WE DON'T NEED NO STAGE

1   Wikipedia article on packet switching. http://en.wikipedia.org/wiki/Packet_switching Retrieved 21 February 2009.

2   Powell, Michael. Quoted by Bazeley, Michael. Post on SIPthat Blog. http://sipthat.com/2003/12/30/fcc-chairman-speaks-on-voip-regulations/ Retrieved 21 February 2009.

3   Zucker, Jeff. Quoted by Stetler, Brian. "Forest Fire: Zucker Sees Strike as an Opportunity for Change." *New York Times.* 29 January 2008.

PROTECTING THE STAGE

1   Cushman, David. June 2008 Presentation. http://www.slideshare.net/davidcushman/why-traditional-ad-models-will-not-work-in-social-networks-and-what-will? Retrieved 28 January 2009.

2   Kelly, Kevin. "We Are the Web." *Wired.* August 2005 issue. http://www.wired.com/wired/archive/13.08/tech.html Retrieved 29 January 2009.

3   New York Times Facebook policy. Quoted by Poynter Online Blog. http://www.poynter.org/content/content_view.asp?id=157136 Retrieved 29 January 2009.

4   Wikipedia article on influencer marketing. http://en.wikipedia.org/wiki/Influencer_marketing Retrieved 28 January 2009.

PERSONAL WALLED GARDENS

1   Burnett, Frances Hodgson. *The Secret Garden*. Originally published in 1910. Now public domain.

2   Arrington, Michael. Post on TechCrunch Blog. "The Personalized Homepage War: Who Matters." http://techcrunch.com/2008/02/24/the-personalized-homepage-war-who-matters/ Retrieved 19 September 2008.

3   "From WWW To Widgets." Sidebar in *Bloomberg Businessweek*. No author listed. http://www.businessweek.com/magazine/content/07_30/b4043074.htm Retrieved 20 September 2008.

THE TWO STAGES OF JOURNALISM

1   Gillmor, Dan. "Who's a Journalist? Does That Matter?" Salon. http://www.salon.com/technology/dan_gillmor/2010/08/26/who_is_a_jour nalist Retrieved 26 August 2010.

2   Hundley, Wendy. "Blogger Feels Stifled By Lewisville Schools' Revised Policy on Media Access." *Dallas Morning News*. 22 October 2009.

THE NEW NEWS CURATOR

1   *Webster's Dictionary*, 2006 edition. Definition of "curator."

2   Jarvis, Jeff. "Death of the Curator. Long live the Curator." Post on buzzmachine.com Blog. 23 April 2009. http://www.buzzmachine.com/2009/04/23/death-of-the-curator-long-live-the-curator/ Retrieved 12 February 2010.

3   Shirky, Clay. Quoted by Juskalian, Russ. "Interview with Clay Shirky, Part I." *Columbia Journalism Review*. 19 December 2008. http://www.cjr.org/overload/interview_with_clay_shirky_par.php?page=all Retrieved 14 February 2010.

SOCIAL MEDIA GUIDELINES

THE CHAOTIC NEW ORDER

1   Arrington, Michael. "The Morality and Effectiveness of Process Journalism." TechCrunch Blog. 7 June 2009. http://techcrunch.com/2009/06/07/the-morality-and-effectiveness-of-process-journalism/ Retrieved 6 August 2009.

2   Jarvis, Jeff. "Product v. Process Journalism." Post on buzzmachine.com Blog. 07 June 2009. http://www.buzzmachine.com/2009/06/07/processjournalism/ Retrieved 7 August 2009.

3   Diagram included is the creation of Jeff Jarvis.

UNDERESTIMATING THE AUDIENCE

1   Wikipedia entry on metanarrative. http://en.wikipedia.org/wiki/Metanarrative Retrieved 11 June 2009.

2   Rosen, Jay. "Audience Atomization Overcome: Why the Internet Weakens the Press." *Pressthink.* 12 January 2009. http://archive.pressthink.org/2009/01/12/atomization.html Retrieved 10 June 2009.

3   Lasica, J. D. *Darknet: Hollywood's War Against the Digital Generation.* Hoboken: Wiley, 2005.

4   Gillmor, Dan. *We the Media: Grassroots Journalism By the People, for the People.* Sebastopal: O'Reilly Media, 2004.

THE WEB'S WIDENING STREAM

1   Malik, Om. "How Internet Content Distribution & Discovery Are Changing." Post on GigaOm Blog. 17 May 2009. http://gigaom.com/2009/05/17/how-internet-content-distribution-discovery-are-changing/ Retrieved 22 May 2009.

2   Borthwick, John. This quote was taken from a blog post for which the archived link is no longer active.

3   Schonfeld, Erick. "Jump Into The Stream." TechCrunch. 17 May 2009. http://techcrunch.com/2009/05/17/jump-into-the-stream/ Retrieved 21 May 2009.

JOURNALISM'S NEW VALUES

1   Smith, Michael. Personal interview.

2   Feldman, Charles S. and Rosenberg, Howard. *No Time To Think*. London: Continuum International, 2008.

3   Bercovici, Jeff. "Mixed Media." Portfolio.com Blog post. 20 October 2008. http://www.portfolio.com/views/blogs/mixed-media/2008/10/20/no-time-to-think-when-faster-equals-disaster?tid=true Retrieved 13 November 2008.

4   Jarvis, Jeff. "The Public Press: Transparency Is Our Goal." Post on buzzmachine.com Blog. 10 June 2008. http://www.buzzmachine.com/2008/06/10/the-public-press-transparency-is-our-goal/ Retrieved 14 November 2008.

5   Anderson, Chris. "What Would Radical Transparency Mean?" Post on The Long Tail Blog. 12 December 2006. http://www.longtail.com/the_long_tail/2006/12/what_would_radi_1.html Retrieved 11 November 2008.

6   McLellan, Michele, and Porter, Tim. *News, Improved*. Washington: CQ Press, 2007.

YOUR PERSONAL BRAND

A REASONABLE VIEW OF TOMORROW

1   Hart, Roderick P.; Jones, Alex S.; Kunkel, Thomas; Lemann, Nicholas; Lavine, John; Mills, Dean; Rubin, David M.; and Wilson, Ernest. "A License for Local Reporting." *New York Times*. 22 December 2007.

2   Kaplan, Ethan. "Reducing Back to Art." Post on blackrimglasses Blog. 12 April 2008. http://blackrimglasses.com/2008/04/12/reducing-back-to-art/ Retrieved 23 April 2008.

3   Sullivan, Danny. "Q&A with Gabe Rivera, Creator of Techmeme." Post on searchengineland.com Blog. 17 January 2007. http://searchengineland.com/qa-with-gabe-rivera-creator-of-techmeme-10278 Retrieved 24 April 2008.

2009: THE GREAT BEGINNING

1   Carr, David. "Stoking Fear Everywhere You Look." *New York Times*. 07 December 2008.

2   Adams, Henry. *The Education of Henry Adams*. Archived online as part of the American Studies Project of the University of Virginia. http://xroads.virginia.edu/~hyper/HADAMS/ha_home.html

CHASING "THE" TRUTH

1   Rosen, Jay. "Audience Atomization Overcome: Why the Internet Weakens the Press." *Pressthink*. 12 January 2009. Retrieved 11 December 2009.

2   Rosen, Jay. "He Said, She Said Journalism." *Pressthink*. 12 April 2009. http://archive.pressthink.org/2009/04/12/hesaid_shesaid.html Retrieved 12 December 2009.

3   Lippman, Walter. *Liberty and the News*. New York: Harcourt, 1920.

THE CHAOTIC NATURE OF CHANGE

1   Adams, Henry. *The Education of Henry Adams*. Archived online as part of the American Studies Project of the University of Virginia. http://xroads.virginia.edu/~hyper/HADAMS/ha_home.html

2   Rosen, Jay. "Audience Atomization Overcome: Why the Internet Weakens the Press." Pressthink. 12 January 2009. Retrieved 11 December 2009.

3   Lurie, Peter. "Why the Web Will Win the Culture Wars for the Left: Deconstructing Hyperlinks." 15 April 2003. http://www.ctheory.net/articles.aspx?id=380 Retrieved 12 May 2010.

4   Pascal, Blaise. *Pensees*. Public domain. Archived online as part of Project Gutenberg. http://www.gutenberg.org/ebooks/18269

PRIVACY DISRUPTED

1   Zuckerberg, Mark. Quoted by Kirkpatrick, Marshall. "Facebook's
     Zuckerberg Says the Age of Privacy Is Over." Post on ReadWriteWeb
     Blog. 09 January 2010.
     http://www.readwriteweb.com/archives/facebooks_zuckerberg_says_the_a
     ge_of_privacy_is_ov.php Retrieved 13 June 2010.

2   Jarvis, Jeff. "Confusing a Public with the Public." Post on
     buzzmachine.com Blog. 08 May 2010.
     http://www.buzzmachine.com/2010/05/08/confusing-a-public-with-the-
     public/ Retrieved 12 June 2010.

3   Rosen, Jay. "Audience Atomization Overcome: Why the Internet Weakens
     the Press." *Pressthink*. 12 January 2009.

THE INTERNET WEAKENS AUTHORITY

1   Arends, Brett. "The Three Biggest Lies About the Economy."
     MarketWatch. 29 June 2010. http://www.marketwatch.com/story/the-
     three-biggest-lies-about-the-us-economy-2010-06-29 Retrieved 11 July
     2010.

2   Rosen, Jay. "Audience Atomization Overcome: Why the Internet Weakens
     the Press." *Pressthink*. 12 January 2009.

THE TROUBLE WITH TWITTER

1   Rosen, Jay. "How the Backchannel Has Changed the Game for
     Conference Panelists." *Pressthink*. 17 March 2010.

THE ORDER OF THE WEB

1   Boles, Ben. Personal Interview.

2   Weinberger, David. *Everything Is Miscellaneous*. New York: Holt, 2008.

THE BACK END'S THE THING

1   Weinberger, David. *Everything Is Miscellaneous*. New York: Holt, 2008.

2   Neilsen, Jakob. Quoted by Croll, Alistair. "What if You Ran An Ad, and Nobody Saw It?" Post on Gigaom Blog. 14 October 2008. http://gigaom.com/2008/10/14/what-if-you-ran-an-ad-and-nobody-saw-it/ Retrieved 08 November 2008.

3   Turner, Fred. *From Counterculture to Cyberculture*. Chicago: University of Chicago Press, 2006.

THE COST OF INTERACTION

1   Day, Don. "How Do We Match Up With Google's Design Principles?" Post on Lost Remote Blog. 01 May 2008. http://www.lostremote.com/2008/05/01/googles-principles-of-design/ Retrieved 22 May 2008.

2   Factor, Sue. "What Makes A Design 'Googley'?" The Official Google Blog. 23 April 2008. http://googleblog.blogspot.com/2008/04/what-makes-design-googley.html Retrieved 23 May 2008.

3   Yelvington, Steve. "Online Newspapers." Post on Yelvington Blog. 15 April 2008. http://googleblog.blogspot.com/2008/04/what-makes-design-googley.html Retrieved 21 May 2008.

ADVERTISING LOSES ITS BALANCE

1   Hagel, John. "Unanswered Questions at Supernova 2007." Post on edgeperspectives.com Blog. 26 June 2007. http://edgeperspectives.typepad.com/edge_perspectives/2007/06/unanswered-ques.html Retrieved 14 February 2009.

2   Yahoo Answers entry on the definition of Wikipedia. http://answers.yahoo.com/question/index?qid=20080516120918AARuFkB Retrieved 13 February 2009.

3   Sullivan, Laurie. "Analyst: Overabundance Will Drive Down Online Ad Channels." Post on Online Media Daily Blog. 09 December 2008. http://www.mediapost.com/publications/?fa=Articles.showArticle&art_aid=96384 Retrieved 14 February 2009.

4   Rothenberg, Randall. "A Bigger Idea." Post on I, A Bee Blog. 05 February 2009. http://www.randallrothenberg.com/2009/02/heartbeats-and-mouseclicks-manifesto-on.html Retrieved 15 February 2009.

5   Lasica, J. D. *Darknet: Hollywood's War Against the Digital Generation*. Hoboken: Wiley, 2005.

THE PROBLEM WITH WEB ADVERTISING

THE HIDDEN DISRUPTION

1   AP story reported on Salon.com. "More Time Spent Online." 29
    December 2009.
    http://www.salon.com/business/2009/12/29/us_watercooler/index.html?sou
    rce=rss&aim=/business Retrieved 11 January 2010.

2   Elkin, Tobi. "Starcom IP Chief: Humans Are God." Online Media Daily.
    4 March 2004.
    http://www.mediapost.com/publications/index.cfm?fa=Articles.showArticl
    e&art_aid=2148 Retrieved 10 January 2010.

3   Custom Publishing Council. No author listed. 17 December 2009.
    http://www.custompublishingcouncil.com/news-industry-
    article.asp?ID=687 Retrieved 11 January 2010.

IT'S ALWAYS ABOUT THE MONEY

1   Lasica, J. D. *Darknet: Hollywood's War Against the Digital Generation.*
    Hoboken: Wiley, 2005.

2   Jarvis, Jeff. "Google Ad Manager: It's Bigger Than It Looks." Post on
    buzzmachine.com Blog. 14 March 2008.
    http://www.buzzmachine.com/2008/03/14/google-ad-manager-its-bigger-
    than-it-looks/ Retrieved 15 March 2008.

FAILURE AT THE TOP

1   Perez-Pena, Richard. "In Deepening Ad Declines, Sales Fall 8% At
    Magazines." *New York Times.* 11 July 2008.

2   Borrell Associates Report.
    http://www.borrellassociates.com/reports?prodID=111

THE FIRST LAW OF SOCIAL MEDIA

1   Battelle, John. "It's Time To Put This Myth To Rest." Open Forum. 25
     November 2008. http://www.openforum.com/idea-
     hub/topics/technology/article/its-time-to-put-this-myth-to-rest Retrieved 27
     November 2008.

2   Wilson, Fred. "Do You Ever Do Any Real Work?" Post on Musings of a
     VC in NYC Blog. 19 November 2008.
     http://www.avc.com/a_vc/2008/11/do-you-ever-do.html Retrieved 26
     November 2008.

3   Godin, Seth. "How To Make Money Using the Internet." 20 November
     2008. http://sethgodin.typepad.com/seths_blog/2008/11/how-to-make-
     mon.html?utm_source=feedburner&utm_medium=feed&utm_campaign=
     Feed%3A+typepad%2Fsethsmainblog+%28Seth%27s+Blog%29
     Retrieved 27 November 2008.

EMBRACING THE DISRUPTION

1   Glaser, Connie. The link to the article in the *East Bay Business Times* is
     no longer accessible.

2   Owens, Howard. Personal e-mail correspondence.

USING FREE TO SELL PAID

1   Anderson, Chris. *Free: The Future of a Radical Price*. New York:
     Hyperion, 2009.

2   TMZ.com press release. Quoted and archived on Futon Critic Blog. 18
     February 2009.
     http://www.thefutoncritic.com/news.aspx?id=20090218wbt01 Retrieved
     28 March 2009.

IS THE MAINSTREAM WINNING?

1   McCracken, Harry. "Whatever Happened to the Top Web Properties of
     April 1999?" Post on Technologizer Blog. 23 April 2009.
     http://technologizer.com/2009/04/23/whatever-happened-to-the-top-15-
     properties-of-april-1999/ Retrieved 24 April 2009.

2   Ziade, Richard. "Big Media's Head Start." Post on Basement.org Blog. 23
     April 2009.
     http://www.basement.org/2009/04/big_medias_big_head_start.html
     Retrieved 24 April 2009.

THE FOUR OPPORTUNITIES OF 2010

1   Kubler-Ross, Elisabeth. *Death and Dying*. New York: Scribner, 1997 edition.

PUREPLAYS AND THE 50% THRESHOLD

1.   Pie charts taken from Borrell Associates reports/projections from 2004 and 2010.

2   Small, Jay. "Too Critical Makes An Odd Criticism." Post on personal Blog. 02 July 2010. http://jaysmall.com/2010/07/02/too-critical-makes-odd-criticism Retrieved 06 July 2010.

3   Sterling, Greg. "Does Groupon Help or Hurt McClatchy?" Post on Screenwerk Blog. 02 July 2010. http://www.screenwerk.com/2010/07/02/does-groupon-help-or-hurt-mcclatchy/ Retrieved 03 July 2010.

INDEX

A

abundance 39, 140, 158, 242-3, 245, 405
acts 16, 18, 21, 32-4, 64, 69, 81, 119, 134, 226, 338, 405, 408
ad-supported content 21, 138, 158, 191, 326, 339-41, 345, 405
Adams 94, 106, 399, 405
   Henry 46, 94, 105, 131, 399
ads 11-12, 60, 65, 137-9, 143-4, 162, 166-70, 182-4, 190-1, 195, 254-7, 263-5, 278-9, 284-5, 310-11, 321
advertisers 19-20, 25-6, 132-3, 138-9, 162-3, 165-9, 174, 176-7, 182-4, 217-18, 221-3, 240, 255-6, 263-6, 318, 390-2
advertising 157-62, 164-5, 172, 176-7, 182-3, 186-7, 220-2, 240-1, 254-6, 285-6, 288, 311-12, 325-6, 340-1, 367-8, 390-1
advertising companies online 405
   traditional 231
advertising industry 150, 157, 166, 182, 232, 255, 262, 353, 355, 405
advertising infrastructure 284-6, 405
advertising online 187, 256, 405
advertising packages 201, 203, 405
Advertising Promotions 175, 405
advertising revenues 57, 167, 191, 405
advertising system 182, 188, 190-1, 357, 405
age ix, 31, 33, 54, 56, 76, 95, 114, 119, 156, 173, 190, 232, 238, 333, 405
Age of Participation 90, 95-6, 116, 405

agencies 160-3, 184, 223, 266, 288, 318-20, 359, 405
aggregation 243, 374, 405
all-time 176, 298, 383, 386, 405
analog dollars 13-14, 218, 321, 324, 405
anchor 134, 150, 224, 405
Anderson 209, 398, 403, 405
AnyAdServerUSA 222, 405
AOL 3, 60, 62, 108, 143, 187, 286, 314-17, 350, 405
Apple 4, 48, 231, 251, 405
application separation 9, 13-14, 405
apps 246, 251, 405
Archived online 399, 405
arrangements 164, 223, 230, 234-5, 405
artists 13, 19, 81, 268, 405
assets 195, 317, 341, 366, 405
atomization 120-2, 405
attention 4, 26-7, 36, 44, 49, 61, 81, 90, 94, 128-9, 157, 166, 213, 220-4, 330, 369-71
attraction 245, 369-72, 375-7, 379, 405
attraction marketing 371-2, 376, 405
audience 4-5, 13-20, 25, 41, 44-5, 49-54, 57, 66-8, 92, 134-5, 151-3, 199, 279, 331-2, 373-4, 389-90
   big 85, 393
   mass 17, 120, 184, 326
Audience Atomization Overcome 51, 98, 107, 113, 116, 120, 397, 399-400, 405
audience problem 81, 196, 213, 405
authenticity 20, 58, 67-8, 70-2, 79, 259, 405
authority 21, 51-3, 55, 66, 69, 71, 98, 107-8, 112-14, 120, 145, 248, 300, 322, 340, 344

B

baggage 114, 203-4, 386, 405
basket approach, all eggs in one 207-8, 210
Batavian 202-3, 405
beliefs 44-5, 54, 80, 98, 105, 116, 135, 176, 180, 207, 231, 239, 242, 260, 321, 336-7
Bernays 54, 405
biases 33, 54, 68, 299, 301, 405
blog format 63, 141-4, 258, 275-6, 405
blog software 141-2, 152, 265, 405
bloggers 20-1, 32, 36, 47, 71, 82-3, 127, 149, 181, 196, 271-2, 321, 333-4, 363, 374, 389-91
blogging 18, 31, 142-3, 197, 271, 292, 312, 376, 389-91, 405
blogs 6, 32, 37, 47-8, 68-9, 113, 127-8, 132, 143, 158, 197-8, 215-16, 270-2, 312, 336-8, 389-91
   buzzmachine.com 396-8, 400, 402
Boles 132-3, 400, 405
Borrell 160-2, 174, 188, 227, 229-30, 320, 365, 405
Boxee 10, 12, 197, 229, 405
brand-extension websites 292, 405
branding, personal 95, 128, 220, 223-4, 242, 292, 303-4
   brands 22, 74-5, 77-9, 177, 187, 204, 217-18, 224-5, 232, 248, 304-5, 309, 324-5, 340, 364, 385-7
   individual 45, 79, 82, 305
   person's 74
Brittany 76, 405
browser 60, 62, 167, 169-70, 207-8, 210, 212-13, 251, 405
browser window 208, 210, 405

405

408

LaVergne, TN USA
10 December 2010

208316LV00002B/1/P